LEGENDARY BOWL

Deciding College Football's G.O.A.T.

LEGENDARY BOWL

Deciding College Football's G.O.A.T.

Michael J. Calabrese

©2024 All Rights Reserved. No portion of this book may be reproduced, stored in a retrieval system, or transmitted in any form or by any means- electronic, mechanical, photocopy, recording, scanning, or other-except for brief quotations in critical reviews or articles without the prior permission of the author.

Published by Game Changer Publishing

Paperback ISBN: 978-1-963793-65-9
Hardcover ISBN: 978-1-963793-66-6
Digital ISBN: 978-1-963793-67-3

www.GameChangerPublishing.com

DEDICATION

For my father, Jimmy.
From the first game I watched on your lap to our last great
sports debate, I treasured our time together.

Read This First

Thanks so much for picking up my book! To show my appreciation, I've got a few freebies for you—no strings attached:

1. A cool, visually engaging tournament bracket.
2. A behind-the-scenes podcast on how the book came together.
3. Another podcast packed with insights from my research.

Enjoy!

Tournament Bracket

Behind The Scenes Podcast

Being A De Facto Selection Committee Podcast

LEGENDARY BOWL

Deciding College Football's G.O.A.T.

A Modern Era Tournament

Michael J. Calabrese

www.GameChangerPublishing.com

Table of Contents

Introduction 1

Author's Note 11

Chapter 1 – 68 Team Overview (Team Capsules) 25

Chapter 2 – The Greatest "What If" Teams of All Time 101

Chapter 3 – The Most Difficult Teams to Select 107

Chapter 4 – Unsung Heroes 113

Chapter 5 – The Tournament - Play-In Games 119

Conclusion 251

Introduction

By Kelley Ford

There were approximately 100 people surrounding a grass field on College Avenue in New Brunswick, New Jersey, on Saturday, November 6, 1869, and they would be forgiven if they failed to fully comprehend the significance of what they were witnessing. After all, the 25 players on the field from Rutgers University and the College of New Jersey (now known as Princeton University) were attempting to kick and bat a soccer ball into a goal at either end of the field using their hands, feet and head. Players were not allowed to carry or throw the ball. At the conclusion of the game, Rutgers was victorious by a score line of 6–4, and the first iteration of what ultimately became known as college football was born.

While nearly everything about the sport of college football has changed since that original College Football Saturday in November 1869, some elements of the sport have persisted through the centuries. History and traditions. Rivalries and upsets. Passion and drama. But perhaps more than anything else, controversies and debates. One week after losing to Rutgers 4–6, the College of New Jersey won the rematch 8–0 in Princeton, New Jersey, and would retroactively be declared 1869 national champions by the National Championship Foundation despite finishing with the same record as their in-state rivals.

For more than 125 years, the process by which the highest level of college football determined its national champion was marred by controversy. Various mathematical formulas created by biased individuals and/or a plethora of subjective polls often resulted in more than one team claiming a national championship in any given year. This remained commonplace until the 1997 season, at the end of which the Associated Press (AP) Poll named Michigan national champions, while the Coaches Poll determined Nebraska was the No. 1 team in the country.

In 1998, the demand for a definitive national champion was seemingly satisfied with the creation of the Bowl Championship Series (BCS). The stated goal of the BCS was to match the top two teams in the country in a true national championship game. However, at the conclusion of the 2003 season, there was another split national championship: LSU defeated Oklahoma in the BCS National Championship Game, but the AP Poll voters decided USC was No. 1 after defeating Michigan in the Rose Bowl. The controversy continued. The 2004 season was also controversial, as three "Power Five" conference champions—USC, Oklahoma and Auburn—all finished 12-0. With only two spots available in the title game, it was the SEC Champion Tigers that were left out. Perhaps the final straw for the BCS was the 2011 season. A mere seven seasons after the SEC had an undefeated champion left out of the BCS National Championship Game, the conference had two teams from the same division compete for the coveted crystal ball. Alabama would go on to avenge its only regular season loss (6-9 in overtime in Tuscaloosa) by taking down LSU 21-0 in New Orleans. It was the third of what would ultimately be seven national championship rings for Nick Saban. While most pundits agreed that the BCS was an improvement on the system it replaced, there was still widespread desire for a playoff, especially after the All-SEC National Championship Game rematch following the 2011 season.

Thus, in 2014, the College Football Playoff (CFP) was created to replace the oft-criticized BCS. It was determined that a selection committee would be charged with selecting the four best teams to compete for the College Football National Championship. The winner of the CFP would be crowned the undisputed national champion. This system was designed, in part, to eliminate the controversies that had plagued the sport since its inception. But this is still college football, after all. Controversies and debates have been woven into the fabric of the game since 1869. As it turns out, the very first year of the CFP ended up being one of the Selection Committee's most controversial decisions of the Playoff era.

TCU was 11-1 and ranked No. 3 in the Committee's penultimate rankings. But while most Power conferences were contesting a conference championship game during the first weekend of December, the Big 12 had not yet adopted that approach for its 10-team membership composition. So, while TCU destroyed previously 2-9 Iowa State by a score of 55-3, reigning national champion and No. 4-ranked Florida State capped off a perfect 13-0 season by squeaking past No. 11 Georgia Tech by a score of 37-35 in the ACC Championship Game. Most expected that to be enough to push the Seminoles ahead of the Horned Frogs on Selection Sunday. What many didn't expect was for No. 5 Ohio State to leapfrog TCU as well after dismantling No. 13 Wisconsin 59-0 in the Big Ten Championship Game behind third-string quarterback Cardale Jones. Furthermore, because the Committee ranks teams in groups of three, for the first time all season, the Committee determined that TCU and Baylor were "comparable" and applied the head-to-head tiebreaker. Baylor knocked off TCU in a classic 61-58 game in Waco in mid-October, leading the Bears to be ranked ahead of the Horned Frogs on Selection Sunday. The fact that a team could be ranked No. 3, win 55-3 on the road, and fall to No. 6 in the rankings during the most crucial week of the season did not sit well with many college football fans. From that moment on, the clamoring for an expanded playoff grew louder and louder. Eventually, the Expansionists got their wish.

In 2022, College Football Playoff officials announced that the postseason event would expand from four teams to 12 teams starting with the 2024 season. In theory, this would eliminate all controversy associated with team selection. (Stop me if you've heard this before.) But for those who valued the four-team era, the 2023 season represented one final glorious season to be cherished. Heading into Conference Championship Game weekend, the Committee's penultimate rankings were as follows, with upcoming conference championship game opponents noted:

- **Georgia (12-0)** [vs. No. 8 Alabama in Atlanta, GA]
- **Michigan (12-0)** [vs. No. 16 Iowa in Indianapolis, IN]
- **Washington (12-0)** [vs. No. 5 Oregon in Las Vegas, NV]
- **Florida State (12-0)** [vs. No. 14 Louisville in Charlotte, NC]
- **Oregon (11-1)** [vs. No. 3 Washington in Las Vegas, NV]
- **Ohio State (11-1)**
- **Texas (11-1)** [vs. No. 18 Oklahoma State in Arlington, TX]
- **Alabama (11-1)** [vs. No. 1 Georgia in Atlanta, GA]

If the four top-ranked teams all won their conference championship games, the Committee's job was seemingly straightforward: for the first time in the CFP era, there would be four undefeated Power Five champions, and those would be the four Playoff participants in the final edition of the four-team format. Washington dispatched Oregon (for a second time that season) 34–31 on Friday night despite being 9.5-point underdogs, and the stage was set for Saturday. Georgia, Michigan, and Florida State were all favorites. This was finally going to be the year that many had envisioned from the onset of the four-team Playoff era: we were finally going to have four undefeated Power Five champions in the Playoff. But as was seemingly always the case with Nick Saban on the sidelines, Alabama had different plans.

The Crimson Tide defeated the Bulldogs 27–24, despite being a 5.5-point underdog, bringing an end to the possibility of the poetic final chapter of the four-team Playoff and propelling the sport into its biggest controversy in at least 20 years—and perhaps longer. Earlier in the day, Texas had blown past Oklahoma State 49–21, and in the evening games, Michigan manhandled Iowa 26–0, and Florida State's defense shut Louisville down in a 16–6 rock fight. Massively important context for the ACC Championship Game is that freshman third-string quarterback Brock Glenn got the start for the Seminoles after starter and Heisman Trophy candidate Jordan Travis was lost for the season two weeks earlier, and backup Tate Rodemaker was ruled out with a concussion. When the dust settled, the Committee was left with the following five teams to consider for four spots:

- **13–0 Michigan** (Big Ten Champions)
- **13–0 Washington** (Pac-12 Champions)
- **13–0 Florida State** (ACC Champions)
- **12–1 Texas** (Big 12 Champions; L 30–34 vs. Oklahoma in Dallas, TX, in early October)
- **12–1 Alabama** (SEC Champions; L 24–34 at home vs. Texas in early September)

Five teams—four spots. Never before had an undefeated Power Five conference champion been left out of the Playoff. Never before had a team ranked outside the Committee's top-six heading into Conference Championship Game weekend made the four-team field. Never before had my own proprietary final Most Deserving Rankings not matched the Committee's final four (in order, no less). But on December 3, 2023, a date that will live in infamy for Florida State fans, all of that changed when the College Football Playoff Committee produced their final rankings:

1. **Michigan (13–0)**
2. **Washington (13–0)**
3. **Texas (12–1)**
4. **Alabama (12–1)**

5. **Florida State (13–0)**
6. **Georgia (12–1)**
7. **Ohio State (11–1)**
8. **Oregon (11–2)**

A 13-person committee in a conference room at the Gaylord Texan Resort in Grapevine, Texas, collectively acted on their expectations: Alabama is likely a better team than Florida State, especially without star quarterback Jordan Travis. My own proprietary KFord Ratings projected the same. However, that means the Committee concluded metrics were more important than what they actually knew: Florida State was 13–0 with an ACC Championship. It's pretty clear how I feel about what happened to 2023 Florida State. But one of the most beautiful aspects of college football is that there are many other fans out there who believe the Committee got it right in 2023. The controversies and debates that are unique to college football are a large part of the sport's mystique.

The reality is that the criteria by which teams are selected for inclusion in the CFP, regardless of size, will always remain a matter of intense debate. Should it be the teams that are surmised to have the best chance of winning a playoff game on a neutral field? Should it be the teams that are determined to be the most deserving based on resumé? Should it be some combination of the two? Using a mathematical model, I am able to generate an objective answer for both approaches.

If you are reading this, it is safe to assume you are a fan of college football. Every fan has an origin story that sparked his or her fandom. Mine begins before I can even remember, was cultivated during my formative years, and was solidified during the 2007 season, which, for me, is the single greatest college football season of my lifetime. Over the course of the 2007 regular season, a ranked team lost to a lower-ranked or unranked opponent 62 times. Top 10 teams lost 29 times. The No. 1 ranked team lost four times. The No. 2

ranked team lost seven times. On three occasions, the No. 1 and No. 2 ranked teams both lost in the same week. And it culminated with LSU becoming the first team in college football history (and still the only one) to be declared national champions with two losses. "The Year of the Upset," as it became known, cemented college football as my favorite sport in perpetuity. The permanent setup in my home features a basement wall with five televisions. Every College Football Saturday, I have all five televisions showing games from noon Eastern time until well after midnight—it truly is an obsession for me.

In 2019, I took my obsession to the next level and created kfordratings.com. Every week during the college football season, I publish my own opponent- and tempo-adjusted college football power ratings, which I call the KFordRatings. There are many college football rating systems in existence, most notably Bill Connelly's SP+ and Brian Fremeau's FEI. To me, Bill and Brian are the godfathers of college football predictive analytics, and their work has paved the way for many others, including myself, to attempt to build on their findings. My KFordRatings are presented on a points per game above or below the Football Bowl Subdivision (FBS) average scale, and they are designed to be purely predictive, or forward-looking. In other words, the KFordRatings can be used to project by how many points Team A would be expected to be favored against Team B on a neutral field if they played tomorrow. But predictive metrics like the KFordRatings are only one piece of the puzzle. To get a sense of the bigger picture, we need a way to quantify a team's resumé. Using the power ratings as the engine, I can generate something I call "Most Deserving Rankings."

My Most Deserving Rankings are just that: a ranking of the most deserving FBS college football teams based solely on what they have accomplished on the football field in the current season. They are a results-oriented, or resumé-based, measure of how a team has performed against its schedule—including scoring margin—relative to how the average Top-25 FBS team would be expected to perform against that same schedule. The inspiration for this ranking system came from ESPN's Strength of Record metric. But unlike Strength of Record, my Most Deserving Rankings also incorporate a team's scoring margin relative to what would be expected of the average Top-25 FBS team given the schedule.

Using predictive analytics like the KFordRatings and descriptive metrics like the Most Deserving Rankings, we can better understand the strength and accomplishments of every college football team. By no means do these two values alone tell the full story of a team. Given my background and specific skill set, numbers are the lens through which I have chosen to initially view college football teams. They provide us a starting point for the conversations and debates that inevitably take place each season.

But conversations and debates in college football are not confined to singular seasons. Want to rile up a group of college football fans? Ask them which team was better: 2019 LSU or 2001 Miami (FL)? 2004 USC or 1995 Nebraska? And then just sit back and enjoy the show. In this book, Michael takes it a step further. He doesn't just pose the question; he takes you on a journey into one of the most hotly contested debates in all of sports: which college football team since 1980 has been the best of all?

As a college football fan, I certainly have an opinion on this topic. And naturally, I lean on my historical numbers, which have been converted from a points-per-game scale to a percentile ranking, as a starting point. Before I dive into Michael's Legendary Bowl bracket, I would be remiss if I did not mention that 1971 Nebraska grades out as the "best" college football team of all time, according to my historical ratings, outranking more than 14,000 other teams with a KFordRating percentile rank of 99.9. While I often simplify this by saying, "1971 Nebraska is the 'best' college football team of all time, per my ratings," it would be more accurate to say, "In 1971, Nebraska was more dominant against the rest of college football than any other team has ever been, per my ratings." That said, due to the differences in the sport from the early 1970s compared to today, it is reasonable to use 1980 as the cutoff for this exercise, as Michael has done.

So, which college football teams have been the most dominant relative to the rest of the field since 1980, per my historical ratings? I simulated the bracket to find out! Overall, I must say that Michael's selection and seeding are closely correlated with my historical ratings. The lowest seed in my Sweet 16 is a 5-seed. My Elite 8 is comprised exclusively of 1-, 2-, and 3-seeds. My simulated Final Four pits 2005 Texas against 2018 Clemson on the left side of the bracket and 2001 Miami (FL) against 2004 USC on the right side of the bracket. My championship game features 2018 Clemson defeating 2004 USC for the Legendary Bowl title. The talk going into the 2018 National Championship Game was how Alabama was on pace to be one of the best teams in college football history. Clemson proceeded to beat the Crimson Tide 44–16, establishing themselves among the all-time greatest teams to ever play the game.

College football is a uniquely American game. And in my judgment, it is the greatest sport known to mankind. As long as we, the fans, the lifeblood of the sport, continue to be passionate about our teams, our rivalries and our traditions, the controversies and debates are sure to rage on well into the 12-team College Football Playoff era and beyond. I look forward to enjoying this journey together.

Author's Note

As a college football fanatic, I wrote this book with three main audiences in mind. The first group includes anyone who has fallen deeply, madly, and hopelessly in love with a college football team. It could be the first team you laid eyes on or the one that you watched when you were in college. Maybe it was your alma mater's best team in program history. Perhaps you had a personal connection with a player or made a cross-country road trip to watch your school in a bowl game. For whatever reason, this team meant the world to you. And unlike the NFL, where a single player like Tom Brady or Patrick Mahomes can provide their fans with multiple shots at a title, the window for greatness in college is very small. In many cases, that perfect window opens for just one season. The potential, the pressure, the raw energy that surrounds a team in the midst of a dream season was once summed up by former college football media personality Elika Sadeghi in this way: "How do people who don't watch college football know what it's like to simultaneously feel alive and like you want to die?"

This book is also for anyone who has embraced the pageantry, the traditions, and the unforgettable moments that make this sport unlike any other on earth. You may not live and die with a single school, but you're keenly aware of the gravitational pull of this crazy game. And you're happy to go along for the ride each autumn.

And finally, this book was designed for anyone who loves to debate sports. College football, since the very beginning, has always been a sport that's been hotly debated. From the 1960s—with 100+ schools playing 10 to 12 games each—until the final season of the original four-team College Football Playoff, where 133 teams played as many as 15 games in a season, the mathematics of scheduling never aligned. As a result, the sport struggled for generations to get the best teams on the field to face off against one another on a yearly basis. In the 1970s alone, 15 different teams claimed national titles. And the debates extended beyond individual teams to questions of regional power, of conference supremacy, and the whims of media rankings from the likes of the UPI and AP. Since its creation, college football has been a convoluted and messy sport to discuss.

As a result, there has always been this lingering feeling of "what if"—what if a team had gotten one more call or bounce of the ball in their favor, or if their star quarterback hadn't gotten hurt, or if their head coach hadn't left for another job before the bowl game? The sport is riddled with these "what ifs."

And unlike other sports, college football has always placed a premium on résumé building and defending. It's not just your final record and the pure math of it; it's about who you played, how you played against them, the style points, the creativity, and the brand of football you play.

This book adds one more dimension to the mix—it stretches across eras. Few debates are more enjoyable than those comparing Michael Jordan to LeBron James. The problem with these debates (much like the one we'll discuss in this book) is: How do you match up schools and players from different eras? Were they as physically imposing? Were the offenses simpler or more complex? This book will pair them up, head-to-head, and showcase what would happen in these hypothetical situations. Because all these debates—whether they occur in barbershops, on television, or just among friends—usually end at an impasse. Simply put, these debates deserve better than to end in a draw. After all, college football hasn't settled for those since 1995, so why should we?

This book gives you genuine results from a process that is as impartial, fair, and balanced as possible. This isn't an algorithm spitting out the average of 10,000 simulations. ChatGPT wasn't consulted. In this book, you'll have the opportunity to experience teams from yesteryear actually playing against one another. Each game will be accompanied by expansive write-ups and box scores detailing the action. And that is going to hopefully spur even more debate and arguments. But at the end of the day, we've dusted off these old teams and created new data points. You're going to experience something that's brand new.

Additionally, it's important to clarify what this book is not. It's not a ranking of the best 68, 75, or 100 teams of all time. While there are many excellent books on these topics, and I encourage readers to explore them, our focus here is different. We're offering a unique opportunity on the virtual gridiron that's never existed before. To put it another way, while many books simply arrange and rank teams of yesteryear like a showroom full of antique cars, we're taking them out for a spin.

Within these pages, you'll hopefully find tributes to your favorite team. The nostalgia factor here is designed to envelop you like a warm blanket. Whether your team won the national championship, pulled off a shocking upset, or launched a single player into superstardom, that team and its players hold a special significance for you. Collectively, they were more than just a team; they helped capture the nation's imagination and provided a moment in time when your school was considered the center of the college football universe. The late Bobby Bowden once said, "College football is the front porch of your university." This is your chance to see your school through that lens once more.

For many, college football or basketball is the primary way they interact with a school. Whether at a tailgate, inside the stadium, or watching on television, fans get to witness the pageantry, the unadulterated excitement, and the energy that radiates from this wonderful game. This buzz, for lack of a better word, reflects positively on the school and, by extension, its alumni and supporters. This deep connection is why people hold such fondness for their teams. This book aims to rekindle the magic created by these players, teams, and coaches by giving them a deserved second spotlight.

Now, one of the first questions I'm often asked is, "Why 68 teams?" In my opinion, March Madness—despite not always identifying the absolute best team on a yearly basis in a single-elimination tournament—certainly maximizes entertainment, excitement, and accessibility. That's the inspiration here. I've adopted that format, including four play-in games, so that once we enter the bracket officially, there are 64 teams, 16 in each region. We'll narrow it down to the final four, the final two, and then crown a champion of the book with a single winner.

Do I genuinely believe a 15-seed could win the entire tournament? As someone striving for impartiality from the start, no. However, I do think such a team could win a game or challenge a top seed, just as we see every spring during March Madness. Once the matchups are set and the games begin, upsets are inevitable. You're going to see outcomes that, at least on paper, seem improbable. And that's just a normal March Madness. In this case, every single team in the field is exceptional in some way, shape, or form. In a lot of cases, we have special quarterbacks who were able to pull rabbits out of their hats time and time again. When you put players like this in a situation against the top seed, there's always a chance for some magic to happen—in this case, an upset.

For the process of picking the teams, I consulted metrics like Sports Reference's SRS rating system and Bill Connolly's SP+ rating systems over the years, which have evolved. I dug through NCAA season-by-season record books, which in recent years have been digitized. But when I went back into the '90s and the '80s, I was literally looking at Xerox copies as though they were the Pentagon Papers. Having access to all this information has been great, and it's led me in the right direction, starting with some of the obvious teams at the very top of the bracket. As for the double-digit seeds, I leaned on articles, books and beat writers, and I stood on the shoulders of great college football historians to guide my way.

When it came to tiebreakers, I often looked for teams that were particularly dominant or had special qualities on at least one side of the ball. Did they run a unique offense? Was there a defensive mastermind calling the plays from the sideline? How did they fare in close games? These were some of the deciding factors that helped me navigate the selection process.

I also made the decision to limit each school to one entry, so you won't find six or seven of Nick Saban's teams in this field.

The Ratings & Simulation Process

> **Tournament Results Generated Through NCAA Football 14 On PlayStation 3**
> **Every Roster Reflects Real-Life Team Composition**
> **Playbooks Calibrated To Reflect Offensive & Defensive Schemes**
> **Coaches Edited To Reflect Conservative/Aggressive Decision-Making Style**
> **Weather, Injuries, Player Ejections, All Included In Simulations**

The legitimacy of this book is rooted in the player rating methodology. I developed a custom rating system for each individual player—all 4,760 who made the field. As a frame of reference, we're simulating this through EA Sports' NCAA Football 14 on PlayStation 3—the last game made in the series before it was sunsetted. We're still awaiting the return of the video game series in the summer of 2024. The 11-year-old game proved to be incredibly useful, as many enthusiasts have kept it alive through custom integrations and updates to both the gameplay and rosters.

My ratings system was a hybrid of many that came before it, leveraging work done by the community on a website called *Operation Sports*. Here, I started with a custom conversion chart for high school recruiting ratings. For teams modern enough to have recruiting ratings for their players, I converted these ratings based on measurables like the 40-yard dash, the number of reps on the 225 bench press, and players' three-cone drill performance.

Beyond this, I considered in-season success for the particular year being examined, including accolades and national awards won. Additionally, if those players had completed their professional careers in the NFL, this provided a gauge for their potential, alongside their collegiate achievements, to inform their ratings.

The older the team, the more comprehensive and objective the rating could be. For instance, backups who might not have seen much field time in 1984 but were in the NFL by 1988 demonstrated potential that was not evident from their college playing time alone.

Therefore, ratings were based on available measurables, in-season success, statistical achievements, awards, and professional prospects, with a reliance on the discernment of NFL scouts and teams for their evaluation of potential. Using conversion charts and detailed analysis, I aimed to assemble a roster that was as accurate as possible. The entire process took five to six hours per team. Hundreds of hours of detailed work transformed these virtual rosters into near carbon copies of their real-life counterparts.

In the end, we were left with a scoring system rated out of 99 for overall performance, offense, and defense.

Now, here are a few notes on the gameplay. As mentioned, we utilize EA Sports' NCAA Football 14 on the PlayStation 3. For anyone who's played it, you're likely aware that simulating head-to-head matchups can introduce some glitches and issues. One notable problem is play-calling; without adjustments, the AI tends to favor screen passes disproportionately. To address this, I meticulously created custom playbooks for all 68 teams in the field, ensuring more realistic play-calling. Additionally, I adjusted the quarter length from the standard 15 minutes (used in all NCAA football games) to 10 minutes. This adjustment was intended to help generate the most realistic data in terms of overall plays, yardage, and points per game. It was painstaking, but over time, I was able to calibrate it finely so that point totals, plays, and outcomes were plausible. Going from 15 minutes to 10 minutes helped accomplish that.

Moreover, setting up each individual team, from player ratings to their custom playbooks, took 6 to 7 hours. This process also involved watching full games from the past. For example, while I was historically familiar with the 1984 BYU team, I hadn't actually watched any of their games. I ended up viewing six of their games on YouTube to better understand their play-calling tendencies, defensive sub-packages, and offensive strategies, particularly which players were targeted more frequently. This depth of research was applied to each team, aiming to ensure the most realistic outcomes possible.

Before running the simulations for the first time, I dedicated tens of hours to fine-tuning the settings. This prevented unrealistic scores on both ends of the spectrum. Such as a high-scoring offense winning a game 10-7 or a defensive-minded team winning a game 63-56. This meticulous calibration gave every team in our field of 68 the best chance for an accurate representation both in victory and defeat.

Finally, the last pieces of human intervention required came from the officiating and special teams front. In addition to the rules hard-wired into the game, I added in targeting penalties that we regularly see called each and every Saturday in the fall. As I sat and watched each simulation, I would consult the replay if a hit on a quarterback looked overly aggressive or if a player was hurt as a result of a big hit. According to the NCAA rule book, *"no player shall initiate contact and target an opponent with the crown (top) of his helmet."* The NCAA also has special protections for defenseless players. If the video replay revealed targeting by that definition, I would award the opposing team 15 yards and an automatic first down while ejecting the offending player.

As for special teams, anyone who has ever played the game can tell you that it's nearly impossible to achieve three separate feats: blocking field goals, blocking punts, and recovering onside kicks. If the game's AI were allowed to simulate these scenarios, we would have seen zero blocked kicks and an onside recovery rate below five percent. To increase the likelihood of these events, I would jump in as a player on the defensive team each time a kick or punt was attempted. As a result, over the course of 67 games, I blocked a handful of kicks (FGs, XPs), three punts, and recovered roughly 10% of all onside kick attempts. This was more in line with actual success rates and added to the realism of the simulations.

Emotional Disclaimer

This is a crucial message for anyone reading this book: your team is almost assuredly going to lose. In any given year, almost every team in college football loses. And keep in mind, that's against a mixed bag of lowly, average and slightly above average competition. Even the very best teams that go on to win national championships may only face three or four top-ten opponents in a given year. In our field of 68, there are no cream puffs, no doormats, no "little sisters of the poor." From top to bottom, this bracket is filled with legendary teams. It might seem almost sacrilegious to critique the 2001 Miami Hurricanes, but I'm going to use them as a guiding reference here to illustrate how closely matched these teams are. The 2001 Hurricanes are viewed, in my opinion, as the odds-on favorite to win. And you'll discover later in the book why I believe that. Their performance against these other teams will certainly stand out. But even the Miami Hurricanes, in 2001, had a game where they failed to score an offensive touchdown (against Boston College in November). Leading 12–7 in the closing seconds, it was only a red zone interception, lateraled to Ed Reed and returned for a touchdown, that prevented their loss to an 8–4 Boston College team. That's how close a legendary team in our book came to losing to a decidedly regular team.

USC, another No. 1 seed in this book (from 2004), won three games by 6 points or less in that year. They narrowly defeated Stanford by 3 on the road. Aaron Rodgers and California nearly nipped them at the Coliseum. Even their rival UCLA, who was not having a great season, put USC on upset alert. With under a minute to go, leading by just 5, USC staved off disaster by intercepting UCLA on the final drive of the game.

My point with this emotional disclaimer is that anything can happen in this book. It's wise to prepare yourself emotionally and mentally before turning the pages to face the outcomes because even the best teams are vulnerable to defeat. Winning six consecutive games against legendary competition is a daunting task.

Why I Wanted To Write This Book

I grew up in the suburbs of Philadelphia, a region fiercely loyal to professional sports teams. To my knowledge, this area was among the first to adopt 24/7 sports talk radio programming. So, debates weren't confined to just the hours before and after a game; they occurred year-round. The Philadelphia Eagles, in particular, were a topic of endless discussion. Fans debated not only the upcoming season or recent performances but also legacies: How does this team rank against the very best? Where does this player belong in history? This culture of framing teams, players, and coaches in a historical context was ingrained in me from a very young age.

If you wanted to be a part of that, you needed to come with receipts, so to speak—whether you wanted to call into the show or even just debate my father in the car. You couldn't just say, "Well, that's what I think," or "I have a gut feeling." You had to have something to back it up from a statistical perspective.

There is one other element of my sports upbringing of note. Even though I was brought up in Philadelphia's blender of sports passion and enthusiasm—and vitriol at times—I was raised by two New Yorkers. They had a love for New York teams, so there wasn't any pressure inside my household to live or die with the Phillies, Sixers, Flyers or Eagles. In a way, it gave me permission to be impartial and enjoy the bigger picture of sports.

The way in which my mother enjoys sports is a great example of this. She has a deep, abiding love for March Madness. She is not just pulling for a single team; she loves the event as a whole. As a corporate lawyer for over 40 years, working six days a week, she reserved the first Thursday and Friday of March Madness as her days off every year. She'd immerse herself in brackets, roping my father and me into her office pool. We would fill out picks together, discussing strategies and predictions, ensuring we chose the right upsets, including the famed 12–5 matchup.

Seeing my mother's passion for March Madness from a very early age made the event special to me. Her love for the game and the competition—not just on the court but also against her coworkers, and in our case, competing against my father and me—left a lasting impression.

On the other side, I had my late father, whose sports life can only be described as charmed. He was a "greatness magnet," having witnessed some of the most remarkable moments in sports history. At seven years old, he was present at Don Larson's perfect game in the 1956 World Series. He recounted that if you had asked him afterward how the game was, he would have said, "It was pretty boring. The Yankees won 3–0, and there were barely any hits!"

At that age, he couldn't fully appreciate the rarity of the event, something that had never happened before and hasn't happened since. Fast forward to 1992, he was there to see Christian Laettner's game-winning shot for Duke against Kentucky in the Elite Eight, arguably the greatest moment in sports history. And to add a cherry on top, he witnessed Derek Jeter's 3,000th hit in person. His knack for being there in big sports moments was downright Forrest Gumpian. If there was an iconic moment, there's a chance he was in the background.

In American sports culture, there's pressure to never be seen as a bandwagon or fair-weather fan. You're expected to live and die with your team. My father certainly checked this box with the New York Yankees. He subscribed to the Major League Baseball television package so he wouldn't miss a single game. But in our house, there was more "appointment television" than just his Yankees. He was fascinated by the greats, from Secretariat to Wayne Gretzky to Michael Jordan, making sure never to miss an opportunity to watch them and often engaging in debates about their legacies and places in the pantheon of sports. This led to us watching and debating the very best in every sport just as much as we watched "our" teams. Looking back, my childhood was filled with these G.O.A.T (greatest of all time) arguments long before they were viewed as "hot takes" or "clickbait."

Critically, my father also instilled in me a deep love for college football. In the Philly area, the focus is squarely on the Eagles. College football plays second banana to the big, bad NFL. But in our house, college football was *the* major event. Every Saturday, we would wake up early, watch College GameDay, and debate who we thought was going to play for the national title that year.

When I was introduced to college football at a very early age—during the pre-BCS era—there was no assurance that the top two teams would even play each other. Nor was there any guarantee that, by the end of the year, there'd be any consensus on who was the best team. For much of the '70s, '80s, and into the '90s, it was not uncommon to have split national champions. This required an emotional adjustment to the fact that, to a large extent, one watches for the love of the game. Winning your conference was a significant achievement. Defeating your rival held special meaning. The regionalism, which has since been diluted by national TV coverage, meant that if you were in the Deep South, you followed the ACC or the SEC, with the primary goal being to beat your neighboring teams.

This was the sports environment in which I was raised, and I absolutely adore the idea that *any* team could have a special season. For instance, Iowa went to the Orange Bowl in 2002, just two years removed from a horrific 3-9 campaign. That dream season didn't come with any national championship hype. In fact, the Hawkeyes lost to their rival, Iowa State, in the third game of that season. That loss essentially barred them from national title contention. Yet, that entire year was about winning the Big Ten, overcoming the major powers in their conference, and finishing undefeated in league play. They upset nationally-ranked Penn State on the road in overtime and destroyed Michigan in "The Big House" by 25 points. That team remains a beacon for students who were on campus at the time or anyone who has ever rooted for Iowa. It's "that" team that they point to and maintain a deep connection with. Mention the names Bob Sanders, Dallas Clark, or Brad Banks to an Iowa fan, and you're sure to put a smile on their face. And that's what I appreciate: it's not just Super Bowl or bust, where there's one winner and 31 losers. In college football, there's room for a team to have a special year without it being at the expense of everyone else.

Many of the teams featured in my book won the national title, shared a portion of it, went undefeated, or are viewed as among the greatest in college football history. While that's significant, this book casts a wider net. It's not solely about the national champions, the All-Americans, the Heisman Trophy winners, or the College Football Hall of Fame inductees. It also celebrates the unsung heroes, the monumental upsets, and those moments where, for one night, you stood at the epicenter of the college football universe because you achieved an unexpected victory or something truly remarkable.

After nearly 30 years of avidly following college football, I feel I've earned the right to moderate this debate, especially as someone without a singular, diehard team allegiance. I attended Loyola University Maryland in Baltimore (a school without college football) and spent a year at the University of Missouri, where I briefly worked as a student assistant for the football team. My love for football has always driven me to be involved, whether through coaching in high school, assisting a seventh-grade football team, covering the sport in college, or engaging in full-time or freelance sports journalism post-graduation. I've contributed to *The New York Post*, *TheScore*, *USA Today*, and *The Action Network*, and appeared on ESPN Radio, covering everything from smaller schools to the powerhouse programs of the SEC.

Throughout my life, I've strived to maintain neutrality in covering the sport, a task made easier by my deep love for the game. Whether it's a Thursday night Sun Belt game or the national championship, I approach every matchup with equal interest, believing that something special can happen every time you watch a college football game. With the NCAA Football 14 video game powering our virtual tournament, I'm confident we'll witness something extraordinary here too.

The last point I want to make is that I've always aimed to be involved with college football in some capacity. My motivation was to find a way to engage with the sport as a writer, commentator, bettor, fantasy/video game player, and simply as a fan who has attended games at 34 separate stadiums across the country. Being part of college football, in my own way, has always been important to me, and writing this book is yet another way I'm extending that connection.

Here is my Legendary Bowl bracket: The Free Gifts version will allow you to visualize the entire tournament in a glance. Scan the QR code to download:

Tournament Bracket

CHAPTER ONE

68 Team Overview (Team Capsules)

'95-Nebraska '19-LSU Tigers
'04-USC Trojans '01-Miami Hurricanes

1 Seeds

1995 Nebraska Cornhuskers

The Cornhuskers ran roughshod over every team they faced in 1995, becoming the only school in the modern era of college football to win every game by two or more touchdowns. When you factor in their blowout of Florida in the Fiesta Bowl, NU finished the year averaging over 400 yards per game on the ground at a clip of 7 yards per carry. Speaking of Nebraska's 62–24 whipping of UF, it was the largest margin of victory for a No. 1 over a No. 2 since Army shut out Notre Dame 48–0 at Yankee Stadium in 1945. Tommie Frazier finished second in the Heisman race, and nine of the team's 22 starters received All-American honors (first, second, third or honorable mention). In total, 27 players would appear on NFL rosters in the coming years. Tom Osborne's stars shone the brightest when facing top competition, walloping the four top-ten teams they faced that season by an average of 30 points per game. You couldn't run on them (2.5 ypc allowed), and opposing quarterbacks completed less than half of their attempts when facing the

Blackshirts. How's this for dominance? The entire season, the Huskers only trailed for 13 minutes and 47 seconds. Despite being a run-heavy offense, they put together scoring flurries with regularity. In 11 of the Huskers' 12 games in 1995, they scored 27 unanswered points. The Nebraska offensive line didn't give up a sack all season long, and only committed six penalties in 12 games. And when it came to consistency, there wasn't a more tried-and-true stalwart than Coach Osborne. Starting as an assistant in 1964, Osborne was a part of the program as a coach, assistant AD, and Athletic Director for 49 years. In that time, he amassed 255 wins as a head coach, three national titles in a four-year span, and oversaw Big Red's move to the Big Ten.

> Record: 12–0 (7–0) | SP+ Rankings OFF: 1st | DEF: 7th
> Record Against Ranked Opponents: 4–0, 196–73 Point Differential

2001 Miami Hurricanes

To quote Dan Le Batard, the 2001 Miami Hurricanes' roster was a "nuclear absurdity." To put their athleticism into perspective, multiple Canes competed on the school's track and field team and appeared at Big East Championship events, including Andre Johnson (100m), Daryl Jones (100m/200m Dash, 4x100m Relay), Willis McGahee (100m), Clinton Portis (200m), Ed Reed (Triple Jump, Javelin), and Vince Wilfork (Shot Put). Seventeen players went on to become first-round NFL Draft picks. As for their on-field exploits in the 2001 season, the Hurricanes were out for vengeance after getting shortchanged by the BCS computers the previous year. In response, Miami obliterated ranked opponents, winning by an average margin of 32.8 ppg. The Canes led the nation in turnover margin, scoring defense, and non-offensive touchdowns with a mind-numbing 11 on the season. Had the Canes failed to score a single offensive touchdown all season long, they still would have won eight games by virtue of their non-offensive TDs, field goals, and safeties. Ken Dorsey won the Maxwell and Bryant McKinnie won the Outland. Five others were finalists for major awards, and Larry Coker took home the Bear Bryant Coach of the Year honor. At the time of publication, Ed Reed and Andre Johnson are already in the NFL Hall of Fame, and it's likely that teammates Frank Gore and Vince Wilfork will be joining them in the next few years. Given their depth, skill position talent, and ball-hawking defense, the Hurricanes enter the tournament as the odds-on favorite to win.

> Record: 12–0 (7–0) | SP+ Rankings OFF: 2nd | DEF: 1st
> Record Against Ranked Opponents: 5–0, 236–72 Point Differential

2004 USC Trojans

Pete Carroll and recruiting coordinator Ed Orgeron assembled a cast star-studded enough for Hollywood. Carroll also served as the Trojans' defensive coordinator, while offensive coordinator Norm Chow pulled the strings of one of the most explosive offenses ever led by an under-center quarterback. The result was a team with zero appreciable weaknesses. Their regular season highlight came in the Coliseum against seventh-ranked Cal, led by Aaron Rodgers. With the game on the line, leading 23–17, the Trojans forced three incompletions and sacked Rodgers once on the final four plays in the red zone, sealing the win and protecting their perfect season. By season's end, six Trojans received All-American honors, Matt Leinart won the Heisman Trophy, and USC waxed No. 2 Oklahoma in the Orange Bowl 55–19 (a game that didn't even feel that close). Southern California became just the second school in college football history to win wire-to-wire, and it did it in style. The defense was top-ranked against the run (79.4 ypg) and led the nation in takeaways with a staggering 38 in 13 games. That fall was also Reggie Bush's coming out party. The Trojans' Swiss Army Knife accounted for 2,330 all-purpose yards and 15 total touchdowns, finishing sixth in the Heisman voting.

> Record: 13–0 (8–0) | SP+ Rankings OFF: 4th | DEF: 4th
> Record Against Ranked Opponents: 3–0, 123–43 Point Differential

2019 LSU Tigers

It's nearly impossible to construct a better offense than what the Bayou Bengals put on the field in the fall of 2019. A Broyles Award-winning coach was the architect behind an offense that featured the Joe Moore Award-winning offense line that blocked for the Heisman Trophy winner who threw to a pair of future Pro Bowl wide receivers. And when Joe Burrow wasn't picking apart opposing secondaries, Clyde Edwards-Helaire was finding the sledding easy running into sub-packages (1,867 total yards, 17 total TDs). Defensively, LSU wasn't perfect under Dave Aranda, but it was disruptive on the back end, leading the nation in pass breakups and finishing fifth in interceptions. Grant Delpit took home the Thorpe Award, and Derek Stingley Jr. became the first true freshman consensus All-American as a position player since Adrian Peterson in 2004. But there's no escaping what made this team truly terrifying, and that was Burrow's unshakable confidence in big games. The Tigers averaged 42.5 points per game against ranked opponents, and in those games, Burrow accounted for 30 total touchdowns against just three turnovers. The Tigers' Heisman Trophy winner now holds two single-season FBS records: touchdowns responsible for (65) and total yards (6,040). In the end, LSU left absolutely zero doubt, becoming the first team in college football history to defeat all of the preseason top four while finishing a sterling 7–0 against top-ten opponents.

> Record: 15–0 (8–0) | OFF: SP+ Rankings OFF: 2nd | DEF: 16th
> Record Against Ranked Opponents: 7–0, 298–190 Point Differential

2 Seeds

2005 Texas Longhorns

Vince Young is the undisputed king of the Rose Bowl, having led back-to-back fourth-quarter comebacks in Pasadena. In addition to his big game heroics, his 2005 campaign marked the first time in college football history that a quarterback threw for over 3,000 yards and rushed for over 1,000 yards in the same season. And keep in mind, Young barely played in the fourth quarter in 2005 because UT blew out so many opponents. Thanks to the Horns' shotgun zone-read attack, Young is the only player in FBS history to rush for 200 yards and pass for 200 yards in the same game twice in the same season (OK State, USC). But this wasn't just the Vince Young show; Mack Brown made sure that VY was surrounded by elite talent. Between 2002 (Vince Young's signing class) and 2005, Brown signed eight five-star recruits and 43 four-star recruits. By 2005, those recruits had blossomed into five All-Americans and nine First Team All-Big 12 performers. The Longhorns' offense averaged north of 50 points per game and was only held below 40 points once the entire season (at Ohio State, Week 2). They became the first team to score 650 points in a single season while ranking in the top four in both passing efficiency and pass-efficiency defense. In the preseason, Coach Brown coined the slogan, "Take Dead Aim." Both Brown and his team were taking aim at the USC Trojans, who entered the 2005 season as the runaway favorite to win the title. And much like the Miami Hurricanes in 2001, Texas played with a chip on their shoulder in pursuit of a national championship. Texas obliterated five opponents by 40 or more points and capped its season with an upset of the aforementioned Trojans, a team that at the time was considered the greatest ever. That snapped USC's 34-game win streak and secured Young's place in college football history.

> Record: 13–0 (8–0) | SP+ Rankings OFF: 2nd | DEF: 11th
> VY 4th Qtrs vs. Ohio State/USC: 15 for 23 for 182 Yds, TD |
> 60 Rushing Yds, 2 TDs

2013 Florida State Seminoles

As a redshirt freshman, Jameis Winston was tasked with reviving a dormant dynasty in Tallahassee. Famous Jameis proved more than capable from the very first game (25 for 27, 356 yards, 4 TDs) and never looked back. It helped that he was surrounded by stars. All 22 of Florida State's starters in 2013 made an NFL roster. Roberto Aguayo, the Noles placekicker, won the Groza Award and became a second-round NFL Draft pick. And even their punter had a cup of coffee in the league before getting cut by the Tampa Bay Buccaneers. It was a complete team led by a Heisman-winning quarterback. The result was 723 points (51.6 ppg) and an average margin of victory of 41.8 points per game when facing FBS opponents. The Seminoles embarrassed ranked opponents by nearly 34 points per game and held half of their competition to 7 points or less. And when Florida State finally faced adversity in the final BCS National Championship Game, the Noles proved up to the task, erasing an 18-point deficit and winning the game in the closing seconds. It was the largest comeback in BCS title game history, putting an end to Auburn's magical season in the process. Seventeen Seminoles received All-ACC honors, 10 made All-American teams, two won major national awards (Heisman, Groza), and Jimbo Fisher won the AFCA Coach of the Year. The Seminoles are one of seven teams in our field to finish a season ranked in the top five in both offensive and defensive rankings, according to ESPN's Bill Connelly.

> Record: 14–0 (8–0) | SP+ Rankings OFF: 3rd | DEF: 3rd
> Jameis Winston's Passing Stats When Tied Or Trailing: 71.8%, 9.9 YPA, 10 TDs, 1 INT

2020 Alabama Crimson Tide

While many teams simply survived the strange and unprecedented COVID season, the Crimson Tide thrived. Alabama's offense was exceptional, from its personnel to its statistical accomplishments. Four of the Tide's five starters along the Joe Moore Award-winning offensive line were drafted into the pros. Three skill position starters went on to become first-round picks in the 2021 NFL Draft (Harris, Smith, Waddle), and John Metchie III and Brian Robinson Jr. went in the second and third rounds, respectively, the following year. On the field in 2020, Alabama executed Steve Sarkisian's offense flawlessly, piling up 48.5 points and 541.8 yards per game. Mac Jones finished with the highest PFF grade in the CFP era and set the NCAA record for passing efficiency in a season (since surpassed by Coastal Carolina's Grayson McCall [2021] and LSU's Jayden Daniels [2023]). The Tide converted third downs at the highest percentage since 2006 (58.9%), and they got on teams early, leading the nation in first-half points (29.4). Just for good measure, Alabama was unflappable on special teams (13th in SP+), thanks to a perfect season from Will Reichard (14/14 FGs) and explosive punt returning courtesy of DeVonta Smith (21.5 ypr). Its defense was solid through and through, finishing in the top 20 in both scoring and run defense, forced fumbles, passes defended, and red zone scoring. This was Saban's second-highest-rated team in terms of overall SP+ ranking, finishing a hair behind his 2012 squad.

> Record: 13–0 (10–0) | SP+ Rankings OFF: 1st | DEF: 15th
> Mac Jones Led The Nation In QBR (96.1), YPA (11.2),
> And Completion Percentage (77.4%)

2021 Georgia Bulldogs

Every single starter and six reserves on the Georgia defense heard their names at the NFL Draft either in 2022, 2023 or 2024. Six of the Dawgs' defensive starters in 2021 became first-round selections, coming up one shy of the all-time record (7-'01 Miami FL). But UGA wasn't just an all-star team on defense—it was a well-oiled machine. According to Jonathan Shapiro, a writer for *Dawg Post*, if you removed all the "garbage-time" points allowed by UGA when its starters had been pulled and factored in the points scored by the Dawgs' defense and special teams, the Bulldogs' defense allowed a net of just 3.7 points per game in 2021. In 15 games, the Georgia defense gave up three rushing touchdowns (2nd), just 5.6 yards per pass attempt (2nd), and fielded the best red zone defense since Alabama in 2011, with opponents scoring on just 62.5% of their opportunities. On offense, Stetson Bennett seemed to save his best for the Dawgs' biggest games, posting an 82.9 QBR against ranked opponents. According to ESPN Analytics, Alabama had a 71.6% chance of beating Georgia with 8:53 remaining in the national title game. Bennett closed that game 4-for-4 for 83 yards and a touchdown. His go-ahead bomb to A. D. Mitchell halfway through the fourth quarter traveled 52 yards in the air, exorcizing 41 years of torment for Georgia fans as it did so.

> Record: 14–1 (8–0) | SP+ Rankings OFF: 4th | DEF: 1st
> Stetson Bennett Against Ranked Opponents: 13-to-2 TD–INT
> Ratio With A 9.2 YPA

3 Seeds

1991 Washington Huskies

Don James, aka "The Dawgfather," fielded one the most balanced and complete college football teams the sport has ever seen. The Huskies' famed eight-man front suffocated opposing rushing attacks, surrendering less than 6 feet per carry (1.9 yards). Six of those eight players up front were drafted into the NFL, including Outland and Lombardi Trophy winner Steve Emtman, who went first overall to Indianapolis. As a unit, Jim Lambright's defense finished top three nationally in takeaways, pass-efficiency allowed, scoring, and rushing defense. Offensively, UW averaged 41.9 points (2nd) and 471.9 yards (7th) per game behind a stellar running game and a big-play passing attack led by All-American receiver Mario Bailey. In total, four Huskies made All-American, and 28 players from this roster went on to the NFL. Dave Hoffmann, a starting inside linebacker for UW, who would go on to protect two U.S. Presidents as a member of the Secret Service, said it best: "At least defensively, we were going to go on a rampage, and we weren't going to stop until we were at the top of the mountain." Seven of the Huskies' 12 opponents failed to hit double digits, and they whipped conference opponents by an average margin of 30.5 points per game (Pac-10 Record). By season's end, the '91 Huskies had set 10 school records and secured a share of the national title by smoking Michigan in the Rose Bowl by 20 points.

Record: 12–0 (8–0) | SP+ Rankings OFF: 1st | DEF: 2nd
Steamroller: Washington Beat Four Opponents By 48+ points

1994 Penn State Nittany Lions

The '94 Nittany Lions rewrote the Penn State record books. Joe Paterno's offense scored 564 points (47 ppg) in 12 games. Kerry Collins won the Maxwell Award and finished fourth in the Heisman voting. Ki-Jana Carter fared even better in New York, ending up as the Heisman runner-up. Carter had a nose for the end zone, finishing the season with 1,695 yards and 26 touchdowns (including his MVP performance in the Rose Bowl). Bobby Engram won the Biletnikoff Award, and Kyle Brady earned All-American honors at tight end. Collins, Carter, and Brady became top-ten NFL Draft picks in 1995, and Engram came off the board in the second round of the '96 draft. Four of the Nittany Lions' five linemen were drafted into the NFL, including a pair of future All-Pro guards (Jeff Hartings, Marco Rivera). According to ESPN's Bill Connelly, the Nittany Lions and '95 Nebraska Cornhuskers were the only teams to field "perfect" offenses in the '90s (99.9 percentile). Even PSU's much-maligned defense saved its best performances for the big stage, holding ranked opponents to just 18 points per game. And just to add to the mystique of this team, Collins led a 96-yard game-winning drive against an elite Illinois defense, capping off a 21-point road comeback. Collins was 7-for-7 on the final drive and Penn State's fullback, Brian Milne, bullied his way into the end zone to preserve Paterno's final perfect season in Happy Valley.

Record: 12-0 (8-0) | SP+ Rankings OFF: 1st | DEF: 29th
Three Yards A Cloud Of Dust? PSU Scored 55+ Points in Five Games

1996 Florida Gators

Steve Spurrier's Fun 'n' Gun wasn't supposed to work in the rough-and-tumble SEC. The best teams in the SEC ran the ball effectively. When Spurrier arrived in Gainesville in 1989, the best passing team in the conference for much of the '80s had been Vanderbilt—which also, coincidentally, was the league's doormat. But Florida was no Vandy, and by 1996, the aerial show at The Swamp was must-watch TV. Danny Wuerffel was magnificent as Spurrier's triggerman, distributing the ball to Reidel Anthony, Ike Hilliard, and Jacquez Green. All three averaged over 18 yards per catch and struck fear into the opposition. By season's end, the Gators averaged 502 yards and 47 points per game. Defensively, they had an outstanding group of linebackers led by James Bates and a terror off the edge in redshirt freshman Jevon Kearse. The secondary featured three All-SEC performers and the defense as a whole was coached up by College Football Hall of Famer Bob Stoops. The Ol' Ball Coach put a hurting on the SEC, decimating conference opponents by 33 points per game. He even got the best of Peyton Manning and Tennessee at Neyland Stadium, knocking off the second-ranked Vols while ending Manning's Heisman campaign before it got started (4 INTs). And in the national title game, Spurrier's Gators looked unstoppable. They ran away from Florida State, 52–20, cementing a spot among college football's greatest teams.

Record: 12–1 (8–0) | SP+ Rankings OFF: 1st | DEF: 10th
Wuerffel Set SEC Single-Season Records in Passing Yards (3,625) And Touchdowns (39)

2018 Clemson Tigers

The Tigers became the first college football team to go 15–0 since Penn… in 1897. Like that ancient Penn team, Clemson led the nation in scoring defense (13.9 ppg). The Tigers' dominance started up front with their defensive line. Dubbed the Power Rangers, their line consisted of Christian Wilkins, Dexter Lawrence, Clelin Ferrell, and Austin Bryant. Wilkins, Lawrence, and Ferell would become first-round NFL Draft picks and Bryant a fourth-round pick after a *ho-hum* 15 TFL senior season. Five defenders in total made All-American teams in 2018, Isaiah Simmons wreaked havoc from his hybrid safety/linebacker position, and the Tigers bottled up a historically good Alabama offense in the national title game, holding the Tide 31 points below their season average. Offensively, Trevor Lawrence came of age as a true freshman on the national scene. Thrust into the starting lineup five games into the season, the 18-year-old slowly progressed before hitting his stride in the College Football Playoff. Against Notre Dame and Alabama, he was flawless, completing 66% of his passes while accounting for 707 total yards. Six passing touchdowns and no interceptions from Lawrence made a previously dominant Clemson team truly unbeatable. A star turn from fellow freshman Justyn Ross in the CFP (12/301/3) combined with the steady play of Travis Etienne and Tee Higgins rounded out one of the most ruthlessly efficient teams of all time.

Record: 15-0 (8-0) | SP+ Rankings OFF: 3rd | DEF: 10th
The Tigers Recorded 136 Tackles For Loss During The Season, An NCAA Record

4 Seeds

1988 Notre Dame Fighting Irish

A name you may not be familiar with when it comes to the '88 Irish is Vinny Cerrato. As ND's recruiting coordinator, he was responsible for bringing quarterback Tony Rice, wide receivers Ricky Watters and Rocket Ishmail, defensive tackle Chris Zorich, linebacker Mike Stonebreaker, and cornerback Todd Lyght to South Bend. In total, the 1988 Fighting Irish sent 34 players to the NFL (32 via the Draft). Their coaching staff was absolutely legendary. Head coach Lou Holtz and defensive coordinator Barry Alvarez are both in the College Football Hall of Fame. Four assistants in total went on to become D-1 head coaches. Joe Moore oversaw their offensive tackles and tight ends, and the Moore Award is now given annually to the nation's best college football offensive line. On the field in '88, the Fighting Irish knocked off four top-ten opponents, dismantling No. 2 USC and No. 3 West Virginia to end the season by a cumulative score of 61–31. But you can't discuss this team without mentioning their most iconic win, a 31–30 triumph over No. 1 Miami on October 15th, 1988. The game, dubbed "Catholics vs. Convicts," was one of the most anticipated collegiate sporting events of all time, and spawned books and documentaries. The Irish pulled off the upset and ended the Canes' 36-game regular season winning streak in the process. The ND defense was fierce (3rd in scoring) and featured three First Team All-Americans in the front seven (Stams, Zorich, Stonebreaker). Offensively, as a run-heavy team that often utilized the option, the Irish still averaged over 32 points per game while featuring game-breakers like Ricky Watters and future All-American Rocket Ismail. As a tandem, they scored four touchdowns in the return game.

Record: 12–0 | SP+ Rankings OFF: 8th | DEF: 7th
Lou Holtz Defeated Four College Football Hall Of Fame Coaches
(Mich., Miami, PSU, WVU)

1998 Tennessee Volunteers

Johnny Majors was hired away from Pitt, following his 1976 national championship with the Panthers. And despite winning 65% of his games, three SEC titles, and posting a record of 3–1 in major bowl games, Majors and the Tennessee program were seemingly always the bridesmaid, never the bride. When Phillip Fulmer took over, that narrative persisted, even as he upgraded the overall talent. A 42–10 record for Fulmer in his first five years had a Steve Spurrier-sized asterisk, as the Vols went winless against the Florida Gators between 1994 and 1997. Those losses came with Hall of Famer Peyton Manning at quarterback, so it was only natural that fans viewed Tee Martin and the '98 Vols as a stepping-stone team. What they got was an undefeated national champion that had a knack for pulling out close wins. The Vols won five one-possession games, four of those coming against ranked opponents. Tennessee's offense, led by the dual-threat Martin, bullied defenses with an elite running game that finished with the second-best yards per carry average (4.9) outside of the service academies. Offensive coordinator David Cutcliffe worked wonders with Martin, who matched Manning's adjusted yards per attempt average (8.5) during No. 16's Heisman runner-up season. Its defense was special, holding ranked opponents to just 17 points per game while ranking sixth against the run, 17th against the pass, and third in turnovers generated with 33. Linebackers Al Wilson (1st) and Raynoch Thompson (3rd) both received All-American honors, while Darwin Walker and Dwayne Goodrich were named to All-SEC teams. The Vols' special teams were anchored by All-SEC placekicker Jeff Hall, future NFL draft pick David Leaverton at punter, and Peerless Price on kick return (27.8 ypr, 1 TD). By season's end, the Vols had upset Donovan McNabb on the road, exercised their demons with an overtime win against No. 2 Florida, and upset Florida State in the very first BCS National Championship Game. This team's legacy grows with every passing year, evidenced by the buttons, shirts, and signs in and around Knoxville that read "It Feels Like '98" whenever Tennessee football is on the rise.

> Record: 13–0 (8–0) | SP+ Rankings OFF: 13th | DEF: 6th
> The Vols Won 3 Games By Scoring in The Final :30 Seconds or in Overtime

2010 Auburn Tigers

Many of the teams discussed in this book were loaded with All-Americans, future pros and legendary coaches. Auburn didn't need all of that. It had Cam Newton. Newton's teammates, on the offensive side of the ball, went on to start just one game, cumulatively, in the NFL. That was right tackle Brandon Mosley, who started once for the New York Giants. Newton was a one-man band, and boy, did he put on a show. He could have won the Heisman based on his rushing stats alone (1,473 yards, 20 TDs), but he was just as deadly through the air in 2010 (30 TDs, 10.2 ypa). Running Gus Malzahn's famed "Hurry-Up, No-Huddle" offense, defenses were powerless to slow down Newton and the Tigers. Auburn averaged 38 points per game... against ranked opponents. It ran it at a 6.12 yards per carry clip, one of the highest averages by an SEC program in modern history. Defensively, it was the Nick Fairley show. The dominant interior lineman took home the Lombardi Trophy and was named a consensus All-American. Three more defensive linemen would end up hearing their names at the NFL Draft in the coming years (Clayton, Lemonier, Ford). As for the rest of the defense, seven players signed contracts as undrafted free agents. Antoine Carter and Josh Bynes were named to the All-SEC second team, and Zac Etheridge received an honorable mention. Was Auburn a two-man team? Basically. Newton and Fairley had the ability to take over games, and they did just that. Newton put the Tigers on his back in big moments, running for 217 yards against LSU, scoring four touchdowns against Alabama during the "Camback," and torching South Carolina for 408 total yards and six total touchdowns in the SEC Title Game.

Fairley finished his season with an absurd 24 TFLs, three coming in the BCS National Championship Game against the historically good Oregon rushing attack. Fairley would be named Defensive Player of the Game. Six wins over ranked opponents and five wins by 3 points or less proved that Auburn was equal parts dominant and clutch.

> Record: 13–0 (8–0) | SP+ Rankings OFF: 3rd | DEF: 27th
> Cam Newton Was The First QB To Lead The SEC in Rushing Since Jimmy Sidle in 1963

2023 Michigan Wolverines

For programs competing for national titles, momentum is paramount. Capturing it, maintaining it and benefiting from it—on and off the field. Under Jim Harbaugh, the Wolverines were ascending in his first two years back at his alma mater. They were 20–4 in his first 24 games and headed to Columbus for "The Game" in November of 2016, with a chance to make the College Football Playoff for the first time. Michigan would lose in heartbreaking fashion, 30–27 in overtime. And for all intents and purposes, they lost the momentum Harbaugh and his staff had created in their first two years on the job. Michigan would suffer through a 29–18 stretch in the next four-plus years. That included losing three more games to its bitter rival by an average margin of 21 points per game. The Buckeyes had won 17 of 19 in the series, and Jim Harbaugh acknowledged his failures by taking a massive pay cut following the disastrous 2–4 season in 2020—roughly 50% of his base salary. In his moment of crisis, he turned to his older brother John, a Super Bowl-winning head coach, for advice and a coaching recommendation. That family meeting brought Mike MacDonald to Ann Arbor. He revived a once proud Michigan defense and presided over a top-ten unit. Critically, it resulted in a 15-point win over Ohio

State, a trip to the CFP and a boatload of momentum. Following the season, MacDonald returned to Baltimore as John's defensive coordinator. Luckily for Michigan, another former (John) Harbaugh protégé from Baltimore came to help the Wolverines, this time Jesse Minter. The rising star in the coaching ranks kept the momentum going on the defensive side of the ball, helping Michigan whip Ohio State for the second straight season while attaining another top-ten defensive ranking, according to SP+. This success was all building to 2023. Under Minter, the Michigan defense became generationally good. The Wolverines finished 2023 first in scoring, total defense, and turnover margin while confusing opponents with exotic coverages. It's said that Minter's sophisticated defense was built on four tenets: block destruction, shocking effort, ball disruption, and obnoxious communication. It helped that he plugged in four All-Americans, two first team members in the secondary (Johnson, Sainristil), and two second team members along the line (Graham, Jenkins). According to Bill Connelly, Michigan is the second-highest-rated defense since 2000, one-tenth of a percent behind 2011 Alabama. And as Cole Cubelic reported, Michigan became the first national champion to lead at halftime in every game since Miami (FL) in 2001. Offensively, the Wolverines were formidable and constructed to protect leads. They bullied teams on the ground, resulting in a program-record 27 rushing touchdowns for All-American Blake Corum. Quarterback J. J. McCarthy battled through an ankle injury and finished the season third in QBR, albeit with less than 200 yards passing per game. In the end, they left no doubt, rising to the occasion in the final six games. They faced five top-16 opponents in that stretch and won by an average margin of 29 to 16.

Record: 15–0 (9–0) | SP+ Rankings OFF: 12th | DEF: 1st
Led The Nation in Stop Rate: Defensive Drives That Ended in Punts, TOs or TOs on Downs

5 Seeds

1980 Pitt Panthers

It's always a good sign for a team if I need to compare its accomplishments with the 2001 Miami Hurricanes to see if they hold a modern record. The Panthers had an astounding 30 NFL Draft picks on the team ('01 Miami had 38). They also took home a lot of hardware, including the Outland (May), the Maxwell (Green), and Lombardi (Green) awards. Oh, did I mention they had a young passer by the name of Dan Marino? Hugh Green finished second in the Heisman Trophy voting, the highest finish by a defensive player at the time. ESPN voted Green the 12th greatest player in college football history during its coverage of the sport's 150-year anniversary. Jackie Sherrill's team had four future NFL Hall of Famers in Marino, Jimbo Covert, Russ Grimm, and Rickey Jackson. On the field in 1980, the Panthers held nine teams to single digits, including South Carolina in the Gator Bowl during a 37–9 beatdown. They beat opponents by an average of 21 points per game and had lots of weapons surrounding Marino and quarterback Rick Trocano. Randy McMillan, a future first-round pick, was a battering ram out of the backfield. Benjie Pryor earned second team All-American honors at tight end, and receivers Willie Collier and Dwight Collins excelled at stretching the field. Collins finished with an insane yards per catch average (27.6) and 10 touchdowns for the Panthers. But it was their elite defensive line that made them so intimidating. Green had 17 sacks and seven forced fumbles on the edge. As a unit, all five defensive linemen made NFL rosters, and the Panthers led the nation in rushing (1.6 ypc) and total defense. Their down linemen finished with a staggering 49 sacks. Pitt's defense took over games and overwhelmed the competition. ESPN's Bill Connelly ranked them the third most dominant defense of the decade (98.9 percentile). Had it not been for awful turnover luck (7) at Florida State in mid-October, the Panthers may have run the table and gone down as one of the sport's very best.

> Record: 11–1 | SP+ Rankings OFF: 4th | DEF: 2nd
> 13 Selectors Picked Pitt As Their 1980 National Champions,
> Including *The New York Times*

1990 Georgia Tech Yellow Jackets

The 2007 college football season takes the cake as the craziest in modern history, but the 1990 campaign wasn't far behind. Top-ranked national brands like Miami (FL), Michigan and Notre Dame were falling left and right that fall, allowing programs like BYU, Georgia Tech, Houston, Illinois, and Virginia to all spend time in the AP Top Five. The Yellow Jackets made the most of their rare opportunity and springboarded from unranked in the preseason to an unbeaten record and a share of the national title. Head coach Bobby Ross made the wise decision to hire George O'Leary as his defensive coordinator in 1987, and by 1990, the Ramblin' Wreck from Georgia Tech was a lockdown unit, holding seven opponents below 14 points. The Jackets didn't allow an offensive touchdown until the fifth week of the season. Ken Swilling, aka "Captain America," was named a consensus All-American after leading the ACC in interceptions. He appeared on the ACC's 50th Anniversary Team with teammate Marco Coleman. Offensively, Shawn Jones was a crafty playmaker for OC Ralph Friedgen, and he saved his best for last, an MVP performance against Nebraska in the Citrus Bowl (318 total yards, 3 total TDs). William Bell eclipsed 1,000 all-purpose yards and punched in seven touchdowns out of the backfield. All-in-all, GT beat four ranked opponents, including a 41–38 upset of then-top-ranked Virginia on the road. The Yellow Jackets were still forced to share the national title with 11–1–1 Colorado, who won a game using a controversial fifth down against Missouri. So for the purposes of this book, I'm happy to crown Georgia Tech as the undisputed national champions of the 1990 college football season.

> Record: 11-0-1 (6-0-1) | SP+ Rankings OFF: 18th | DEF: 3rd
> GA Tech Remains The Last Team Unranked in The Preseason
> To Win A National Champion

2000 Oklahoma Sooners

On January 1st, 1988, the Sooners lost by 6 to the Miami Hurricanes in a de facto national title game in the old Orange Bowl. At the time, it appeared that OU would challenge for Big 8 and national titles on a regular basis. But the combination of scandal and Barry Switzer's departure in the coming years set the once proud program on a downward trajectory. After treading water for a few years while on NCAA probation, the Sooners went 37-40-3 from 1992-1998. Enter Bob Stoops. In short order, Stoops changed the culture and retooled the roster and coaching staff while embracing a version of the Air Raid offensively. From 5-6 in 1998 to 13-0 in 2000 with three consensus All-Americans (Heupel, Calmus, Thatcher), the '00 Sooners are one of the most impressive turnaround stories in college football history. Stoops' Sooners blasted four top 15 teams by 10+ points, including an undressing of Texas on national television (63-14). As a team, they scored seven non-offensive TDs (5 Pick-Sixes, 2 PR TDs) while holding six opponents to 275 yards or less. Four future FBS head coaches were on the staff: OC Mark Mangino (Kansas), co-DC Brent Venables (OU), co-DC Mike Stoops (Arizona), and Passing Game Coordinator Chuck Long (SDSU). The Sooners capped off the season by shutting out the Florida State offense in the Orange Bowl, surrendering just 2 points when a snap sailed over punter Jeff Ferguson's head late in the fourth quarter. Their 13-2 triumph was the program's seventh national title and their first since 1985.

> Record: 13–0 (8–0) | SP+ Rankings OFF: 5th | DEF: 4th
> Against Top-25 Opponents: 6–0, Average Margin Of Victory 35–19

2002 Ohio State Buckeyes

Jim Tressel arrived in Columbus in January of 2001 with the hope of unlocking Ohio State's potential. The program had spent the previous 13 seasons under John Cooper's leadership. Cooper did three memorable things: he won 70% of his Big Ten games, amassed an incredible amount of talent year in and year out, and, most notably, finished 2-10-1 against Michigan. Despite three top-six finishes in the AP Poll in his final six seasons, Cooper was out. Tressel, an Ohio native, had spent 24 of his last 26 seasons coaching in the Buckeye State in some capacity. After a three-year stint as a position coach at Ohio State, he led the D-1AA Youngstown State Penguins to 10 playoff berths and an unprecedented run in which he won four national titles in 7 years. In short order, he remade Ohio State and transformed a previously underperforming program with blue-chip recruits into a rugged blue-collar team that skillfully developed its players. He plucked Maurice Clarett from nearby Youngstown, and the feature back became the main driver of the Ohio State offense. The former Mr. Football in the state of Ohio became a freshman All-American while rushing for 1,237 yards and scoring 18 touchdowns. But it was Tressel's defense that won the day and, ultimately, the school's first national championship in 32 years. Five starters from the nation's top defense were selected in the 2003 NFL Draft and another five in the following two drafts. Future first-round draft picks A. J. Hawk and Bobby Carpenter were reserves. The defense was special, holding six teams to single digits and the famed Miami Hurricanes to just 17 points in regulation in the BCS National Championship Game. As 11.5-point favorites, the Canes were riding a 34-game winning streak, which is still the longest in the modern era (1980 onward). The Buckeyes were the beneficiaries of a questionable pass interference call in overtime, but they did hold Miami 16.5 points below its regular season scoring average that night in Tempe. It may not always have been pretty, but the Buckeyes and their coach certainly knew how to win.

> Record: 14–0 (8–0) | SP+ Rankings OFF: 37th | DEF: 4th
> The Buckeyes Were 5–0 Against Ranked Opponents And 7–0 in One-Possession Games

6 Seeds

1984 BYU Cougars

The last team outside of a true "power conference" to win a national championship was the '84 Cougars. LaVell Edwards' best team was remembered for its record-setting pass-first offense, but it was their play on both sides of the ball that made this perfect season possible. Defensively, Kyle Morrell was named a First Team AP All-American and headlined a playmaking secondary. Brigham Young's linebacking corps was led by a pair of future NFL stalwarts who would each start in a Super Bowl in the coming years (Kurt Gouveia and Leon White). The Cougars took the ball away 32 times in 13 games and finished 10th in total defense. But in their biggest games, the ball and their national title hopes were in the hands of Robbie Bosco. He didn't disappoint under pressure, finishing the season as the nation's leader in passing yardage and second in passer efficiency behind Heisman Trophy winner Doug Flutie. You couldn't zero in on a single receiving target because Bosco spread it around expertly. By season's end, six players had 30+ receptions, and running back Lakei Heimuli pitched in with 796 yards on the ground and 10 total touchdowns. The Cougars were productive and skilled up and down this roster, as evidenced by the 15 players from that team who were drafted into the NFL. But what made this team unforgettable was how it elevated its play in the clutch. A goal line stand against Hawai'i, which required Morrell to "Superman" over the Rainbows' offensive line, ended up saving the day for the Cougs on the road in Honolulu. And in the Holiday Bowl, a hobbled Bosco was there to spark a come-from-behind victory in the fourth quarter. Despite six turnovers on the night and digging a 10–17 hole, Bosco led two fourth-quarter touchdown drives, connecting with Glen Kozlowski and Kelly Smith in the end zone. Marv Allen capped the comeback with an interception in the final minute. That pick sealed the national title argument for BYU, who finished the season as the only undefeated team in the country.

> Record: 13–0 (8–0) | SP+ Rankings OFF: 4th | DEF: 22nd
> The Cougars Were 5–0 in One-Score Games And Won
> The Other Eight By 31 PPG

1999 Virginia Tech Hokies

Frank Beamer was a quintessential program builder. After a successful stint at Murray State in the mid-1980s, Beamer returned to his alma mater to build something special in Blacksburg. Virginia Tech, at that time, was a middling program with zero 10-win seasons and just one bowl win to its credit. It had no conference affiliation and was viewed as a stepping-stone job. It took time, but by 1993, Beamer had put the pieces in place for the Hokies to go on a run. Beamer Ball, as it would come to be known, was built around rock-solid defense and exceptional special teams. The Hokies blocked 63 kicks in the 1990s (31 punts, 18 XPs, 14 FGs), the most in Division I-A. That 1993 season was Beamer's launching pad, a 9–3 campaign that finished with a ranking in the final AP Poll for the first time in 7 years. By 1999, his defense was playing at an elite level, finishing the regular season ranked first in scoring (10.5 ppg) and third in total defense (247.3 ypg). Corey Moore, a unanimous First Team All-American, won the Bronko Nagurski Trophy and Lombardi Award at defensive end. Five other Hokie defenders received All-Big East honors. Molding that defense, alongside the legendary defensive coordinator Bud Foster, was enough to compete for a Big East title, but it was the signing of Michael Vick that took this team to the next level. The Newport News product was vacillating between Syracuse and Virginia Tech as National Signing Day approached in the spring of 1998. Syracuse's offense at the time was tailor-made for Vick, who idolized Donovan McNabb. But Virginia Tech's proximity and Vick's mother's preference that he stay close to home sealed the deal. Vick was both ruthlessly efficient (1st in Passing Efficiency) and a big play waiting to happen for VT in '99. Not only did he lead the nation in yards per attempt (12.1), he scored four rushing touchdowns from 45+ yards out. No other quarterback has reached that yards per attempt average since Vick did in 1999. And on the sport's biggest stage, Vick put on a show for the ages. As 6-point underdogs to No. 1 Florida State in the 2000 Sugar Bowl, Vick accounted for 322 yards and two touchdowns against the lightning-quick Seminole defense (8th SP+). On that night, he made Florida State look slow and put the fear of God into them for three quarters. Virginia Tech led 29–28 in the fourth quarter before Peter Warrick and the Seminoles pulled away. But for 3 hours on January 4th, 2000, the nation wondered if Virginia Tech had the greatest quarterback under center in college football history. As Bobby Bowden prophetically said of Vick before the Sugar Bowl, "That's the quarterback of the future."

Record: 11–1 (7–0) | SP+ Rankings OFF: 4th | DEF: 7th
Hokies Beat Nine Teams By 20+ Points And Scored Eight
Non-Offensive Touchdowns

2007 West Virginia Mountaineers

The '07 Mountaineers were an absolute thrill ride dropped smack dab in the middle of the craziest season of college football on record. They were led by a dual-sport star at quarterback, who was selected in the fourth round of the Major League Baseball Draft by the Anaheim Angels and told by a handful of SEC programs that he'd be a great fit... at wide receiver. West Virginia was the only D-1A school to offer Pat White a scholarship as a quarterback. That turned out to be a fantastic decision. White ran RichRod's famed spread option to perfection. In 2007, among quarterbacks, he finished first in rushing yards (1,335), second in rushing touchdowns (14), and third in QBR. He was a magician of the read option, and his backfield mates Steve Slaton, Noel Devine, and Owen Schmitt each brought something special to the ground attack. Slaton was a decisive one-cut runner with elite vision and great hands. Devine was one of the shiftiest runners in the country and had acceleration like a Ferrari. And then there was the "Runaway Beer Truck," Owen Schmitt. The 'Neers battering ram was an effective weapon in short yardage. When you put it all together, this was the most terrifying rushing attack to hit college football since the '95 Nebraska Cornhuskers—if not the most creative. West Virginia's defense, while playing second fiddle to its high-scoring offense, finished eighth in scoring and "cranked up the havoc" before it was even a football term. The Mountaineers finished 7th in total defense, collected three sacks per game (15th) and forced 20 fumbles. They capped the season with a blowout of Oklahoma in the Fiesta Bowl, but their legacy remains tied to that fateful Backyard Brawl against Pitt, with a national title game appearance hanging in the balance. White went down with an injury, and WVU was upset 13-9 as the nation's No. 2 team. RichRod would leave a mere 15 days later for Michigan, and the program has yet to rekindle the kind of magic that was brewing in Morgantown back in 2007.

> Record: 11–2 (5–2) | SP+ Rankings OFF: 9th | DEF: 11th
> WVU Averaged 3.77 Rushing TDs Per Game. No Power Five Team Has Topped That Since

2014 Oregon Ducks

Chip Kelly built Oregon into a national power, amassing a 46–7 record in four seasons in Eugene as the Ducks' head coach. But when the NFL came calling, Kelly bolted, leaving the program in the hands of its offensive coordinator, Mark Helfrich. In his first season, like Kelly, Helfrich couldn't get the Ducks over the hump, dropping games to Stanford and Arizona in November. But in 2014, things were finally different. With Marcus Mariota at the controls, the Oregon offense was truly unstoppable. It finished fourth in scoring, third in total offense, and Mariota personally ranked first in passer rating, yards per attempt, TD–INT ratio, and QBR. He swept every major award, from the Heisman and Maxwell to the Walter Camp and Davey O'Brien. Three other Ducks joined him on the All-American Team, and another ten made first, second or honorable mention Pac-12 All-Conference teams. With the exception of an early season loss to Arizona, the Ducks were a juggernaut for most of the season. They decimated the three ranked opponents they faced in the regular season by an average score of 46–28. The Ducks routed Arizona 51–13 in a rematch in the Pac-12 title game and leveled Florida State in the College Football Playoff by 39 points, ending the Seminoles' 29-game win streak. Helfrich's team performed well against Ohio State for three quarters before Ezekiel Elliott and the Ohio State offensive line took over down the stretch. Despite that disappointing performance in the national title game, the high-flying Ducks are remembered as the best Oregon team of the modern era due to Mariota's brilliance, a defense that would send seven players to the pros, and three convincing wins over teams that finished the season in the AP Top 10 (Florida State, Michigan State, UCLA).

> Record: 13–2 (8–1) | SP+ Rankings OFF: 2nd | DEF: 24th
> Ducks Had Depth: Six Players With 400+ Receiving And Four Freshman All-Americans

7 Seeds

1987 Syracuse Orangemen

In the early and mid-80s, Syracuse ran a fairly vanilla I-formation offense. But offensive coordinator George DeLeone wanted to add a wrinkle that had gained prominence at Wichita State, of all places. It was called the "freeze option" because a subtle step by the quarterback and/or running back froze second-level defenders. This false step, oftentimes in the opposite direction of where the play was headed, allowed the Orangemen and quarterback Don McPherson to attack flat-footed defenses. The results were staggering. In 1985, Syracuse finished 60th in offensive SP+. It installed the freeze option and let McPherson cook, and by 1987, Syracuse had climbed to 10th in scoring offense. For his efforts, McPherson won the Maxwell Award and finished second in the Heisman race. But this wasn't a one-man show: 19 players from the '87 team were drafted into the NFL. The Orangemen offense was perfectly balanced, averaging over 210 yards on both the ground and through the air. Robert Drummond, Daryl "Moose" Johnston, and Michael Owens all averaged over 5 yards per carry and combined to punch in 17 total touchdowns. Syracuse smoked the defending national champion Penn State by 27 points in the Carrier Dome. It won 9 games by double digits and, as an underdog, played Auburn to a 16–16 tie in the Sugar Bowl on New Year's Day.

This was Dick MacPherson's best team and one of the best teams of the 1980s not to play for a national title. Syracuse finished fourth in both the Coaches and AP polls, the high water mark for the program since 1960.

> Record: 11–0–1 | SP+ Rankings OFF: 8th | DEF: 3rd
> Syracuse Won The Lambert Trophy, Given To The Best Team in The East, Its First Since '66

2004 California Golden Bears

The only quarterback that got the best of those mid-2000 USC Trojans, once they had ascended to "dynasty level," was Vince Young in the BCS National Championship Game. But the second-best performance by a quarterback against USC in that 2004 to 2005 window came from Aaron Rodgers. The future Hall of Famer completed 85% of his pass attempts in a 23–17 loss at the Coliseum on a beautiful October afternoon in 2004. Three of his five incompletions on the day came in a goal-to-go situation at the end of the fourth quarter, including a pair that grazed the hands of his receivers. But '04 Cal was more than that near miss against USC. The Golden Bears were well-balanced, well-coached, and incredibly deep. Beyond the magical combination of QB-whisperer Jeff Tedford and his JUCO transfer Rodgers, this roster featured a 2,000-yard rusher (J. J. Arrington), eight total selections to the All-Pac-10 first team, and 14 future NFL Draft picks. Rising superstars like Marshawn Lynch and Daymeion Hughes played complementary roles in 2004 and demonstrated the Bears' depth. Sonny Dykes, an AP Coach of the Year winner, was an assistant at Texas Tech and coached against that Cal team in the 2004 Holiday Bowl. He remarked in recent years that Cal "was as talented a college football team as I've seen in a long, long time. When Marshawn Lynch is your third team tailback, you're a pretty good football team." Cal was good enough to win nine of its ten games by 17+ points, but not good enough to impress enough AP voters at the eleventh hour. As a result, Texas edged past Cal in the final BCS rankings, costing Cal a Rose Bowl bid, which would have been its first in 45 years. The Bears enter our field with a chip on their shoulder and a soon-to-be Hall of Fame quarterback, making them one of the most dangerous teams in our 68-team field.

> Record: 10–2 (7–1) | SP+ Rankings OFF: 11th | DEF: 10th
> Cal Had A Better Point Differential In Pac-10 Play Than
> USC (+184 to +168)

2010 TCU Horned Frogs

Starting in 2006, non-automatic qualifying conference champions (the forerunner to the Group of Five) finally had a direct path to a major bowl game. If they were the top-ranked non-AQ team, finished in the Top 16 of the final BCS rankings, and were ranked ahead of at least one AQ conference champion, they were invited to a major bowl game. The stipulation that they needed to finish ahead of one AQ champion went out the window if they finished in the Top 12 of the final BCS rankings. These "BCS Busters" were often plucky underdogs like the 2006 Boise State Broncos of "Statue of Liberty" fame, or the 2007 Hawaii Warriors, who completed the program's first undefeated regular season in 82 years. These schools were the college football version of a "March Madness Cinderella." The '10 TCU Horned Frogs may have been lumped into that BCS Buster conversation, but they were wolves in underdog's clothing. Gary Patterson's team featured four All-Americans and a quarterback, Andy Dalton, who would go on to start 167 games in the NFL, including playoff appearances. In total, nine Horned Frogs from this roster were drafted into the NFL, 13 were recognized as first or second team All-Mountain West honorees, and they made a clean sweep of the MWC POY honors (Offense, Defense, Special Teams). They started the season ranked sixth in the AP Poll, and by its end, they'd climbed all the way to No. 2. TCU knocked off three ranked teams along the way, including No. 4 Wisconsin in the Rose Bowl, besting the Badgers when Tank Carder batted down their last-gasp 2-point conversion attempt in the closing minutes. The "Immaculate Deflection" secured an iconic 21–19 win in Pasadena. All three of TCU's ranked wins came away from Amon G. Carter Stadium, and it held those opponents to an average of 280 total yards while generating 14 tackles for loss and 13 pass breakups. As for the rest of its schedule, TCU was merciless, dropping opponents by an average score of 44 to 11. In the past 17 seasons, only the 2011 Alabama Crimson Tide and 2010 TCU Horned Frogs finished a season as the nation's leader in all of the following defensive categories: total yardage, passing yardage, scoring, and opponent third down conversion percentage. This team ground its opponents to dust and had staked a claim as the greatest BCS Buster/Group of Five team of all time.

> Record: 13-0 (8-0) | SP+ Rankings OFF: 12th | DEF: 10th
> Secret Service Protection: TCU Allowed Just Nine Sacks in '10,
> And 0 To J. J. Watt in Rose Bowl

2011 Oklahoma State Cowboys

When Mike Gundy announced his choice for offensive coordinator in February of 2011, there was legitimate concern that the Pokes' offense would fall off without their wunderkind play-caller on the sideline. Offensive coordinator Dana Holgorsen had pumped electricity in a previously lackluster Oklahoma State attack. The Pokes jumped from 28 points per game in 2009 to 44 in 2010 and finished third nationally in total offense. Holgorsen was hired as West Virginia's head coach in December of 2010, so the pressure was on Gundy to hit a home run with his replacement. He did. Todd Monken only improved upon Holgorsen's work and unleashed a borderline-perfect offense against the Big 12 in 2011. The passing game was lethal, with former New York Yankee draft pick (second round) Brandon Weeden slinging the ball all over the yard. His favorite target, two-time Biletnikoff winner Justin Blackmon, was a certified YAC monster, displaying game-breaking speed and physicality reminiscent of a young Terrell Owens. By season's end, Brandon Weeden held the school's passing record for career yardage and touchdowns (since broken), and Justin Blackmon had six multi-touchdown games to his name, including an absurd 8/186/3 line in the Fiesta Bowl against No. 4 Stanford. Just for good measure, the Pokes finished 10th in yards per carry average behind a stellar season from Joseph Randle (1,482 all-purpose yards, 26 total TDs). ESPN's Bill Connelly rated them the only perfect (99.9 percentile) offense of the 2010s. But just like West Virginia 4 years prior, Oklahoma State came up just short, with a rare opportunity to play in the national championship game on the table. As 27-point favorites, Oklahoma State traveled to play Iowa State. The 5–4 Cyclones fell behind 24–7 early in the third quarter, and it appeared that Oklahoma State was just one win away from a perfect regular season. But then things began to unravel in Ames. The Cyclones parlayed a big kick return into a six-play touchdown drive. Then they caught the Pokes napping with a surprise onside kick. After trading fumbles, Zach Guyer banged home a chip-shot field goal to draw ISU within 7. The fourth quarter brought more good fortune for Iowa State, which continued its run and tied the game at 24 when it forced Weeden into a rare interception and coaxed two more punts out of the Oklahoma State offense. But every upset needs a bit of luck, and the Cyclones got it when Quinn Sharp, previously 15 of 16 inside of 40 yards, pushed a 37-yard kick wide right. After trading touchdowns in overtime, the decisive play of the game came when linebacker Jake Knott tipped the ball away from Blackmon and into the arms of Ter'Ran Benton. The interception sent the crowd into a frenzy, and air raid sirens blared across Jack Trice Stadium. The Cyclones ran it twice on the ensuing drive before Jeff Woody plunged into the end zone for the game-winning touchdown. This would be as close as Oklahoma State would get to a national title game appearance in the program's proud history which stretches back to 1901.

> Record: 12–1 (8–1) | SP+ Rankings OFF: 1st | DEF: 60th
> 12 Players Earned All-Big 12 Honors, A Program Record

8 Seeds

1982 SMU Mustangs

The Pony Express was more than a catchy nickname. The SMU running game could beat you between the tackles, on the perimeter with surprising speed, or deceptively with a magician-like option quarterback. Including in the Cotton Bowl win over Pitt, Eric Dickerson ran for 1,741 yards, and Craig James racked up 1,195 all-purpose yards. But the tricky part about defending SMU was dealing with its sawed-off quarterback, Lance McIlhenny. He was lightning-quick and could get off a pitch at the last second. Defensively, the Mustangs held eight opponents to 14 points or less and nearly shut out Dan Marino and the Pitt Panthers in their bowl game. Each level of their defense had future professional football stars (NFL and CFL). Michael Carter anchored their five-man front and is one of the most accomplished athletes in American history. Not only did he earn All-American honors at SMU before making three All-Pro teams in the NFL, he also won a silver in the shot put at the 1984 Olympics. At linebacker, Gary Moten made the All-SWC first team and was a tackling machine, and safeties Russell Carter and Wes Hopkins became high draft picks, with Hopkins making the NFL's All-Pro team in

1985. Had it not been for a 17–17 outcome against Arkansas in the season finale, SMU would have been unanimously selected as 1982's national champion. But Jeff Harrell pushed his 52-yard field goal attempt wide right, and that tie would come to haunt Bobby Collins and the Mustangs. They would finish second in both polls, behind a one-loss Penn State.

> Record: 11-0-1 (7-0-1) | SP+ Rankings OFF: 19th | DEF: 5th
> Dickerson Surpassed Earl Campbell As The SWC's Career Rushing King in 1982

2004 Utah Utes

Before Urban Meyer won three national titles in a 9-year span, he was an up-and-coming coach with a unique offense and a chip on his shoulder. At Bowling Green, his offenses put up a ton of points and exceeded expectations but fell just short of special seasons, failing to make it to a bowl game in his two seasons in the MAC. But at Utah, his teams had an edge. In his first year in Salt Lake City, the Utes bagged a pair of wins over Pac-10 programs and lost by 2 at Texas A&M. The following year, he had something special. His spread option offense was piloted by future No. 1 overall draft pick Alex Smith. Interior lineman Chris Kemoeatu was named an All-American, as was all-purpose weapon Steve Savoy (17 total touchdowns). Defensively, six starters made All-MWC teams, and the Utes dominated the turnover margin and field position elements of the game. Utah ended 2004 third in turnover margin (+1.25 per game), third in net punting, and fifth in kickoff return average (26.2 ypr) and blocked an astounding seven kicks. And when the lights shone the brightest, Utah dominated. During the regular season, the Utes faced three power conference opponents (Texas A&M, Arizona, North Carolina), winning by an average score of 37 to 14. In those contests, Alex

Smith completed 70% of his passes, racked up 998 total yards, accounted for 12 total touchdowns, and turned the ball over just once. Utah finished the regular season No. 6 in the BCS rankings, securing a berth in a major bowl as the first "BCS Buster." It drew Pittsburgh in the Fiesta Bowl and manhandled the 19th-ranked Panthers. Utah outgained Pitt by nearly 200 yards and converted 80% of its third down attempts while still leaving room for some razzle-dazzle. On the Utes' final touchdown of the night, Alex Smith connected with Steve Savoy on a quick bubble screen, but instead of following his blockers back inside, Savoy pitched to Paris Warren out of the backfield. Warren raced down the sidelines, cut it back at the 3-yard line, and hurdled into the end zone. After the score, Brent Musburger remarked, "That was brand new, wasn't it?" Utah won 35–7, Smith won game MVP, and Warren finished with 15 catches for 198 yards and two scores. Urban Meyer would ride off into the sunset (Florida), and Utah entered the discussion as college football's greatest "Cinderella."

> Record: 12–0 (7–0) | SP+ Rankings OFF: 3rd | DEF: 45th
> Four Utah Assistants Became Head Coaches: Andersen, Mullen, Sanford, Whittingham

2010 Stanford Cardinal

Andrew Luck became a college superstar in 2010. He finished second in the Heisman race behind Cam Newton, was named the Pac-10's Offensive Player of the Year, and led the Cardinal to its first major bowl win in nearly 40 years. He was accurate (70.7%), surprisingly mobile both inside and outside the pocket (453 rushing yards, 3 TDs), and he pushed the ball downfield effectively (9.0 ypa). And in its fourth year under Jim Harbaugh, Stanford finally had a talented supporting cast. Two-way throwback Owen Marecic won the Paul Hornung Award, given to college football's most versatile player. He started at both linebacker and fullback, routinely logging 100 snaps. He joined Luck as a Heisman vote-getter, nabbing three first-place votes. Three Cardinal offensive linemen were named to the Pac-10's first team all-conference (Martin, DeCastro, Beeler), and all three left The Farm as All-Americans by the end of their college careers. Doug Baldwin and Coby Fleener both nabbed second team all-conference honors as pass catchers, and a young Zach Ertz started his career with a bang (5 TDs). It was a bit of a "no-star" defense coached up by mastermind Vic Fangio, who later became the highest-paid defensive coordinator in NFL history. His aggressive 3–4 scheme generated 36 sacks (12th), 30 turnovers (12th), and rarely got beat with the big play. He did all of this without a single First Team All-Pac-10 selection, although Richard Sherman would continue to improve in the coming years, blossoming into a perennial All-Pro cornerback and member of the NFL's All-Decade Team (2010s). Stanford's only loss of the season came to Oregon, who would play for the BCS National Championship. After drubbing Virginia Tech 40-12 in the Orange Bowl, Stanford legend and 1970 Heisman Trophy winner Jim Plunkett would say, "They've bounced back from some terrible years and put Stanford back on the football map." Stanford would finish the season fourth in both polls, the school's best finish in 70 years.

> Record: 12-1 (8-1) | SP+ Rankings OFF: 5th | DEF: 7th
> Turnaround Town: Stanford 2006: Five Losses By 28+ |
> Stanford 2010: Seven Wins By 28+

2012 Texas A&M Aggies

College football accomplishments, both individual and team-based, are often evaluated through the lens of expectation. That's what made Johnny

Football's breakout Heisman season in 2012 so spectacular. Texas A&M had just entered the SEC after a 26–25 run under Mike Sherman in the Big 12. It hadn't won a conference title in 14 years. The last major bowl win for the Aggies came in 1987 when Jackie Sherrill's squad hammered Notre Dame in the Cotton Bowl. So when they started the 2012 season with a narrow defeat to Florida, expectations were low. But then offensive coordinator Kliff Kingsbury cut Johnny Manziel loose. All of a sudden, Manziel's wild improvisational skills were creating big plays left and right. In the next five games following the loss to the Gators, the Aggies averaged 53 points per game. But another narrow home defeat to LSU threw cold water on the Aggies and their supporters. Luckily, Manziel was saving his best for the second half of the season. After the 24–19 defeat to LSU, Manziel started to play hero ball, generating 790 yards of total offense and seven touchdowns in back-to-back wins over Auburn and No. 17 Mississippi State. With a trip to Tuscaloosa on deck to face the mighty Alabama Crimson Tide, few people believed that he could keep the good times rolling. Alabama had the nation's top-ranked defense at the time and a 13-game winning streak. As two-touchdown underdogs, Texas A&M marched right down the field and scored on its opening drive. On its second drive, Manziel reached into his bag of tricks. His now-famous touchdown pass set the tone for the game: he fumbled the ball into the air, recovered it, and fired a perfect pass to Ryan Swope off of his back foot. The Aggies would stretch the lead to 20–0 before hanging on late for a dramatic 29–24 victory. Two blowouts later and Manziel broke Cam Newton's SEC record for total offense. Despite being the first freshman Heisman finalist since Adrian Peterson, Manziel edged out Manti Te'o for the prestigious award. To cap the season, A&M annihilated Oklahoma 41–13 in a Big 12 South reunion at the Cotton Bowl. By season's end, donation dollars were flooding in for renovations to Kyle Field, Kevin Sumlin got a $1.1 million contract bump per season, and three assistant coaches were on their way to FBS head coaching jobs of their own (Beaty, Kingsbury, Polian). That was the Manziel effect. It should be noted, however, that it wasn't just Manziel who helped the Aggies shock the world in 2012 en route to a No. 5 finish in both polls. The entire offensive line played in the NFL, three of them coming off the board in the NFL Draft's first round (Joeckel, Matthews, Ogbuehi). Future Pro-Bowler receiver Mike Evans was named a freshman All-American, and Damontre Moore was a consensus All-American and Ted Hendricks Award finalist. If A&M had been afforded an opportunity to play in an expanded playoff, no one would have wanted to see Manziel and the "Wrecking Crew" defense.

> Record: 11–2 (6–2) | SP+ Rankings OFF: 5th | DEF: 12th
> This Was The Aggies' First Top-Five Finish in The Polls in 56 Years

9 Seeds

1996 Arizona State Sun Devils

Unless you're a blue blood, it's hard to buy credibility in college football. Programs like Alabama, Notre Dame, Ohio State, and USC have gotten the benefit of the doubt in the polls for generations. And when college football's nouveau riche put together dream seasons, they're often picked apart by pundits and pollsters. But in 1996 The Sun Devils had something that was undeniable: a blowout win over Nebraska. The top-ranked Cornhuskers had won two straight national championships under Tom Osborne and were riding a 26-game win streak into the desert in late September of 1996. Jake Plummer threw for 292 yards, and the Sun Devil defense held the famed Nebraska option attack to just 130 yards. That 19–0 shutout victory catapulted Arizona State from 17th in the polls to sixth overnight. From there, Plummer and the dazzling ASU offense (fourth in total offense, third in scoring) pummeled six more opponents by 15+ points and finished the season a perfect

11–0 overall and 8–0 in the Pac-10 for the first time in school history. Offensively, receiver Keith Poole and left tackle Juan Roque joined Plummer as All-Americans. Terry Battle and J. R. Redmond were dangerous all-purpose weapons that impacted the return game as well. Defensively, Derrick Rodgers was named a consensus All-American off the edge and was joined in the defensive box by future Pac-10 DPOY Pat Tillman. As Pac-10 champs, Arizona State squared off against No. 4 Ohio State in the Rose Bowl with a shot at the national title on the line. In the closing minutes, a defensive battle gave way to dramatic late-game scores. Plummer delivered a fourth down strike to keep the Sun Devils' season alive with 3 minutes remaining. His long completion to Lenzie Jackson set up a goal-to-go situation against an aggressive Ohio State defense. Facing a heavy blitz, Plummer snaked his way through the line, past the linebackers, and dove into the end zone to give ASU a 17–14 lead with 1:40 remaining. But the veteran Joe Germaine calmly led Ohio State down the field and, with 19 seconds remaining, found David Boston on a whip route in the end zone. The heartbreaking loss put a damper on its season, but ASU still finished fourth in both polls, marking its best finish since 1975.

> Record: 11–1 (8–0) | SP+ Rankings OFF: 2nd | DEF: 27th
> Jake "The Snake" Plummer Was Inducted Into The College
> Football Hall of Fame in 2023

2006 Louisville Cardinals

Lamar Jackson's Heisman season of 2016 has been Louisville's high water mark in the last 10 years. But you don't have to go that far back to find a season in which the Cardinals actually controlled their national championship destiny. In 2006, Bobby Petrino's Cardinals opened the year ranked 13th in both polls due in large part to their roster continuity (17 returning starters) and the surprising return of Michael Bush. The senior running back had just completed a 24-touchdown campaign in 2005. But right away, disaster struck as Bush broke his leg in the opener against Kentucky. This would prove to be Petrino's best coaching performance because, despite the loss of his preseason All-American running back, the Louisville offense remained elite. It ranked fourth in scoring and second in total offense, and Brian Brohm and Hunter Caldwell were ruthlessly efficient through the air (fifth as a team). Brohm recovered from an early season injury to his thumb and played lights out against West Virginia in arguably the biggest game in Louisville program history. The fifth-ranked Cardinals hosted the third-ranked Mountaineers in a battle of undefeateds at Papa John's Cardinal Stadium. The Thursday night standalone game drew the second-largest TV audience for a college football matchup in ESPN's 27-year history. Brohm threw for 354 yards and a touchdown, leading the Cardinals to a decisive 44–34 victory. The win moved them up to third in the BCS Standings, and since Ohio State and Michigan were ranked one and two, respectively, and were set to meet at the end of the regular season, Louisville just needed to win to reach its first national title game. Unfortunately for UofL, it would enjoy its newfound success for all of one week, blowing a 25–7 lead over Rutgers on the road on November 9th. The Cards would rebound, winning the Big East championship and soundly defeating Wake Forest by 11 points in the Orange Bowl. This secured the program's best finish in either poll (6/5). Eleven Cardinals made All-Big East teams, including seven to the first team, the most in the league. Art Carmody won the Groza Award after making 21 of 25 attempts, and both defensive tackle Amobi Okoye and offensive guard Kurt Quarterman made All-American teams. But that fateful night in Piscataway remains one of college football's biggest "what ifs," for not just Louisville football but also the Big East, which would disband just 7 years later.

> Record: 12–1 (6–1) | SP+ Rankings OFF: 4th | DEF: 22nd
> Ten Offensive Players From This Roster Were Drafted Into
> The NFL Between '07–'09

2007 Missouri Tigers

Head coach Dan Devine presided over the Golden Age of Missouri football before heading off to the NFL in 1970. The following three decades were forgettable for the Tigers, who burned through five head coaches by 2000. But in 2001, Mizzou hired Gary Pinkel, a Don James protégé. He'd won big at Toledo, going 11–0–1 in 1995 and 10–1 in 2000, before Mizzou brought him in to resurrect its program. A 22–25 start to his time in Columbia forced Pinkel to think outside the box. As a result, he opted to open up his offense in 2005, utilizing elements of Urban Meyer's offensive philosophy at Bowling Green and Utah. He had faced Meyer twice as Mizzou's head coach, losing both times. Those humbling losses made an impression. During their last meeting in 2002, Bowling Green scored 51 points on the Tigers. Josh Harris, the BGSU quarterback, accounted for 411 total yards and three total touchdowns. Pinkel wanted to bring that offense to Columbia. Doing so would ultimately save his job. In 2005, Brad Smith proved what a dual threat could do in this offense, passing and running for 230+ yards against Nebraska. He would cap that season with a monster performance in the Independence Bowl, which saw Mizzou wipe out a 21-point deficit against South Carolina. In 2006, Chase Daniel took over at quarterback and showed great promise, but it wasn't until 2007 that all of the pieces would come together for the Tigers. Pinkel had picked it up on the recruiting trail and bagged four-star recruits such as running back Tony Temple, tight end Chase Coffman, and all-purpose superstar Jeremy Maclin. With Daniel leading a perfectly balanced spread attack and a defense filled with All-Big 12 performers—nine defenders made first, second, HM—Mizzou was primed for a breakout season. It opened the season with impressive wins over Illinois, Ole Miss, and Nebraska. It beat the Cornhuskers by 35, their biggest beatdown of NU since 1947. The Tigers fell to Oklahoma by 10 in Norman but regrouped and rattled off five wins in a row, setting the stage for a No. 2 vs. No. 3 battle against Kansas at Arrowhead. Mizzou would take the Border War 36–28 and climb to the top of the polls for the first time since 1960. Unfortunately, a rematch with OU in the Big 12 title game prevented them from playing for the school's first national championship. The Sooners handled Mizzou 38–17, and the Tigers had to settle for the Cotton Bowl. Tony Temple scored four rushing touchdowns, and Mizzou hammered Arkansas by 31. The Tigers would rank fourth in the final AP Poll, which remains their best finish in program history. Four Tigers made All-American teams (Daniel, Maclin, Moore, Rucker) thanks to their explosive playmaking. Mizzou finished top eight in scoring offense (39.9 ppg), total offense (490.3 ypg), third down conversion rate (53%), turnovers generated (33), and non-offensive touchdowns (7). And just to cement their place in history, the Tigers' win over Kansas was immortalized by a *Sports Illustrated* cover that read, "Mizzou, That's Who."

Record: 12–2 (7–1) | SP+ Rankings OFF: 1st | DEF: 46th
Jeremy Maclin Was The Only Player To Score Four Ways in 2007
(Rec, Rush, KR, PR)

2010 Boise State Broncos

Picking a top Boise team to include in this field was difficult, but the 2010 Broncos simply had too much talent to ignore. Twenty-three of their 24 starters from the 14–0 Fiesta Bowl-winning team returned in 2010, including six players who earned first, second, or honorable mention All-American honors. With a loaded supporting cast, Kellen Moore's 2010 season was the third most efficient by a passer in the history of college football at the time. He completed 71.3% of his passes, which is massively impressive given his yards per attempt (10.0, 2nd). He accounted for 37 total touchdowns and was magnificent against ranked opponents (10 TDs, 1 INT). He would finish fourth in the Heisman voting. Eleven Broncos joined Moore on the All-WAC first team, with Nate Potter (LT), Billy Wynn (DE), and Titus Young (WR) also earning third team All-American honors. Ten Broncos from this team would be drafted into the NFL between 2011 and 2013. And unlike the 2009 Broncos, Boise was consistently tested against quality competition in 2010. It opened against No. 10 Virginia Tech at FedEx Field in Landover, MD, and outlasted the Hokies 33–30 in a classic. Then the Broncos hosted nationally-ranked Oregon State and beat the Beavers by 13 points. In total, they faced seven bowl teams and went 6–1, winning by an average of 23.5 points per game. In their lone defeat, Chris Petersen's team led by 17 late in the third quarter and missed a 26-yard field goal that would have won them the game on the final play of regulation. That miss from Kyle Brotzman, Boise State's all-time leader in made field goals, and his subsequent miss in overtime gifted Nevada and Colin Kaepernick a miraculous upset.

> Record: 12–1 (7–1) | SP+ Rankings OFF: 4th | DEF: 22nd
> Kellen Moore Was Named An All-American in Back-To-Back Seasons By Major Outlets

10 Seeds

1994 Colorado Buffaloes

While the Buffaloes won a share of the national championship in 1990 at 11-1-1, its most complete team took the field in 1994. The Buffaloes were led by Kordell Stewart, a dual-threat quarterback far ahead of his time. He was more of a game manager for the Buffaloes, but he played that role perfectly, accounting for 17 total TDs against just three interceptions. He completed 62% of his passes, rushed for 818 yards before accounting for sack yardage, and was a seasoned veteran running the speed and power option. He would set the NFL record for the Combine 40-yard dash by a quarterback (4.52s), become the NFL's very first 20/10 QB (20 passing TDs, 10 rushing TDs), and earn the nickname "Slash" because he was capable of playing quarterback, running back, and wide receiver. Despite his athleticism, he wasn't even the most dangerous player in his own backfield. That distinction rested with the Heisman Trophy winner, Rashaan Salaam. The Buffs No. 19 was the perfect blend of speed and power and the focal point of CU's entire offense. Utilizing 12 personnel (single back, two tight ends) Colorado bludgeoned opponents, and Salaam finished with an absurd season stat line of 2,349 all-purpose yards and 24 touchdowns. When teams did crowd the box, CU had a pair of future first-round draft picks at wide receiver (Westbrook, Carruth) and, in Christian Fauria, a third team All-American to throw to at tight end. And while its defense wasn't quite as elite, it had loads of talent. Seven starters were drafted by NFL teams, and another seven reserves had their names on cue cards at Madison Square Garden's Paramount Theater between 1995 and 1997. Chris Hudson won the Thorpe Award, and Ted Johnson and Matt Russell would finish their careers in Boulder as top-five tacklers in program history. In Bill McCartney's final year, CU was consistently playing on the sport's largest stages. It upset No. 4 Michigan with a 64-yard Hail Mary toss from Stewart to Michael Westbrook and faced six ranked opponents before

November. The Buffs' lone blemish on their 1994 résumé was a 24–7 road loss to Nebraska, the eventual national champion. Outside of that, they knocked off five ranked opponents and obliterated Notre Dame 41–24 in the Fiesta Bowl to finish third in both polls. No Colorado team has finished higher in the polls since.

> Record: 11–1 (6–1) | SP+ Rankings OFF: 6th | DEF: 13th
> McCartney Inducted Into The CFB Hall Of Fame With 93 Wins And Three Top-4 Finishes

1998 Kansas State Wildcats

When Kansas State brought its A-game in 1998, the Wildcats were as dominant as any team in our field. Bill Snyder, a College Football Hall of Famer, swept nearly every major National Coach of the Year honor. Quarterback Michael Bishop finished second in the Heisman race to Texas' Ricky Williams after leading the nation's highest scoring offense (48 ppg). Its defense finished in the top 10 against the run and the pass while holding opponents to fewer than 14 points per game. And just for good measure, the Wildcats were lights out on special teams. The reigning Lou Groza Award winner, Martín Gramática, set the D-1A record for scoring by a kicker in a season with 135 points. David Allen was a game-changing force in the return game, leading the nation in both punt return average (22.1) and touchdowns (4). Both Allen and Gramática were consensus All-Americans. Kansas State drew three top-20 opponents during the regular season and edged out Colorado, Nebraska, and Mizzou in hard-fought battles. The Nebraska win was a true "We've arrived" moment for Kansas State. The Wildcats had lost 29 straight to Big Red, including the last three by a combined 90 points. With College GameDay on hand, the Wildcats flipped the script on Nebraska, scoring 13 points in the final 5:25 to secure a 40–30 win, as well as 29 first-place votes in the AP Poll and the top spot in the Coaches Poll. But the Big 12 Title Game proved to be a bear trap for K-State. The Wildcats blew a 27–12 fourth-quarter lead to Texas A&M and headed to overtime with a trip to the first BCS National Championship Game on the line. After trading field goals in the first overtime, Gramática banged home a 25-yarder in the second OT period to give KSU a 33–30 lead. The defense stiffened and backed A&M into a corner. Facing a 3rd and 17, backup quarterback Branndon Stewart found running back Sirr Parker on a quick slant route. Parker caught it in stride, raced past a defender, stiff-armed Kansas State's Lamar Chapman, and stretched the ball over the goal line. Parker's touchdown cost K-State a shot at the national title, but the 'Cats are still fondly remembered as the most dynamic, complete, and fun-to-watch team of Synder's illustrious career in Manhattan.

> Record: 11–2 (8–0) | SP+ Rankings OFF: 3rd | DEF: 7th
> Honor Roll: 15 NFL Draft Picks, 12 All-Big 12, Four All-Americans, Two College Football Hall of Famers

2013 South Carolina Gamecocks

The Ol' Ball Coach won 11 games three straight times in Columbia. That made picking the best Gamecocks team between 2011 and 2013 rather difficult. But the deciding factor here was Connor Shaw. As a senior, he accounted for over 3,000 total yards, 31 total touchdowns, and—most impressively—only one of his 284 pass attempts were intercepted. The offense relied on Mike Davis (1,535 all-purpose yards, 11 TDs) and a stout defense that featured future No. 1 overall NFL Draft pick Jadeveon Clowney. The Gamecocks were top 20 in total defense, points allowed, and takeaways. Four starters were named first or second team All-SEC, including defensive tackle Kelcy Quarles, who joined Clowney as an All-American. This team got better as the season rolled along, knocking off No. 5 Mizzou on the road in overtime and turning No. 6 Clemson over six times in a two-touchdown Palmetto Bowl triumph. As underdogs to Wisconsin in the Capital One Bowl, the Gamecocks fought back in the second half, erasing a 4-point deficit and winning by 10. The pollsters were impressed enough by the win to elevate Spurrier and his team to No. 4 in both polls, the program's first season that ended in the top five (and still the only one to do so). Clowney had become the face of this program and left college as a two-time All-American with 47 career tackles for loss and nine forced fumbles, which remains a school record. The native son of South Carolina was the only consensus No. 1 recruit to ever sign with USC and is credited with the wave of talent that washed over Columbia between 2011 and 2013. The 33 games that USC won in those three years are far and away the most in a three-year span in school history.

> Record: 11–2 (6–2) | SP+ Rankings OFF: 20th | DEF: 5th
> OSKIE! South Carolina Generated 13 Turnovers in Its Final Three Games

2017 Central Florida Knights

Whether you believe UCF was the best team in the country in 2017 or not, three things about them were undeniably true. The first was that its shotgun spread attack was absolutely phenomenal. McKenzie Milton was the perfect triggerman of the nation's highest scoring team (48.2 ppg), flashing pinpoint accuracy (67.1%) and shifty running ability (613 yards, 8 TDs) in equal proportions. The second element of UCF's dream run in 2017 was the "havoc" its defense generated. The Knights finished second nationally in takeaways and top 20 in forced fumbles and passes defended. And the final piece of UCF's "We Belong" argument is that it got better as the season progressed, even when the competition improved. The Knights feasted on non-bowl and FCS competition early, beating those opponents by an average score of 55–22. But down the stretch, they faced five bowl teams in their final six games, including three ranked opponents in succession to close the season. The War On I-4 between UCF and USF proved to be a thriller, with the Knights outlasting the Bulls 49–42 at The Bounce House. The following week, its offense won the day again, prevailing in double overtime 62–55 against No. 20 Memphis. This set the stage for a Peach Bowl meeting with No. 7 Auburn, who beat the two teams that would ultimately play for the national title (Alabama, Georgia). As 10.5-point underdogs, UCF did what it had done all season long: Scott Frost's team racked up yards, scored a lot of points, and turned its opponent over. The result was a shocking 34–27 upset, which was enough to score them a share of the national title, thanks to the Colley Matrix. As a recognized championship selector for the FBS level by the NCAA, the Colley Matrix legitimizes UCF's title talk. Sixteen Knights made the first or second All-AAC team, another six were drafted into the NFL, and two more signed as undrafted free agents. In terms of this tournament, their résumé is comparable to other national champions, and they have the makeup of a Cinderella that could make a deep run.

Record: 13-0 (8-0) | SP+ Rankings OFF: 2nd | DEF: 73rd
Taste Test: UCF vs. Top-25 Teams in Final Rankings 4-0 (+12 ppg) | Alabama 4-1 (+4.8 ppg)

11 Seeds

1985 Air Force Falcons

The triple option is college football's great equalizer. When run effectively, teams with inferior talent can hang around with the big boys by eating up the clock and moving the chains on long, methodical drives. But every once in a while, a Service Academy mixes the triple option with premium talent. In 1985, Air Force's wishbone attack had a veteran triggerman at quarterback, power runners in its backfield, a deep threat specialist at wide receiver, and a defense with multiple All-American-caliber players. Bart Weiss knew when to pull it, when to pitch, and when to keep it. He ran for 1,024 yards and 12 touchdowns and threw for 1,449 and eight more scores through the air. His 2,481 total yards in '85 were the second most in program history at the time, while his 10.3 yards per attempt stood as the highest mark in school history until 2015 (min. 125 attempts). Defensively, Terry Maki and Chad Hennings were terrors in the front seven and would go on to receive All-American honors in '86 and '87, respectively. Maki made 30 tackles (school record) while blocking a fourth-quarter field goal, which was returned for the game-winning score in its 6-point upset of No. 15 Notre Dame. But the true heartbeat of the team in '85 was consensus All-American safety Scott Thomas. Not only did he score three different ways (interception, kickoff return, punt return), but he was known as the hardest hitter on the team. His legendary toughness extended to his military duty, where he flew F-16s in combat zones. He survived being shot down in the Gulf War and was awarded the Distinguished Flying Cross. Both Thomas and Hennings are now members of the College Football Hall of Fame. Following an 8-point win over Texas in the Bluebonnet Bowl, Air Force finished fifth in the Coaches Poll, the best final ranking for a Service Academy in the past 60 years. For his efforts, head coach Fisher DeBerry won the FWAA Coach of the Year Award.

> Record: 12–1 (7–1) | SP+ Rankings OFF: 1st | DEF: 31st
> Defense And Special Teams: AF Picked Off 28 Passes And
> Featured An All-American Punter

2000 Oregon State Beavers

Oregon State was once a college football hotbed, with six AP Poll top-20 finishes between 1941 and 1968, three Rose Bowl berths, along with a Heisman (Terry Baker, 1962) in its trophy case. But then a deep freeze set in for the Beavers. Simply put, Oregon State was lost in the college football wilderness for 30 years, failing to make a bowl game between 1968 and 1998. But then College Football Hall of Famer Dennis Erickson was hired as the program's head coach in 1999. The two-time national champion immediately breathed life into the dormant program, and by 2000, it was ready to beat anyone. Thanks to Erickson's recruiting and player development, the Beavers suddenly had studs all over the roster. Five players were named to the Pac-10's all-conference first team in 2000. At receiver, Oregon State featured Chad Johnson and T. J. Houshmandzadeh, a pairing that would go on to catch 126 touchdowns in the NFL. The program sent just eight players to the NFL Draft in the 1990s, but this team alone sent 10 players to the draft between 2001 and 2004. Ken Simonton carried the offense with 1,559 yards and 19 rushing touchdowns. The Beavers ranked in the top 20 in both scoring and total defense and finished with 32 takeaways (10th). Dennis Weathersby anchored an elite secondary that finished second in the Pac-10 in pass-efficiency defense. The Beavs' only setback was a 33–30 loss at Washington against a Husky team that would win the Rose Bowl and finish No. 3 in both polls. The Beavers would end the season with a 10-point win over No. 5 Oregon in the Civil War and a 41–9 thrashing of Notre Dame in the Fiesta Bowl. Those two wins were enough to push Oregon State to No. 4 in the final AP Poll, its best finish in school history.

> Record: 11–1 (7–1) | SP+ Rankings OFF: 10th | DEF: 5th
> "Dam" Right: The Beavers Beat Three Top-10 Opponents By 10 Or More Points

2007 Kansas Jayhawks

Kansas was a founding member of the Missouri Valley Intercollegiate Athletic Association, dating back to 1907. The MVIAA would later become the Big Six, the Big Eight, and then finally the Big 12. Over time Kansas built rivalries with schools like Kansas State, Missouri, Nebraska, and Oklahoma. And while Kansas built a powerhouse program on the hardwood, its football teams were regularly nothing more than a speed bump for national powers in the Midwest. From 1970 through 1994, it won exactly one bowl game and never won nine games in a single season. With the exception of its 1995 campaign under head coach Glen Mason (10–2), there wasn't much to cheer about until 2007. Then, seemingly out of nowhere, Kansas started beating everyone. And not just beating them, but truly hammering them. In the month of September, KU defeated opponents by a combined score of 214 to 23. Pollsters still weren't convinced, leaving KU unranked. The Jayhawks then upset No. 24 K-State in Manhattan and squeezed out two more road wins at Colorado and Texas A&M before they made their mark on the 2007 season. Nebraska had beaten Kansas 36 straight times between 1969 and 2004, often humiliating the Jayhawks by 40, 50, even 70 points as it did in 1986, so it was shocking to see KU installed as 19-point home favorites. As it turned out, that wasn't a high enough line. The Jayhawks racked up 572 yards of total offense, Todd Reesing threw a school-record six touchdowns, their defense forced five NU turnovers, and KU shellacked the Cornhuskers 76–39. Reesing and a high-powered offense had the Jayhawks off to a school record 11–0 start and positioned KU to potentially play in the BCS National Championship Game. But a 36–28 loss to bitter rival Mizzou at Arrowhead derailed its dream season. Kansas would rebound in the Orange Bowl, upsetting No. 5 Virginia Tech by 3 thanks to an Aqib Talib pick-six and a big night from receiver Dexton Fields. For the first time in school history, KU had won a bowl game and finished inside the top 10 in both major polls. Talib and offensive tackle Anthony Collins were named First Team All-Americans, six of their teammates made first or second team All-Big 12, and head coach Mark Mangino was the Consensus National Coach of the Year. He is the only coach in college football history to win both the Broyles Award (top assistant) and the AP Coach of the Year Award as a head coach. And just to add to this team's mystique, the Jayhawks did receive one first-place vote in the final AP Poll, which had never happened in their 117-year history up until that point.

> Record: 12–1 (7–1) | SP+ Rankings OFF: 6th | DEF: 18th
> Payback Time: The Former Doormat Beat Seven Teams
> By 31+ Points

2008 Texas Tech Red Raiders

When Mike Leach took over the program in Lubbock in 2000, it was far from a gut job. Spike Dykes had built a consistent winner in the Hub City, but even at his best (2x nine-win seasons), the Red Raiders played second fiddle to in-state rivals Texas and Texas A&M. Mike Leach set out to change that, and in 2008, he had the firepower to do it. Leach had signed Graham Harrell, a four-star passer out of Ennis, Texas, and the program's highest rated quarterback recruit to date. He was the Gatorade Player of the Year in Texas and held just about every major high school passing record at the time. He was paired with an unheralded two-star recruit named Michael Crabtree, who was actually first offered a basketball scholarship at Texas Tech by Bobby Knight. The Air Raid legends will go down as one of the best duos in the history of college football, connecting 231 times for 3,127 yards and 41 touchdowns in '07 and '08. The pair helped TTU race out to an 8–0 start to the '08 season, setting the stage for an epic showdown with the nation's No. 2 team, the Texas Longhorns. With College GameDay on hand, the Horns and Red Raiders played one of the best games in college football history, culminating with a Harrell-to-Crabtree touchdown with 1 second remaining on the clock. Texas Tech won 39–33 and rose to No. 2 in the AP and BCS Standings, which remains its highest ranking in program history. By season's end, Tech split the Big 12 South Title, sent four players to All-American teams, and the late Mike Leach was honored with the Woody Hayes Trophy. Graham Harrell won the Johnny Unitas Golden Arm Award, and Crabtree took home his second straight Biletnikoff Award. The Red Raiders will forever be linked by that special November night in Northwest Texas when Lubbock felt like the center of the college football universe.

> Record: 11-2 (7-1) | SP+ Rankings OFF: 3rd | DEF: 64th
> Against Top-25 Opponents: 42.6 Points Per Game, 527.8 Yards, 6.82 Yards Per Play

2010 Nevada Wolf Pack

Chris Alt is a college football pioneer, having popularized the use of a brand-new offensive formation. The "Pistol" may look similar to the common "Shotgun" formation, but it gave opposing defenses fits. By aligning the running back directly behind the quarterback, defenses were behind the eight ball in two separate ways. The first was visually identifying where the running back was, and Alt routinely utilized undersized backs to hide them. In 2010, for example, his lead rusher was Vai Taua, who stood barely 5'10". Taua terrorized defenses for 1,836 total yards and 21 total touchdowns. The second issue was that, by aligning behind the quarterback, Nevada could run read plays or options in either direction. This meant on any given play, Nevada could key any defender along the line of scrimmage, hoping to put them in conflict. This offense was always effective under Alt, but it was borderline unstoppable once he paired up with Colin Kaepernick. The three-sport star showcased insane athleticism in high school and was viewed as a potential professional star on the diamond. He tossed two no-hitters in high school and hit 94 MPH on the radar gun. But his heart belonged to football, and he was given a chance to start for four years by Alt and his staff. Kaep got better each season, and his 2010 campaign was one for the record books. As a passer, he was efficient (64.9%) and capable of stretching the defense with deep shots (8.4 ypa). He finished the season with 3,022 yards passing and 21 touchdown tosses. But on the ground is where he was a lethal weapon. He ran for 1,206 yards and 20 touchdowns, becoming just the third player in FBS history to join the 20–20 club. But stats alone wouldn't get Nevada into this field—it needed a marquee win. And on Black Friday 2010, it got just that: upsetting No. 3 Boise State in Reno. After falling behind 24–7 by halftime, Kaep orchestrated a massive comeback, punctuated by a 7-yard touchdown completion to Rishard Matthews with 13 seconds left in regulation. With the game tied, Boise would complete a pseudo-Hail Mary to get into field goal range, only for Kyle Brotzman to miss a 26-yard chip-shot at the final gun. He would choke once again in overtime, missing a 29-yard kick. Anthony Martinez capitalized and connected on his kick from 34 yards out, securing the program's only win over a top-five-ranked opponent.

> Record: 13–1 (7–1) | SP+ Rankings OFF: 11th | DEF: 55th
> The Wolf Pack Scored 52 Rushing Touchdowns And
> Ran For 4,091 Yards

2013 Michigan State Spartans

The "No Fly Zone" secondary was absolutely phenomenal in East Lansing. In terms of accolades, the Spartans' secondary was as good as we've ever seen in college football. Three of their four defensive backs were named to the Big Ten's All-Conference first team, and Darqueze Dennard won the Thorpe Award (Top DB). Sparty's fourth starter, Trae Waynes, won the team's Tommy Love Award (most improved defender) and would grow into a first-round NFL Draft pick (11th overall). The Spartans grounded opposing passing attacks, finishing in the top five in nearly every meaningful pass-defense metric. They held eight of their 14 opponents to two touchdowns or less and upset undefeated Ohio State in the Big Ten Championship game by 10 points. Had it not been for some questionable officiating on a September afternoon in South Bend (ND 17–MSU 13), it would have been Michigan State facing Florida State in the Rose Bowl for the national championship, and not Auburn. Jeremy Langford may have been Sparty's offensive engine (1,579 total yards, 19 total TDs), but Connor Cook was dynamic in their biggest wins over No. 2 Ohio State and No. 5 Stanford, throwing for 636 yards and five touchdowns in those two marquee victories.

> Record: 13–1 (8–0) | SP+ Rankings OFF: 51st | DEF: 1st
> Opposing QBs Rating 92.28 (1st), Completion % 47.5 (2nd),
> 165.6 YDS (3rd)

12 Seeds

1984 Boston College Eagles

The '84 Eagles are woven into the very fabric of college football, having pulled off one of the most iconic game-winning plays in the history of the sport. "Hail Flutie," as it would come to be known, was the 48-yard touchdown pass thrown by Doug Flutie and caught by Gerard Phelan against the Miami Hurricanes. The last-second prayer, which actually traveled 63 yards in the air, all but sealed BC a major bowl bid and the Heisman Trophy for Flutie (although most votes had already been cast). The notoriety of that single play is widely credited with a 16 percent surge in applications to their school the following year. But the "Miracle in Miami" wasn't BC's only highlight that season. Gerard Phelan and Tony Thurman were named All-Americans alongside Flutie. Thurman tied the single-season record for interceptions at the time with 12, and freshman Bill Romanowski put together a breakout rookie campaign, culminating in Defensive MVP honors in the Cotton Bowl against Houston. The Eagles finished the year fourth in the Coaches Poll, its best finish in program history. Had it not been for a second-half collapse against No. 20 WVU (21–20), BC could have lobbied pollsters for a share of the 1984 national title with BYU.

> Record: 10–2 | SP+ Rankings OFF: 1st | DEF: 65th
> BC's Defense Led The Nation in Interceptions With 23 in 12 Games

1997 North Carolina Tar Heels

It's never easy to win at a basketball school, nor is it easy to break through in the world of college football without the benefit of a unique offensive system led by a special quarterback. But Mack Brown proved to be the perfect man for the job in Chapel Hill when he took an ACC afterthought and built them into a perennial contender in a conference dominated by Bobby Bowden and Florida State. The '97 Heels featured a special defense coached up by Broyles Award finalist Carl Torbush. His defense finished top five in scoring, rushing, and passing defense. They held eight of their 12 opponents to 14 points or less and decimated Virginia Tech 42–3 in the Gator Bowl. Over the course of the season, UNC faced three top-40 scoring offenses (FSU, NC State, Va Tech) and held those three teams below their scoring averages by 22.8 points per game. NFL general managers certainly noticed because 10 of UNC's 11 defensive starters were drafted into the league. Greg Ellis, Vonnie Holliday, and Brian Simmons were all first-round picks, and two-time Consensus All-American Dré Bly was a second-round pick in 1999. Nine Tar Heels were named first or second team All-ACC, including legendary center Jeff Saturday. Mack Brown would use this breakout campaign to secure a dream job at the University of Texas before returning 22 years later to Tobacco Road as North Carolina's head coach.

> Record: 11–1 (7–1) | SP+ Rankings OFF: 19th | DEF: 2nd
> Layer Cake: UNC Featured Consensus All-Americans
> At All Three Levels Of Its Defense

1999 Wisconsin Badgers

Barry Alvarez is a member of the College Football Hall of Fame, and his best team came to embody everything he believed a team should be on both sides of the ball. The Badgers were dominant defensively, ranking fifth in both scoring and passing efficiency defense. ESPN's Bill Connelly ranked them the third most dominant defense of the entire decade (98.8 percentile). And offensively, the Badgers never beat themselves, turning it over just 11 times the entire season (t-1st). And then there was Ron Dayne, the focal point of the Badgers' offense. When he got it going, the Badgers offense operated like an eighteen-wheeler rolling downhill. The Dayne Train could run through you or away from you, which was shocking given his size. At 5'10", Dayne weighed 270 pounds and ran the 40-yard dash in 4.5s. Once he got up a head of steam, he was a defensive back's worst nightmare. On the season, he ran for 1,834 yards and 19 touchdowns. He tacked on 200 yards and a touchdown in their Rose Bowl victory over Stanford, which helped them finish fourth in both polls, the school's best finish in the past 61 years. It's important to keep in mind that this team was more than Mr. Heisman at running back. The entire Wisconsin offensive line played in the pros, with four punching meal tickets as NFL Draft picks. In total, 21 Badgers were drafted off of this roster, including five first-rounders between 2000 and 2004. They were deep, tough, and rose to the occasion when facing quality opponents. Wisconsin finished the season 5–1 against ranked opponents behind gutty quarterback play from Big Ten Freshman of the Year, Brooks Bollinger.

> Record: 10–2 (7–1) | SP+ Rankings OFF: 15th | DEF: 1st
> Jamar Fletcher - Member Of The Big Ten All-Decade Team,
> Led The Conference in Picks (7)

2021 Cincinnati Bearcats

In the four-team College Football Playoff era, it wasn't good enough to go undefeated if you were a Group of Five program. You not only needed to run the table, but you also needed to show consistent dominance over multiple seasons while testing yourself with marquee non-conference opponents. Cincinnati set the table for its run in 2021 by winning every regular season game during its COVID-shortened season in 2020. When they got an opportunity to play Georgia in the Peach Bowl, it gave the Bulldogs a four-quarter fight, eventually falling 24–21. The Bearcats' reward was a 2021 preseason ranking of No. 8 in the AP Poll. Cincy exceeded its lofty preseason goals by becoming the first Group of Five team to appear in the CFP. Cincinnati knocked off No. 9 Notre Dame by 11 in South Bend and held seven opponents to 14 points or less. By season's end, 16 Bearcats were named to All-AAC teams (first, second, HM), and both starting cornerbacks were named First Team All-Americans. Its famed "Blackcats" defense was led by Coby Bryant (who won the Thorpe Award as the nation's best cornerback) and Sauce Gardner (who later became the fourth overall pick in the NFL Draft and the 2022 NFL Defensive Rookie of the Year). Cincy led the country in opposing passer rating allowed, finished fourth in interceptions and red zone defense, seventh in passes defended, and 10th in team tackles for loss. The Bearcats were as fearsome a pass defense as college football has seen in the modern era. Offensively, they spread teams out, baked RPOs heavily into their game plan, and relied on Desmond Ridder to make the right decision with the football in both the run and pass games. He was particularly effective against ranked opponents, accounting for six touchdowns and just one turnover in his three matchups with ranked foes. Despite a sound 27–6 defeat to Alabama in the Cotton Bowl, Cincy is remembered as a G5 pioneer and soon moved up the ladder, joining the Big 12 just 19 months later.

Record: 13–1 (8–0) | SP+ Rankings OFF: 12th | DEF: 10th

Draft Bears: Nine Cincy Players Were Selected in the 2022 NFL Draft, A G5 Record

13 Seeds

1998 Tulane Green Wave

Tommy Bowden was a rising star in the coaching ranks before he even secured his first head coaching job. As the son of Bobby Bowden, he was well-connected, and he made the most of assistant coaching opportunities at schools like West Virginia, Florida State, Alabama, and Auburn. But when he arrived at Tulane in '98, the job was daunting, even for a talented young coach. The Green Wave had posted a record of 12–55 in the six seasons preceding his arrival. Luckily for Bowden, he hit two home runs that would change the trajectory of his career and the fortunes of Tulane football. He hired little-known head coach Rich Rodriguez from D-II Glenville State in West Virginia and placed his faith in the erratic and undersized junior quarterback Shaun King. Before Bowden arrived in the Big Easy, King had been running a traditional offense and failed to connect on 50% of his passes. He'd thrown more interceptions (14) than touchdowns (10) and run for all of 6 yards in 19 games. Rich Rodriguez, the pioneer of the zone read and spread option offense, unlocked every ounce of King's potential. He blossomed into one of the very first true dual-threat quarterbacks in college football history. In 1998, he became the first player to throw for 300 yards and rush for 100 yards in the same game and finished 10th in the Heisman race after posting gaudy numbers (4,149 total yards, 49 total TDs). He guided the Green Wave to a perfect season and countless offensive records. Tulane beat 11 of its 12 opponents by double digits, finished second in scoring (45 ppg), four in total offense, and fifth in turnover margin. Bowden would parlay his success into a 10-year stint at Clemson. RichRod followed Bowden to Clemson before getting a head coaching job at West Virginia, and Shaun King was drafted in the second round of the 1999 NFL Draft. He started 24 games in the NFL and led the Tampa Buccaneers to the 2000 NFC Championship Game as a rookie.

> Record: 12–0 (6–0) | SP+ Rankings OFF: 1st | DEF: 78th
> King Set The NCAA Record For Passer Rating (183.3),
> Which Stood For Eight Seasons

1998 UCLA Bruins

A tongue-in-cheek way to describe this Bruins squad would be to call them a "half team." Their offense was a well-oiled machine, particularly through the air. UCLA averaged over 40 points per game (fifth) and performed even better against Top-25 competition (43.3 ppg). Its defense, however, left a lot to be desired. You could run (70th) or pass (51st) on the Bruins, which is why they gave up nearly 28 points per game (65th). But UCLA's leaky defense could do one thing consistently, and that was turn teams over. It forced 33 turnovers (t-third), an element of its game that bailed them out for much of the season. The roster was brimming with talent, evidenced by seven Bruins being named to the Pac-10 conference's first team in 1998 and 11 hearing their names at the NFL Draft over the next four years. Cade McNown was masterful as Bob Toledo's triggerman. The southpaw had the ability to rainbow deep balls over the defense, and his receiving duo of Brian Poli-Dixon and Danny Farmer struck fear into opposing secondaries. Carrying a 20-game winning streak into the Orange Bowl at the end of the '98 regular season, UCLA was on the verge of something special. Had the Bruins not blown a 17-point second-half lead against the Miami Hurricanes, they would have met the Tennessee Volunteers in the very first BCS National Championship. This remains the closest UCLA has been to a national title since 1954.

> Record: 10–2 (8–0) | SP+ Rankings OFF: 2nd | DEF: 55th
> McNown Received The Most Heisman Votes By A Bruin
> Since Gary Beban in 1967

2015 Houston Cougars

When it comes to the little guy in college football, there's usually a steady build-up before a breakout season. For example, before Boise State's 13–0 season and shocking Fiesta Bowl upset of Oklahoma in 2006, the Broncos had won 45 games in the previous four years. But Houston wasn't interested in a slow build-up, so it fired Tony Levine following a 7–5 regular season and signed Tom Herman in mid-December of 2014 in the hopes of bringing the team back to its SWC glory days. Houston hadn't finished a season ranked inside the AP Poll top 10 since 1979. Herman was viewed as a rising star and offensive innovator, but even the most bullish "Cougar backers" couldn't have foreseen the instant turnaround he orchestrated in H-Town. The Cougars stormed out to a 10–0 start to the Herman era. The offense was dubbed the "smashmouth spread," utilizing H-backs as de facto fullbacks, a heaping helping of RPOs, and traditional triple-option elements. The result was a perfectly balanced offense led by a super athletic quarterback (Greg Ward) who would run for 1,100 yards and 21 touchdowns before making it in the NFL as a wide receiver. Defensively, Houston was havoc-minded, generating a nation-leading 35 turnovers. It flew around the football, particularly in the secondary, and sent six defenders to the All-AAC first or second teams. When UH got its shot to prove the AAC truly was a "Power Six" conference, it showed out against Florida State in the Peach Bowl. The Seminoles' Dalvin Cook was held to 33 rushing yards, and Houston forced five turnovers in a 38–24 triumph. The Cougs finished the season eighth in both polls, and Herman took home FWAA First-Year Coach of the Year honors.

> Record: 13–1 (7–1) | SP+ Rankings OFF: 9th | DEF: 51st
> The Cougs Went 4–0 Against Ranked Opponents, Winning
> By An Average Score of 37–25

2015 Ole Miss Rebels

For generations, the battle cry in Oxford, Mississippi, has been "We may have lost the game, but we've never lost the party." The Grove remains one of the sport's greatest tailgating scenes, but in 2015, Ole Miss and its fans had more than cocktails to cheer about. Hugh Freeze certainly colored outside the lines (recruiting violations), but in the end, he assembled one of the most talented rosters in program history. Four starters would go on to become first-round NFL Draft picks in 2016 and 2017, and eight would be named first or second team All-SEC in 2015. That talent was enough to take down five nationally-ranked opponents, including Alabama, who would go on to win the national title that season. Chad "Swag" Kelly set 25 separate school records, including single-season records for passing yards (4,042), total touchdowns (41), completion percentage (65.1), passing efficiency (155.9), and 300-yard passing games (8). His top target, Laquon Treadwell, was a Biletnikoff Award finalist, caught a touchdown in six straight games, and capped his college career with three scores in the Sugar Bowl against Oklahoma State. The Landshark Defense hung its hat on "Havoc." Ole Miss ranked second in passes defended, third in pick-sixes, eighth in TFLs, and 18th in forced fumbles. Had it not been for an insane 4th and 25 conversion by Arkansas in overtime, which required a no-look, over-the-shoulder lateral, Ole Miss would have won the SEC West for the first time ever and been right in the mix for a College Football Playoff bid. When you put it all together, it was easily one of the most entertaining and controversial teams of the modern era.

> Record: 10–3 (6–2) | SP+ Rankings OFF: 24th | DEF: 14th
> Roster Composition: 15 NFL Draft Picks, Four Five-Stars
> (Most in Program History)

14 Seeds

2002 Iowa Hawkeyes

As of publication, Kirk Ferentz is the longest-tenured FBS head coach, which is kind of amazing given his rocky start in Iowa City. He won just four games in his first two seasons combined and endured a 1-4 skid in the middle of his third year. But Iowa Athletic Director Bob Bowlsby gave Ferentz time to figure things out, and that proved to be a fantastic decision. Using the team's 2001 Alamo Bowl victory as a springboard, Ferentz had momentum headed into 2002, and more importantly, he had a deep and talented roster. Fifteen players from this roster were drafted into the NFL, fourteen made the first or second All-Big Ten team, six were named to All-American teams, and three won national awards: Banks (O'Brien), Clark (Mackey), Kaeding (Groza). Iowa finished the season undefeated in Big Ten play for the first time in school history, with only a 36-31 non-conference blemish to in-state rival Iowa State, keeping it from a potential berth in the national championship game. Despite losing to USC by three touchdowns in the Orange Bowl, this Iowa team is remembered as the most dynamic of its generation. Brad Banks' dual-threat ability carried him to a runner-up finish in the Heisman race, Dallas Clark showcased his skills and paved the way for Iowa to be considered "Tight End U," and Bob Sanders intimidated ball carries with a 100+ tackle season that featured four forced fumbles. For a blue-collar program, this team had an edge and an "it" factor, which is why the 2002 squad is universally beloved among Hawkeye alumni.

> Record: 11–2 (8–0) | SP+ Rankings OFF: 7th | DEF: 26th
> Iowa Finished Eighth in The AP Poll, Its Highest Final
> Ranking Since 1960

2007 Hawaii Warriors

When June Jones took over in Honolulu, he had his work cut out for him. The Rainbow Warrior program had fallen on hard times and bottomed out in 1998, finishing 0–12. In six of the next nine seasons under Jones, Hawai'i won nine games or more, culminating in 2007 with an undefeated regular season and a berth in the Sugar Bowl. This remains UH's only major bowl game appearance in program history. Speaking of firsts, Colt Brennan became the school's first Heisman finalist while breaking Ty Detmer's career passing touchdowns record (since surpassed). The 'Bows won half of their regular season games by a single possession, including two overtime thrillers on the mainland (LA Tech, SJSU). The overtime classic against San José State deserves its own 30 for 30. Down 35–21, on a muddy, rain-soaked field, Brennan was picked off with 8:54 remaining in the game. And despite a defensive stop, SJSU pinned Hawai'i down at its own 3-yard line with a perfect punt. Brennan proceeded to orchestrate an eight-play, 97-yard touchdown drive. With under 3 minutes left, the Warriors forced a fumble—the Spartans' first lost fumble of the season—and gave the ball back to Brennan near midfield. They would convert a pair of third down conversions before Brennan took a quarterback sweep into the end zone, tying things up at 35. Brennan found Jason Rivers for a 9-yard touchdown in overtime, and Myron Newberry made the Warriors' defensive play of the year, picking off SJSU's Adam Tafralis in the end zone to secure the victory. Just for good measure, Hawai'i erased a 21–0 deficit in its season finale against Washington, preserving the program's perfect regular season. Toss in the late-night kickoffs (six games started at 12 a.m. or later EST), and it's easy to see why this team had a cult-like following.

> Record: 12–1 (8–0) | SP+ Rankings OFF: 15th | DEF: 80th
> Passing Attack: 473.3 ypg (2nd), Three 1,000+ yd receivers

2011 Baylor Bears

Art Briles developed his famed "Veer and Shoot" offense in the 1990s at Stephenville High School in Texas. One of its calling cards was utilizing ultra-wide receiver splits, putting receivers outside the numbers, just feet from the sidelines. Defenses, in turn, were forced to spread out when defending this offense. Critically, it removed defenders from the box. The next tenet of this offense was to run it hurry-up, no-huddle. This made it even more difficult for defensive coordinators to vary their calls because simply lining up and playing a vanilla scheme was difficult enough. And finally, Briles embraced the mentality of "Haymakers until the final bell" when designing his play calls. He took deep shots, both from traditional play calls and tags/RPOs onto his running game. Most teams add bubble screens or quick slants onto their run plays, but Briles took shots downfield with post and fly route tags. His offense was innovative and easy to run, but it wasn't truly diabolical until he teamed up with Robert Griffin III. The Heisman Trophy winner was the perfect triggerman for his offense, mixing Olympic-level speed with an accurate deep ball. Defenses had no choice but to pick their poison when facing Baylor. The Bears generated 587 yards per game offensively. No Power Five school has surpassed that number since 2011, with the exception of Briles' Baylor 2013 squad. RGIII, Kendall Wright, and Terrance Ganaway were a big play waiting to happen, and it happened a lot. The Bears exploded for 12 plays of 60 yards or more from scrimmage. Baylor knocked off three ranked opponents, including No. 5 Oklahoma, and capped the season with a 67–56 victory over Washington in the Alamo Bowl. Despite a non-existent defense, Baylor finished with 10 wins and a final ranking of 12th in the Coaches Poll, the program's best in 25 years.

> Record: 10–3 (6–3) | SP+ Rankings OFF: 2nd | DEF: 104th
> Baylor And Washington Set A Bowl Record For Combined YDS At 1,377 in The Alamo Bowl

2014 Mississippi State Bulldogs

A fun trivia question to trot out at the bar is, "Who was the top-ranked team in the very first College Football Playoff rankings in 2014?" The answer, of course, is Mississippi State. Despite opening the season unranked, the Bulldogs knocked off three top-eight teams in a row to open SEC play. They upset No. 8 LSU in Death Valley as a touchdown underdog. Then they destroyed No. 6 Texas A&M by 17 points at Davis Wade Stadium. The following week, the cowbells were louder than ever as the Bulldogs drilled No. 2 Auburn by 15 points. The Bulldogs' offense was reminiscent of the scheme the Florida Gators built around Tim Tebow—no surprise, considering MSU made Dan Mullen, the Gators' offensive architect, their head coach the year following Florida's national championship in 2008. It took Mullen nearly five years to find an ideal fit at quarterback to run his offense, but once Dak Prescott got his feet wet, there was no stopping him. He finished the 2014 season top 20 in QBR, passing yards, passing touchdowns, passing efficiency, and yards per attempt. But what made him special was his nose for the end zone and his ability to pick up first downs with his legs. He scored 14 rushing touchdowns (second among QBs) and picked up 24 first downs with his legs on third or fourth down. Defensively, Mississippi State was the epitome of "bend but don't break," leading the nation in red zone defense. Preston Smith (DE) and Benardrick McKinney (LB) both made the All-SEC second team and were drafted in the second round of the 2015 NFL Draft. Three more defenders joined them as pro players, including NFL All-Pro Chris Jones. While this team wilted down the stretch, losing three of its last four games, it still finished the season 11th in the AP Poll, the program's best finish since 1963.

> Record: 10–3 (6–2) | SP+ Rankings OFF: 19th | DEF: 12th
> Prescott Finished Eighth in The Heisman Race, The Best Ever Finish For A Bulldog

15 Seeds

1991 East Carolina Pirates

The ECU Pirates opened the '91 season on the road against a Big Ten opponent. They dropped a shootout to Illinois 38–31 and then proceeded to win 11 games in a row. The Pirates knocked off a 10-win Syracuse team at the Carrier Dome and then another nationally-ranked team in Pitt the very next week. As the momentum began to build, the ECU crowd would regularly break into "We Believe" chants to urge on their team in pivotal moments. The Pirates averaged 34 points per game (12th) and generated enough takeaway to finish fourth in turnover margin. Jeff Blake finished seventh in the Heisman race and was named a second team All-American. If you include his bowl performance, Blake threw for 3,451 yards and accounted for 36 total touchdowns. Speaking of that bowl game, it was an absolute classic. East Carolina trailed NC State 34–17 in the fourth quarter of the Peach Bowl before offensive coordinator Steve Logan let Blake operate from the shotgun on the final three drives. That was a wise move because Blake caught fire, completing 15 of 21 passes for 148 yards on the final three drives with three total touchdowns. Blake completed the comeback when he found tight end Luke Fisher over the middle at the NC State 14-yard line. Fisher broke two tackles and dove into the end zone for the game-winning score with 1:32 remaining. He finished the game with 12 catches for 144 yards. That 37–34 win remains one of the most iconic in ECU history. In total, four Pirates earned All-American honors: Blake, Fisher, and Tom Scott (OT) offensively, and Robert Jones at linebacker. They finished the season ninth in both polls, the best final ranking for any Pirate team.

> Record: 11-1 | SP+ Rankings OFF: 20th | DEF: 84th
> No Quarter: ECU Treated Ranked Opponents Badly,
> Manufacturing Three 4th Qtr Comebacks

1993 Arizona Wildcats

It's usually a good sign when your defense is given a nickname. In the case of the '93 Wildcats, their "Desert Swarm" defense became so iconic it landed the program a No. 1 preseason ranking from two outlets and a *Sports Illustrated* cover in August of 1994. How did a basketball school get that much buzz? The '93 team beat teams to a pulp—that's how. The late Dick Tomey's "Double Eagle Flex" defense confused opposing offenses and allowed his front seven to play fast. The result was the best run defense in the modern era. The Wildcats gave up 2.7 feet per carry (.9 yards). Opponents mustered just 30 yards per game on the ground. They shut out two teams, held three more to 7 points or less, and took the ball away 34 times in 12 games. Defensive tackle Rob Waldrop won three major awards (Bednarik, Nagurski, Outland) and was named a consensus All-American. Tedy Bruschi and Sean Harris joined

Waldrop on the All-Pac-10 first team in Arizona's front seven, and cornerback Tony Bouie finished the season with six picks. Its offense was underwhelming but effective on the ground, taking full advantage of the ideal field position it was gifted by its record-setting defense. Arizona remains just one of four teams to win a major bowl game via shutout in the modern era, routing Miami (FL) 29–0 in the Fiesta Bowl.

> Record: 10–2 (6–2) | SP+ Rankings OFF: 39th | DEF: 1st
> Arizona Led The Nation in Yards Allowed Per Play At Just 3.5

1997 Washington State Cougars

Mike Price nearly swept every single Coach of the Year honor in 1997 because he accomplished something special at Washington State: he won big. The Cougars football program hadn't been to a Rose Bowl since 1931 and hadn't won 10 games since Herbert Hoover was in the White House. After modest success in his first six years on the Palouse, Price and the Cougs had stalled, going 3–8 in 1995. But that's when lightning struck in the form of a 6'5", 235-pound savior from Great Falls, Montana. Ryan Leaf seized the job in 1996, and the offense took flight. By 1997, Wazzu's offense was something to behold. It entered bowl season second in both scoring and total offense. Leaf finished second in passing efficiency rating and was surrounded by a perfect assortment of skill position weaponry. Michael Black gobbled up 1,300 all-purpose yards and 12 total touchdowns at running back. Kevin McKenzie and Chris Jackson caught 21 touchdowns between them, and Shawn Tims, who held the team record for the vertical jump at 37 inches, returned punts and reeled in 35 passes as Leaf's third option. Defensively, the Cougars had tons of skill on the defensive line, which was headlined by the late Leon Bender and Dorian Boose. Steve Gleason led the team in tackles at linebacker, and freshman Lamont Thompson led the Pac-10 in interceptions with six. They were a complete team, led by a fiery Heisman candidate at quarterback, that hung with the national champion for four quarters in the Rose Bowl. Its 21–16 defeat to Michigan didn't come without some drama, as Leaf spiked the ball in the closing seconds to set up a final play from the Michigan 26-yard line. They ruled on the field that the clock had expired, and the game was over. Had they been afforded one more play (as replays show they should have been), the Cougars were a Leaf touchdown pass away from immortality and a likely second-place finish in both polls.

> Record: 10–2 (7–1) | SP+ Rankings OFF: 4th | DEF: 39th
> Ryan Leaf's Third Place Finish in The Heisman Race Remains The Best in Program History

2000 Purdue Boilermakers

This special Boilermaker bunch broke the program's 34-year Rose Bowl drought. Joe Tiller's "basketball on grass" spread attack was ahead of its time and was the antithesis of the traditional ground-and-pound Big Ten offense. Drew Brees, overlooked by national powers out of high school, became Tiller's point guard and was simply magnificent in 2000. The future Hall of Fame quarterback won the Maxwell Award and finished fourth in the Heisman race thanks to his gaudy stats (4,195 total yards and 32 total TDs). Tim Stratton joined Brees as a national award winner, taking home the very first Mackey Award as the nation's top tight end. And three of Brees' starting linemen were drafted into the NFL, including three-time Super Bowl champion Matt Light. That superior offensive line gave Brees time to work, and he picked apart the Big Ten all season long. Purdue knocked off Big Ten powers Michigan, Wisconsin, and Ohio State en route to a share of the conference title and sent a program-record 19 players to the NFL. Already considered the program's best team of the modern era, the 2000 Boilermakers could have accomplished even more had it not been for a pair of 2-point losses (at Notre Dame, at Penn State). Notre Dame drilled a walk-off, game-winning field goal, and Purdue's Travis Dorsch missed a would-be game-winner against Penn State.

> Record: 8–4 (6–2) | SP+ Rankings OFF: 15th | DEF: 42nd
> Twelve All-Big Ten Selections (1st/2nd/HM), Awards: Brees (Maxwell), Stratton (Mackey)

16 Seeds

1999 Marshall Thundering Herd

When most people think about Marshall in the 1990s, visions of Randy Moss treating defenders like small children come to mind. The quarterback throwing him most of those touchdown passes was Chad Pennington, and in 1999, he set out to prove that he was more than a footnote in Randy Moss's illustrious career. Despite racing out to a 22–4 record as a new D-1A member in '97 and '98, Marshall was still in search of respect. Marshall didn't receive a single vote in either the AP or Coaches preseason polls in August of 1999. But in its first game, it upset Clemson on the road and then went on the warpath. The Thundering Herd stampeded over the competition by an average margin of 30 points per game in the next ten games. In the MAC Title Game, as the nation's 11th-ranked team, they finally faced adversity. Trailing 23–0 in the third quarter, Pennington put the team on his back. He threw three second-half touchdowns, including the game-winner with 4 seconds remaining. It was also his 100th touchdown toss as Marshall's quarterback. Marshall capped its dream season with a convincing 21–3 win over No. 25

BYU in the Motor City Bowl. It finished the season ranked 10th in both polls and joined Florida State as the only other undefeated team at the D-1A level that season.

> Record: 13-0 (8-0) | SP+ Rankings OFF: 24th | DEF: 23rd
> Only Virginia Tech And Marshall Finished Top 10 in Both Total Offense And Defense in '99

2006 Rutgers Scarlet Knights

Before Greg Schiano's arrival in 2001, Rutgers was on a 15–51 run. The program had become both a punching bag and a punchline in the world of college football. Schiano's rebuild was methodical, but by 2005, he had them back in a bowl game for the first time in 27 years. In 2006, Rutgers was peaking thanks to a perfectly constructed roster that emphasized toughness and grit over flash and bravado. The Scarlet Knights backfield featured All-American Brian Leonard at fullback and Big East Player of the Year Ray Rice at running back. Defensively, they were one of the best units in school history, embodying Schiano's "Keep Choppin'" mentality. Eric Foster earned All-American honors at defensive tackle, and 13 of his teammates made All-Big East teams. Schiano was honored as the National Coach of the Year by five separate outlets, including the Walter Camp Football Foundation. But this team is remembered for one magical evening in Piscataway, New Jersey. Rutgers started 8-0 for the first time in 30 years and hosted a third-ranked Louisville team at home. It entered as 6-point underdogs and hadn't beaten a ranked opponent since 1988. Despite a raucous crowd pulling for them, Rutgers had dug themselves a 7–25 hole midway through the second quarter. It appeared to be more misery for the Rutgers faithful, but Schiano's team refused to quit. It erased its 18-point deficit and had the ball on its own 9-yard line in the waning minutes of the game. Mike Teel and Ray Rice helped Rutgers march the ball down the field, and placekicker Jeremy Ito banged home a 25-yard game-winning kick after being granted a do-over by the Louisville special teams when it committed an offsides penalty on his previous miss. Ito calmly drilled his second chance and turned and pointed to the Skycam. Moments later, tens of thousands of success-starved fans stormed the field for what Rutgers Radio Network's Chris Carlin dubbed "Pandemonium in Piscataway."

> Record: 11–2 (5–2) | SP+ Rankings OFF: 13th | DEF: 19th
> Rutgers' Upset Of No. 3 Louisville Remains The School's Highest-Ranked Win

2007 Appalachian State Mountaineers

The '07 Mountaineers were the very first FCS/Division 1-AA program to receive votes in the final AP Poll. That's why they're the only FCS team to crack the field of 68. In arguably the greatest upset in college football history, App State shocked No. 5 Michigan 34–32 at the Big House to start the season. That win propelled quarterback Armanti Edwards to superstardom and eventually two Walter Payton Awards (FCS Heisman). Six players off of this roster would be drafted into the NFL, and a staggering 11 made the FCS All-American team as a first, second, or third team honoree. The Mountaineers led the nation in total offense with 488 yards per game, utilizing a spread attack that was ahead of its time. They would go on to win the 2007 FCS National Championship, obliterating Joe Flacco and Delaware 49–21. It was the program's third straight national championship and capped a three-year stretch in which the Mountaineers won 39 games.

> Record: 13-2 (5-2) | FCS Rankings Total OFF: 1st | Total DEF: 70th
> Spread To Run: App State Averaged 287 Yards Per Game On The Ground

2012 Northern Illinois Huskies

Beginning in the mid-90s, Joe Novak slowly built the Huskies into a formidable MAC program. He peaked between 2002 and 2004, winning 27 games and the program's first bowl game in 21 years. But it took two coaching changes before NIU had the coach and the roster to take things to the next level. Dave Doeren rode senior Chandler Harnish to an 11-3 record in his debut. Little did fans know it at the time, but Harnish's monster season (4,595 total yards, 39 TDs) was just a preview of what was to come. In 2012, Jordan Lynch went thermonuclear, flirting with the first 3,000-yard (passing)/2,000-yard (rushing) season in college football history. He would *only* account for 4,953 total yards and 44 touchdowns. Lynch was matched on the other side of the football by future first-round pick Jimmie Ward at safety. After a 1-point loss to Iowa on the road in its opener, NIU reeled off 12 straight wins before fading in the second half against Florida State in the Orange Bowl.

> Record: 12-2 (8-0) | SP+ Rankings OFF: 30th | Total DEF: 52nd
> High-Powered: The NIU Offense Averaged 45 PPG in MAC Play (Second Best Ever, '03 Miami)

2015 Navy Midshipmen

Football is the ultimate team game, but every once in a while, a single player elevates an entire program to a new level. In 2015, Keenan Reynolds did just that. The senior quarterback was named the AAC Offensive Player of the Year and a third team All-American. He accounted for 1,203 yards through the air and 1,373 on the ground. Reynolds tallied 32 total touchdowns and amazingly, despite having the ball in his hands on nearly every offensive snap, he only turned it over twice all season (1 INT, 1 Lost Fumble). For his efforts, he finished fifth in the Heisman vote, and Navy rose to 18th in the final polls—head coach Ken Niumatalolo's best finish in Annapolis. It was easily the most dynamic Service Academy offense of the modern era, and three other Midshipmen made first or second team All-AAC. And most importantly to Navy men and women everywhere, the Mids won the 116th meeting between Army and Navy, the program's 14th straight win in the series.

> Record: 11–2 (7–1) | SP+ Rankings OFF: 14th | Total DEF: 49th
> Born To Run: The Mids Finished Second Nationally With 326 Yards Per Game Rushing

2020 Coastal Carolina Chanticleers

One of the silver linings of the strange COVID season was that a small program from South Carolina was introduced to the nation. The Coastal Carolina Chanticleers burst onto the scene with a diverse spread offense that featured the pistol and a variety of 20- and 21-personnel looks. Grayson McCall was absolutely surgical with the ball in his hands, completing north of 68% of his passes (27 TDs, 4 INTs) and burning defense on the ground (569 yards, 10 TDs). Coastal got two cracks at Top-25 competition and pulled out a pair of upsets over Louisiana and BYU in the famed "Mormons vs. Mullets" game. The Chanticleers' lone blemish on the season was a 37–34 bowl game loss to Liberty, but at that point, they had earned the nation's respect as a quality team with a star-in-the-making head coach (Jamey Chadwell). Three players from the 2020 squad were drafted into the NFL, and McCall went on to become the first player to win three consecutive Sun Belt Player of the Year awards.

> Record: 11–1 (8–0) | SP+ Rankings OFF: 30th | Total DEF: 24th
> McCall's Raw QBR (82.2) Was Higher Than First-Round Picks Justin Fields And Trevor Lawrence

CHAPTER TWO

The Greatest "What If" Teams of All Time

College football national titles are an exclusive club. Those shiny trophies are surrounded by a velvet rope with a sign that reads *"bluebloods only."* It has a decidedly country club vibe. But the 2007 season was the opposite. If it was a club, it was more of a "$10-all-you-can." Everybody was allowed in. It was complete and utter chaos. Teams were dropping left and right in 2007. Just for a frame of reference, five schools went from unranked to being ranked in the top two of the AP Poll, including Boston College, Kansas, Mizzou, Oregon, and South Florida, which was still within the first ten years of even having a Division 1 program. On three occasions within an 8-week span, the No. 1 and No. 2 teams lost in the same weekend. An event like that is usually reserved for once a decade, and it happened three times in 2 months. Seven times in a 9-week span, the No. 2 team in the country lost.

Which brings us to West Virginia.

Number 1: West Virginia, 2007. The Mountaineers were perfectly balanced and finished eighth in offensive efficiency and eighth in defensive efficiency, according to the SP+ rankings. They had a spread option offense with ideal personnel. When coaches talk about perfectly constructing a roster for the spread option, they point to the 2007 Rich Rodriguez Mountaineers.

They had a lightning-quick quarterback who protected the football. They had a pair of home run hitters at running back. And they had a runaway beer truck for a fullback.

Defensively, their 3-3-5 look bewildered opponents and led to a lot of negative plays. They held six teams to 14 points or less during the season, and by season's end, four starters were honored on the All-Big East team. They led the Big East in scoring and scoring defense and won eight of their 11 games by 20 points or more. But with a spot in the national title game on the line, they were upset by their rival, Pitt. That 13-9 loss remains one of the most gut-wrenching in the history of college football. But it also comes with a massive asterisk: Pat White, their star quarterback, was injured in that game, and as a result, the offense stalled, making this team one of the biggest what-ifs of all time.

He would end up returning for the Fiesta Bowl, and West Virginia, as an underdog, blasted Oklahoma. They beat them 48-28 in a game that wasn't even that close. Had it not been for his thumb injury on that night in Morgantown, West Virginia, the Mountaineers would have beaten Pitt and advanced to the BCS National Championship Game, and the ripple effects keep going from there. They probably would have won that game, which meant that they would have kept their head coach, Rich Rodriguez, in Morgantown instead of him leaving for the University of Michigan. And that is why this is the No. 1 team, in my eyes, for the what-if category.

Number 2: Central Florida, 2017. So let's get the elephant in the room out of the way right away. Central Florida won a share of the national championship in 2017. This is something that is argued about ad nauseam in college football. There are plenty of jokes made by the bigger programs that, "Oh, UCF got a participation trophy national title." The reality is the Colley Matrix, a recognized championship collector by the NCAA, ranked the Knights number one in the country after the bowl game. So yes, in fact, they are national champions. And Colley is not some oddball rating system that is giving out national titles all willy-nilly. Between 2014 and 2022, they were in concurrence, awarding the winner of the College Football Playoff with their No. 1 ranking. The only exception was in 2017, when they viewed UCF's perfect record, complete with three Top-25 wins, as enough to tip the scales in their favor.

In 2017, the Knights were undeniably dynamic on offense. Piloted by McKenzie Milton, they led the country in scoring with 48.2 points per game. They ran the table. They whipped three ranked opponents in a row to close out the season. And their last win, a 34–27 victory over No. 7 Auburn, truly validated them as an elite team. Remember that Auburn had beaten Alabama and Georgia that season, the two teams that played in the national title. But they still remained an elite team on the outside looking in at the College Football Playoff Committee. They never took them seriously. They started them off in the rankings at 18th. They were only able to move up to 12th before the bowl game. It was insulting. Their ranking never matched their on-field performance. They defeated everyone in 2017 but not the pollsters.

Their roster, additionally, was loaded. They had nine First Team All-AAC performers and another seven second team members. Six players from this team were drafted into the NFL, and another two were signed as undrafted free agents. So now that we have some time to view this team through a historical lens, they truly were worthy of national championship consideration. That's what makes them a perfect what-if candidate.

Number 3: Penn State 1994. For those who are unfamiliar with the way college football used to be, we used to have split national champions. And in 1994, Penn State deserved to share the national title as much as any team in the history of college football. Their offense has a good case for being considered the greatest pro-style, quarterback-under-center offense in college football history. They averaged 47 points per game. They buried traditional powers USC, Michigan, and Ohio State by an average score of 44 to 17. Their offense featured five All-Americans and a future NFL All-Pro at guard.

And when the chips were down, they proved no moment was too big for them. Kerry Collins orchestrated a 96-yard game-winning drive against Illinois. The Fighting Illini's defense featured a pair of top-three NFL draft picks in their front seven, making the sledding difficult for the Nittany Lions. Collins was perfect on that game-winning drive (7-for-7), which demonstrated that Penn State was not only good, but they were clutch. They ended the season perfectly, going 12-0. They won the Rose Bowl definitively over Oregon. This was also Joe Paterno's best offense by a wide margin. Paterno generally was viewed as one of those coaches who wanted to grind games out, preferring to rely on his defense and field position. But when viewed purely as a coach between the white lines, he was always capable of preparing his teams for the big games. This is evidenced by his bowl record (24-12-1) and performance in national title games. He finished 2-1 with the national title on the line despite being an underdog in two of those three games. He lost by 7 to Bear Bryant in the '79 Sugar Bowl. He knocked off Herschel Walker and Georgia in the '83 Sugar Bowl to win the national title, and he pulled off an all-time upset to shock Miami in the '87 Fiesta Bowl.

That experience, plus the otherworldly talent they had on offense, makes me believe they would have outscored Nebraska in a hypothetical head-to-head in 1994. But it does land them here on the what-if list because they were not awarded a share of the national title, which, in my opinion, is incredibly unfair to Penn State.

Number 4: TCU, 2010. This was Gary Patterson's best team, and it was also his most balanced. He had a future NFL quarterback in Andy Dalton calling the shots, leading an offense that scored 41 points per game while bullying opponents on the ground. Defensively, TCU was the nation's best in terms of scoring, passing, and total defense. When given the opportunity to shine in the regular season, they knocked off nationally-ranked Oregon State at Jerry World and murdered No. 6 Utah, 47 to 7 in Salt Lake City. But that alone would not have been enough to land them on this list. They had to go to the Rose Bowl, an opportunity for a team that, for most of its history, was viewed as not having a seat at the table in a major conference.

Playing in the Rose Bowl was a huge deal in 2010, and the stage never seemed too big for the Horned Frogs. They took on a traditional power in Wisconsin, ranked fourth nationally at the time. Leading 21–19 with 2 minutes left in the game, TCU needed to make a stand on the two-point conversion to secure the win. Tank Carder deflected the 2-point conversion pass, preserving the win for the Horned Frogs. Who knows what would have happened if there had been a College Football Playoff in 2010? Gary Patterson, one of the greatest coaches of all time in college football, and this being his best team, absolutely deserves to be on the what-if list.

And our final "what if" team: **Number 5: Utah, 2004.** Urban Meyer turned Utah into world beaters overnight. He inherited a 5–6 football team when he first got to Salt Lake City. And in the next two years, he posted a total record of 22–2 with two bowl wins, the last of which was a dominant 35–7 Fiesta Bowl win over Pitt, securing a perfect 12–0 season. This Utah team, even though they were not in a major conference, featured the number one overall pick in the NFL draft, Alex Smith, and seven other future NFL draft picks.

Three Utes made All-American teams, 10 made the All-Mountain West Conference team, and Urban Meyer won a handful of Coach of the Year honors. Their offense was unique at the time, taking some elements of the spread, five-wide looks, lots of motion, and plenty of designed quarterback runs. It gave opponents fits. In 2004, USC ran away from Oklahoma in the national title game, bottling up an offense that at the time was content operating from under center and just handing the ball to Adrian Peterson. That played right into the Trojans' hands. USC had the best run defense in the nation at the time. So playing an offense as diverse and complicated to prepare for as Utah would have made for a better national title game, no question, and that's why Utah has made this list.

CHAPTER THREE

The Most Difficult Teams to Select

Having started this G.O.A.T. debate on Twitter (now X) countless times, I can assure you the biggest point of contention will not be who wins this 68-team tournament. Instead, it will be who I've left out of the field. There will be a contingent of fans who scream that I've selected the wrong Ohio State team or invalidated the entire process by leaving out Tim Tebow. This was bound to happen when I opted to cap each program at one team apiece. Many schools like Alabama, Florida, Miami (FL), Florida State, and Ohio State presented several viable options to choose from. But in the end, it was incumbent on me to select just one. And I can tell you, it wasn't easy.

We'll start with **Ohio State**. The Ohio State team that I selected was from 2002. In my opinion, there were *seven* teams that were worthy of consideration to be Ohio State's selected team in my tournament: the '96 team, which won the Rose Bowl; the '98 team, which won the Sugar Bowl; the 2012 team that received a postseason ban; the 2014 team that won the national title; the 2015 team that won the Fiesta Bowl; and the 2019 team that lost in the Fiesta Bowl. Ohio State, in general, is at the absolute head of the table in terms of college football history, accomplishments, and its importance to the game. You can't tell the story of college football without mentioning Ohio State and its impact. The Buckeyes have had legendary coaches. They've produced 55 consensus All-Americans. They've had Heisman Trophy winners. And in the case of selecting which Ohio State team to include in this tournament, there were so many worthy teams.

When I think back on the '90s and John Cooper's teams, you had a clown car of studs on both sides of the ball, particularly in '96, when they had an embarrassment of riches. Yet, they couldn't get over the hump against Michigan when it mattered the most. Then, when you get into the 2010s, they were stacked once again but only won one national title. And in many cases, it was a single loss that bit them. But from a pure talent perspective, 2019, led by Justin Fields, is often considered to be the most talented Ohio State team of all time. The reason why I went with 2002 is that they went undefeated, they beat their rival, and they also beat one of the greatest college football teams of all time, the 2002 Miami Hurricanes. Miami was riding a 34-game winning streak, which included 12 wins over ranked opponents by an average of 20.5 points per game. They were a fearsome dynasty at the peak of their power. This explains why they were a massive favorite in the Fiesta Bowl to repeat as national champions. But Ohio State shocked them in double overtime in a game that is viewed as one of the top five college football games ever played. I take into account not only your overall talent but also what you accomplish at the end of the day. It's the magnitude of the moment. And the 2002 Ohio State team delivered on that.

Next up, **Florida State**. The team I selected here was the 2013 Florida State Seminoles. And this was difficult for a lot of reasons. For starters, Bobby Bowden regularly fielded elite teams. From 1987 through 2000, Florida State finished in the top four of the final AP Poll every single year. It's one of those records that is likely to never be broken in college football history. Even before NIL and the transfer portal, it was difficult to keep college kids motivated with their eyes on the prize in one given season, let alone nearly 14 straight years of dominance. But that's exactly what Bowden was able to do. Another factor that made it difficult was that two of those teams in that window, in 1993 and 1999, were iconic. Both of those teams were national champions. The '93 team was led by Charlie Ward, running their unique "fast-break" offense. He won the Heisman Trophy. They played in the Game of the Century against Notre Dame and lost. But when they had an opportunity to play for the national title in the Orange Bowl later in that season, they were able to pull it out against Nebraska for Bowden's first national title.

In '99, they were perfect. There are a lot of stats that get thrown around in college football, but wire-to-wire champion is one of the most unique accomplishments a team can claim. Only a very small fraternity of teams have ever pulled it off. In 2004, USC completed the feat, and in '99, Florida State was able to do it, becoming the first since the 1940s. In '99, Florida State's roster was as star-studded, and they were dominant. However, when they got to the national title game, it wasn't a "fait accompli" that they would win because a generational quarterback led Virginia Tech in Michael Vick. They played a phenomenal game and led the Seminoles by a single point, 29-28, at the end of the third quarter. Then Florida State pulled away with a performance for the ages by their number nine, Peter Warrick. He had a punt return for a touchdown and caught a TD late in the fourth quarter that basically broke the game wide open. They had swagger; they had playmakers at every level, and they had excellent quarterback play from future Heisman winner Chris Weinke. That '99 team made the decision very difficult. But as you'll see later in this book, when you go through the roster for 2013 Florida State, they had future pros at essentially every position on the field. They, too, were led by a Heisman Trophy-winning quarterback, and their offense was historically good and essentially only had one bad half in the entire season. It was this that tipped the scales in favor of the 2013 team.

In the case of **Alabama**, I selected the 2020 team, but dating back to 1980, there were about six teams that, in my opinion, were worthy of inclusion here. In 1992, they returned to glory, went 13-0, and won the national title. In 2009, Nick Saban was in his third year, and they went 14-0, a perfect season and a national title. Then the rings came in flurries. In 2011, they went 12-1, winning it all; 2012, 13-1, and Saban's third national title with the Tide; 2015, 14-1, a fourth national title; and 2017, 13-1, Saban's fifth national title in Tuscaloosa. The theme here is national titles just stacked on top of one another.

Really, since Nick Saban came into the picture, the 2009 team arguably had the best defense in college football history, but they had some issues offensively. They were run-heavy. This was before Saban and his staff embraced where college football was going from an offensive standpoint. He wanted to lean on his defense, which made perfect sense in 2009 because his defense was so good. The 2020 team, by contrast, was a perfectly oiled machine offensively: led by a quarterback who completed over three-quarters of his passes, a wide receiver who won the Heisman Trophy, a super dynamic running back who was a first-round NFL draft pick, and a play-caller in Steve Sarkisian who was in a perfect position at the right time to be dialing up these plays. But their defense was also phenomenal that season. They made a lot of top plays for Saban and his staff. In terms of overall dominance, other than the SEC Title Game against Florida, they walloped everybody. From a head-to-head standpoint, I'd prefer to go with Alabama's greatest offense of all time because when you're facing off against some of these other teams in this tournament, you need to be elite in that department.

My *Florida* selection is likely to be the most contentious. I could have gone with the 2006 team that went 13-1 in Urban Meyer's second year and won the national championship. They stomped Ohio State as an underdog in the Fiesta Bowl. But really, the argument here is the 2008 team versus the 1996 team. 2008 went 13-1 with Tim Tebow holding the reins. Their lone blemish was a midseason game to Ole Miss. He famously gave a speech where he promised that no one would work harder or play better down the stretch. And he was right. The entire team played essentially perfect football from that moment on and beat an undefeated Alabama in the SEC Title Game, went to the national championship, and shut down a historically good Oklahoma offense. They didn't have any appreciable weaknesses. They had an offensive mastermind in Urban Meyer with perfect pieces to play smashmouth football or spread you out and use the speed of players like Percy Harvin. Defensively, they had so many future pros and so much talent that they simply overwhelmed everyone they played. They also played with an edge. They were so aggressive that they were able to shut down some of the top offenses they played.

All that being said, I'm sticking with the '96 Florida team. For whatever reason, they've slipped through the cracks when people discuss the greatest teams of all time.

They were led by Steve Spurrier at the height of his powers. He was always an offensive savant, but this team was his masterpiece, top to bottom. The way in which he constructed the roster was eerily similar to the 2008 team that I mentioned. They had a Heisman Trophy quarterback. They had a great backfield led by Fred Taylor, a future Pro Bowl running back. They had three wide receivers that were absolute problems for the defense.

They were masters of yards after the catch. As soon as you got the ball to them in space, they could beat you. They had an opportunity to play a really good Florida State team in the '96 Sugar Bowl, and they trounced them. They scored 50 plus in a national title game—that's rarefied air. They looked unstoppable in that game. Defensively, even though there weren't a ton of pros, there were a ton of high-end, high-achieving collegiate defenders on that team.

The secondary was loaded and experienced. A young Jevon Kearse was a situational pass rusher. They had a great linebacker corps, headlined by Johnny Rutledge and James Bates. They really pushed teams to the limit, to the edge. When you look at Steve Spurrier's impact on the game of football, I think it's only fitting that the very best team of his coaching career ended up making this list.

And then finally, staying in the SEC one last time, I'm going with **Auburn** in 2010. They were led by Cam Newton, who is arguably the most impactful player in college football history. You could make the argument for two other teams. In 2004, they went undefeated, and they won the Sugar Bowl. Many people believed that they should have played for the national championship against USC. Instead, they are left as a "what if" team of their own. Had they had that opportunity, they were perfectly balanced. They were led by an NFL quarterback and had two NFL running backs. Holistically, they were a better roster than the 2010 team that I selected. In 2013, this was the miracle Auburn Tigers. Not only did they win with the "Prayer at Jordan-Hare," a Hail Mary completed to beat Georgia, they also won on the "Kick Six," a 109-yard missed field goal return for a touchdown by Chris Davis to upset Alabama in the Iron Bowl.

They played for the national title, and they had a lead in the final minute of that game. But they lost two games that year, and pointedly, their defense just wasn't up to snuff. They gave up so many points in big games that year that I think it's reasonable to say that you want to go with either the '04 or '10 Tigers. Why the 2010 team? Quite simply, Cam Newton was a transformative generational quarterback who was able to take over games with his arm or with his legs in a way that no other player, Bo Jackson included, has ever done in all of football history. He is one of those players that you just need to put ten guys around him, and special things are going to happen. For that reason, I went with 2010 Auburn.

CHAPTER FOUR

Unsung Heroes

Owen Schmidt, West Virginia, Fullback, 2005 through 2007. Schmidt consistently defied the odds. He was born with a cleft palate. He endured three surgeries to fix it, the final reconstruction coming in fourth grade. Because of this, he was constantly bullied at school. But instead of developing issues in terms of his self-confidence, this went in the other direction and developed a hardened toughness about him.

To put it mildly, Schmidt's mailbox wasn't full of recruiting letters. In fact, he was overlooked not only by Division 1 schools but also by the D-II ranks. He started his college career at Wisconsin River Falls in 2003, a sleepy Division III school about a half-hour drive outside of the Twin Cities. In his first year as a freshman, he ran for over 1,000 yards, which caused his coaches to urge him to make a move to the Division 1A level. So he ends up walking on at West Virginia in 2005, and this is the beginning of his Paul Bunyan-esque story. He was a brutal blocker and a perfect addition to a finesse spread offense that West Virginia had at the time.

Some college football players are described as Swiss Army knives. Their ability to help their team win in so many different ways makes them special. If Reggie Bush was a Swiss Army knife, Owen Schmidt was a sledgehammer. A lot of stats are thrown around in this book, and sometimes it can be difficult to suss out what those stats mean and how they relate to other great performances, great players, and great teams. This stat is not like that: Owen Schmidt broke 10 facemasks during his time at West Virginia. That rarely ever happens to a player even once in their entire career, but he broke 10 of them. West Virginia's training staff had to experiment with different metals and alloys to prevent it from happening. He found the end zone 15 times in his college career, but he was so impactful as a player that even though his stats were pretty modest from a running perspective, he still found himself on the cover of *Sports Illustrated* before the 2006 season with a few of his teammates. In his last game as a Mountaineer, he cemented his legendary status with a 57-yard touchdown run against Oklahoma in the Fiesta Bowl. His long run set the stage for a West Virginia rout. As he lumbered down the sideline, play-by-play announcer Matt Vesker called him "a runaway beer truck." Absolute legend—an unsung hero.

Next up on the list is **Hunter Renfrow**, Clemson wide receiver from 2015 to 2018. Renfrow was on the end of one of the greatest plays in Clemson football history. He caught the game-winning touchdown pass from Deshaun Watson to beat Alabama with 1 second remaining in the 2017 College Football Playoff National Championship Game.

Renfrow, a former walk-on, meant much more to the Clemson program than that one catch. He ended his career as a two-time All-ACC selection and won another national championship as a senior. In terms of his impact on the game and the receiving corps at Clemson, he was purely a route-running machine. He used subtle footwork, an array of arm and head fakes, and perfect body positioning to get open time after time after time. He needed to, because his measurables were all underwhelming. He stood less than 5'11". He ran the 40-yard dash in 4.6 seconds. By wide receiver standards, he had small hands, and he couldn't bench press to save his life. Yet he was a two-sport star in high school, getting Division 1 offers for both baseball and football. He ended his Clemson career with 186 receptions, 2,133 yards, and 15 touchdowns. Renfrow once again beat the odds by making it to the NFL. He's entering his sixth year with the Las Vegas Raiders after they made him a fifth-round pick in 2019.

Next one up, and probably my favorite on the list, **Keenan Reynolds**, Navy quarterback from 2012 to 2015.

I'll get this out of the way off the top. There should probably be a statue of Keenan Reynolds outside of Navy's football stadium, and he should be mentioned in the same breath as Heisman Trophy winners, national champions, and number one overall draft picks in the NFL draft because he was, without a doubt, one of the greatest pure football players to ever play the sport. As a triple-option quarterback, he finished as a third team All-American. He was fifth in the Heisman race his senior season, the best finish by a Service Academy player in 32 years. He is the all-time rushing leader in the history of college football in terms of touchdowns, with 88. That's 11 better than the second-place finisher (Wisconsin's Montee Ball). It has the feel of one of those records that may never be broken. He's also the all-time leading rusher as a quarterback with 4,559 career yards.

Keenan Reynolds started his career as a high school football player. He was dynamic. He was a dual threat, but he was undersized. And because he was undersized, he only received three other Division 1 offers: Air Force at the FBS level, UT Martin, and Wofford at the FCS level. It's ridiculous because, by the end, he was a Heisman-caliber quarterback. He led Navy to arguably its best season since the '60s and is included in this field because he was one of those players that, anytime he had the ball in his hands, something good was going to happen for the Midshipmen. Keenan Reynolds, unsung hero number 3.

Next up, **Jimmie Ward**, Northern Illinois safety from 2010 to 2013. Jimmy was just a two-star kid coming out of high school who consistently defied the odds in one way, and that was aggression. For lack of a better word, he was a badass. He still is a badass. He was a big hitter. He had phenomenal ball skills. He finished his college career with 320 tackles and 11 interceptions, showing off his versatility. He holds the school record in Northern Illinois for blocked punts, and he was a third team All-American in his final season in college. He helped Northern Illinois finish the regular season 12-1 with a berth in the Orange Bowl in 2012, the program's only major bowl game in school history. He played so well in that game against Florida State that he recorded a game-high 14 tackles, landing him on the NFL's radar.

That season helped his head coach get a massive promotion. He left Northern Illinois for NC State, where he's still coaching. Two years later, Ward would become a first-round NFL draft pick. And by the end of his current contract with the Houston Texans in 2025, he will have made a little over $61 million in his career. Not bad for a two-star kid.

And finally, the last one on the list is **Greg Ward**, Houston quarterback from 2013 to 2016. I spoke earlier about the idea of Swiss Army knives and how important they can be to a college football roster. Ward was just that. He was a receiver. He was a kick and punt returner. He was a quarterback. In capital letters, he was a Football Player. And when he received the opportunity from Tom Herman and the staff to play quarterback, he never looked back. He was the son of a preacher, and he proved to be Houston's savior. As a program that was downtrodden for so many years, he was able to bring them back and restore some glory for a former Southwest Conference Program.

He guided Houston to the Peach Bowl, and as touchdown underdogs, they dominated Florida State by 14 points. They finished 13-1 and were rewarded with their best ranking in the AP Poll since 1979. In that season, he threw for almost 3,000 yards. He rushed for over 1,000 yards, had 21 rushing touchdowns, and completed 67% of his passes. He was everything to that team offensively. He was an absolute headache for any team to play. But because he played so many positions in college, because he transitioned to wide receiver in the NFL and was a jack of all trades, once again, people forget how dominant he was during his last two years as a starter. That run for Houston doesn't happen without him, which doesn't get Tom Herman, his coach, the head coaching job at Texas. There were so many people who benefited because of his play. He certainly benefited as a professional football player, receiving multiple contract opportunities. But for just that window of time, I believe that he was an unsung hero and one that should be remembered in the annals of college football history.

CHAPTER FIVE

The Tournament - Play-In Games

(16) '06 Rutgers vs. (16) '15 Navy
Brooks Stadium | Conway, SC

Navy 24 – Rutgers 23
(Navy) Reynolds 26 CAR, 171 YDS, 2 TDs | (Rutgers) Leonard 97
All-Purpose YDS, REC TD
Rushing Totals: Navy 371 Yards – Rutgers 222 Yards

A seesaw battle between the Scarlet Knights and Midshipmen was decided in the closing minutes. On 4th and goal at the 2-yard line with 2:27 remaining in the game, Keenan Reynolds pulled the ball, faking to Chris Swain on the A-gap dive, and burrowed into the line. The play was ruled a touchdown on the field and was upheld upon review. Rutgers's Mike Teel was 3-for-5 on the final drive, connecting with Kenny Britt with 7 seconds remaining to help Rutgers move into field goal range. Jeremy Ito's 46-yard field goal sailed wide left as time expired, and Navy advanced to the Round of 64.

(16) '20 Coastal Carolina vs. (16) '07 Appalachian State
Yulman Stadium | New Orleans, LA

> Coastal Carolina 35 – Appalachian State 31
> (Coastal) McCall 317 Total YDS, 4 TDs | (App State) Edwards 388 Total YDS, 3 TDs, 2 INTs
> Boom-or-Bust: App State 5 Plays of 40+ Yards, 4 Turnovers (2 Fumbles, 2 INTs)

The quarterback showcase between Grayson McCall and Armanti Edwards was electric. Edwards, the two-time Walter Payton Award winner, threw for 297 yards and a touchdown and tacked on 91 yards and two scores on the ground. McCall didn't hit as many big plays, but he was ruthlessly efficient in the red zone, tossing a pair of TDs inside the Mountaineers' 20 and taking a QB draw into the end zone in the fourth quarter. The game-deciding play came with 4:35 remaining when Edwards was strip-sacked by Tarron Jackson. The fumble was recovered by Teddy Gallagher and the Chants ran the clock out to preserve a 4-point victory.

(11) '85 Air Force vs. (11) '00 Oregon State
Stanford Stadium | Palo Alto, California

> Oregon State 31 – Air Force 20
> (Ore St) Johnson 6 REC, 137 YDS, 2 TDs | (Air Force) Chad Hennings FUM REC TD
> Total Yards: OSU 477 – AF 291

The Falcons' famed run defense bottled up Ken Simonton in the first half, and a Jonathan Smith fumble was returned 37 yards for a score by College Football Hall of Famer Chad Hennings. Even with the non-offensive touchdown, Oregon State led 13–10 at halftime before Chad Johnson and T. J. Houshmandzadeh scored back-to-back third quarter touchdowns from 46 and 39 yards, respectively. The Beavers bottled up Air Force quarterback Bart Weiss on 4th and goal from the 3 late in the fourth quarter to put an end to Air Force's comeback hopes. The Beavers' reward for shutting down one of the greatest Service Academy teams of all time? Michael Vick and the '99 Virginia Tech Hokies in the Round of 64.

(11) '10 Nevada vs. (11) '07 Kansas
Apogee Stadium | Denton, Texas

Kansas 40 – Nevada 30
(Kansas) Briscoe 5 REC, 122 YDS, 3 TDs | (Nevada) Kaepernick 406 Total YDS, 4 TDs
Track Meet: Kansas YPP 9.3 – Nevada YPP 7.9

Both teams struck quickly, scoring 14 points apiece in the first quarter before the Kansas defense settled in and began corralling Colin Kaepernick. Joe Mortensen blocked a 44-yard field goal attempt in the second quarter, spurring a 17–0 run for the Jayhawks. Todd Reesing picked apart the Nevada pass defense and found Dezmon Briscoe on a broken play just before halftime. Their 45-yard touchdown connection was the second of three on the day for Briscoe. The Wolf Pack fought back in the second half but, down 38–24, were pinned near their own goal line midway through the fourth quarter. A fumbled exchange between Kaepernick and Vai Taua led to a dogpile in the end zone and a safety, salting the game away for KU.

Round of 64 - East

(1) '01 Miami (FL) vs. (16) '99 Marshall
Michie Stadium | West Point, New York

> Miami (FL) 27 – Marshall 6
> (Miami, FL) Portis/Gore 27 CAR, 198 YDS, 2 TDs | (Marshall)
> Grace 13 TK, 2.5 TFLs, FF, FR
> Marshall Third Down Conversions 3 for 14

Playing through a light rain and moderate winds off the Hudson River, this was a slobberknocker of a game from the get-go. The Hurricanes' first two drives stalled after just six plays each, and the Thundering Herd ended the first quarter with just one first down. A Najeh Davenport fumble was recovered by John Grace at the start of the second quarter, setting up the first score of the game, a 48-yard Billy Malashevich field goal. From there, the Hurricanes found their stride, outscoring the Herd 27–3 the rest of the way. A 27-yard touchdown run from Clinton Portis was followed up by an 88-yard punt return touchdown from Phillip Buchanon just before halftime. Leading 14–3 midway through the third quarter, a pass from Chad Pennington was deflected at the line of scrimmage and fell into the arms of James Lewis, putting Marshall's upset bid to bed. His interception gave the Canes their best field position of the game, and Frank Gore cashed in with a 6-yard touchdown run on the following drive. Miami would continue to live in the Marshall backfield down the stretch, ending the game with an eye-popping 11 tackles for loss.

(8) 12 Texas A&M vs. (9) '06 Louisville
Michie Stadium | West Point, New York

> Texas A&M 45 – Louisville 35
> (A&M) Manziel 404 Total YDS, 5 TDs | (UL) Douglas 11 REC, 164 YDS, 2 TDs
> Tug of War: 6 Lead Changes, Game Was Tied 35–35 With 7:08 Left

To put the fireworks from this game in perspective, from the 7-minute mark of the second quarter through the end of the third quarter, each drive ended with a score (although one was a UofL pick-six). The Cardinals' pass rush seemed powerless to stop Manziel from improvising outside the pocket. Case in point: on a 3rd and 13 at the end of the first half, Amobi Okoye had Manziel in his grasp before he spun away from him and hurled a pass off his back foot to Uzoma Nwachukwu in the corner of the end zone. Brian Brohm played hero in the final quarter, tying the game at 35 with a play-action touchdown pass to Gary Barnidge. But his heroics were short-lived, thanks to an answer from Manziel and Mike Evans just four plays later. Their touchdown hookup gave the Aggies a touchdown lead before Brohm was intercepted on the following drive at the A&M 5-yard line by Deshazor Everett. That pick was returned 64 yards, setting up the game-sealing field goal from Taylor Bertolet with 38 seconds remaining. Manziel's night ended with four passing touchdowns (Evans 2x, Nwachukwu, Swope) and a rushing score (77 rush yards).

(5) '90 Georgia Tech vs. (12) '21 Cincinnati
Lane Stadium | Blacksburg, Virginia

> Cincinnati 28 – Georgia Tech 13
> (Cincinnati) Beavers 10 TK, 2 TFLs, 2 FFs | (GT) Bell 22 CAR, 83 YDS
> Georgia Tech Only Ran 9 Plays Inside Cincinnati Territory

The Yellow Jackets were no stranger to upsets, having upset three ranked opponents in 1990, including No. 1 Virginia on the road. But in this game, they had the target on their back, and they ran headfirst into a phenomenal Bearcat defense and slick field conditions at Lane Stadium in Blacksburg. After Scott Sisson banged home a 51-yard field goal on the opening drive, Georgia Tech found the sledding difficult offensively. Its next six drives ended with four three-and-outs, a pick-six (Sauce Gardner), and a lost fumble. Desmond Ridder completed 76% of his passes, and Jerome Ford broke three 20+ yard runs on his way to a big day (179 yards, 2 TDs). If it were not for a 40-yard Emmett Merchant touchdown reception in the third quarter, made possible by a blown coverage when Ja'von Hicks slipped in the secondary, this game would have been one of the biggest blowouts of the Round of 64.

(4) '88 Notre Dame vs. (13) '13 Ole Miss
Lane Stadium | Blacksburg, Virginia

> Notre Dame 26 – Ole Miss 20
> (ND) Ho 4 for 5 FGs, Long 48 YDS | (Miss) Treadwell 9 REC, 117 YDS, TD
> Notre Dame Red Zone Defense: 5 Ole Miss Trips, 13 Total Points

The headline here was a contrast in style. Hugh Freeze's spread offense was predicated on putting linebackers in conflict by utilizing RPOs and what he has defined as a "three-man surface." Essentially, he used tight end motion to add an additional blocker to his wide receiver screens on the perimeter, so an outside hitch-screen has not one, but two blockers (Slot + TE). That would be tagged onto most of his QB read options, putting ND's Wes Prichett and Michael Stonebreaker into a bind on nearly every play. Suffice it to say, this complexity helped Ole Miss run the ball very effectively between the 20s against the Fighting Irish. Notre Dame, likewise, dialed up option and counter elements to use the Land Shark defense's speed against it. Both the Rebels and Irish ran for over 200 yards in this game, but each offense got bogged down in the red zone. Tony Rice avoided red zone turnovers and found tight end Derek Brown in the back of the end zone late in the third quarter for a go-ahead score. Leading 23–20 midway through the fourth quarter, Reggie Ho hammered home his fourth field goal of the day from 36 yards out to extend the Irish lead to 6. Ole Miss's final drive of the game was overwrought with drama. With 2:37 remaining, Chad Kelly was picked off at mid-field by George Streeter, but a roughing the passer penalty and subsequent targeting call (Flash Gordon) gave the Rebels second life. Three plays later, Kelly found Quincy Adeboyejo along the sideline for a 38-yard touchdown, but replay revealed that his right foot was out of bounds when he caught the ball. On 4th and 2 at the Notre Dame 38, Kelly connected with Evan Engram on a crossing route, but the Ole Miss tight end was leveled by Michael Stonebreaker, and the fumble was recovered by the Irish's Pat Terrell. The Irish would run out the clock and advance to meet an elite defense ('21 Cincy) in the Round of 32.

(6) '07 West Virginia vs. (11) '08 Texas Tech
The Bounce House | Orlando, Florida

> West Virginia 55 – Texas Tech 48
> (WVU) Devine 208 All-Purpose Yards, 2 Total TDs | (TTU)
> Crabtree 14 REC, 155 YD, 2 TDs
> Pick Your Poison: Three WVU Runners Ran For Over
> 80 Yards (White, Slaton, Devine)

Texas Tech's 61st-rated run defense was powerless to stop West Virginia's spread option. The Mountaineers rushed for 217 yards—in the first half. Pat White took a quarterback draw to the house from 41 yards out on the opening drive. Steve Slaton got in on the action in the second quarter, breaking three tackles on a 61-yard run. Two plays later, Owen Schmitt met TTU's Brian Duncan at the goal line and bulled his way in for 6. While Texas Tech's defense struggled from the get-go, it only took two drives for Graham Harrell and the offense to get on the same page. After digging a 0–10 hole, Harrell went to work. At one point in the first half, he connected on nine straight passes. By halftime, the shootout was on, with WVU leading 24–17. The second half featured a series of haymakers from both offenses. Michael Crabtree "Mossed" Antonio Lewis for a 27-yard touchdown halfway through the third quarter, giving the Red Raiders their first lead at 27–24. Then lightning struck for RichRod and the Mountaineers. Noel Devine took the subsequent kickoff to the house, nabbing the lead right back for WVU. Then, Ryan Mundy recovered a Baron Batch fumble three plays later. Leading 31–27, Pat White found Tito Gonzales on a play-action pass, and the junior walked into the end zone from 18 yards out. Texas Tech would score on an Eric Morris touchdown reception in the final minute, but Donnie Carona's onside kick was recovered by Darius Reynaud, securing the high-scoring win for West Virginia.

(3) '96 Florida vs. (14) '02 Iowa
The Bounce House | Orlando, Florida

> Florida 27 – Iowa 21
> (UF) Taylor 113 All-Purpose Yards, 2 TDs | (Iowa) Dallas Clark 5 REC, 62 Yards, TD
> Head On A Swivel: UF – 10 TFLs, 2 FFs, 2 INTs | Iowa – 5 Sacks, 2 FFs, INT

Danny Wuerffel never got fully comfortable in this game. The Heisman Trophy winner was sacked five times, was briefly knocked out of the game in the second quarter, and put the ball on the Bounce House turf twice. But despite the Hawkeyes' relentless pressure, Florida found ways to break big plays. Jacquez Green got the scoring started on a tunnel screen in the first quarter, spinning out of a hit from Fred Barr and weaving in and out of defenders for a 37-yard touchdown. Iowa relied heavily on Fred Russell and Brad Banks on the ground early on. The pair converted three third downs on Iowa's opening drive, which ended with a Banks pop pass to Dallas Clark in the end zone. A critical turning point in the game came with 37 seconds remaining in the half. Iowa led 14–10 and was angling for more points when a Banks pass was batted at the line of scrimmage and intercepted by Thorpe Award winner Lawrence Wright. That turnover was converted into points when Bart Edmiston banged home a 46-yard kick to end the half. The third quarter belonged to Fred Taylor and the Gators' defense. Taylor received 12 touches in the third quarter alone and scored from 3 yards out and on a screen pass. Then it was up to the Florida defense to hold onto a 27–14 lead in the fourth quarter. Banks masterfully converted a pair of fourth downs and took a quarterback draw into the end zone on 3rd and goal to make it 27–21 with 6:07 remaining in the game. Hoping to salt the game away, Spurrier gambled on 4th and 2 from the Hawkeyes' 35-yard line, but Wuerffel was sacked by Jonathan Babineaux. Iowa would get as far as the Florida 27-yard line in the final minute before a desperation heave from Banks was knocked to the ground by Fred Weary in the end zone.

(7) '87 Syracuse vs. (10) '17 UCF
Scott Stadium | Charlottesville, Virginia

> UCF 38 – Syracuse 27
> (UCF) Milton 28 for 34, 299 YDS, 3 TDs | (SU) McPherson 277 Total Yards, 2 TDs, 2 TOs
> Finishing Drives: UCF 4 for 4 in Red Zone, 4 TDs | SU 3 for 4 in Red Zone, 2 FGs, TD

The Knights' hurry-up attack was too much for the Orangemen to contain in Charlottesville. Scott Frost's "Blur" Offense ran 82 plays and converted when it mattered most. McKenzie Milton was surgical on third downs, completing 9 of his 10 attempts. The Knights as a team were also a perfect 3-for-3 on fourth down conversions. Adrian Killins got the scoring party going in the first quarter with a 33-yard rushing touchdown. Defenders vacated the middle of the field on a jet sweep fake to Dredrick Snelson, parting the sea for Killins to burst through the defense. Syracuse responded with a scoring drive of its own but had to settle for a field goal when a Tommy Kane touchdown reception was overturned by replay on the following drive. Leading 7-3, UCF responded with an 11-play drive, in which they converted a backbreaking 3rd and 16. Despite Ted Gregory being right in Milton's face, UCF's quarterback found a streaking Tre'Quan Smith down the sidelines for a 30-yard hook-up. The Orangemen kept pace through the second quarter but had to settle for another Tim Vesling field goal in the red zone after Don McPherson was tracked down by Shaq Griffin on a naked boot inside the 5-yard line. Leading 24–13 at halftime, UCF blew the game wide open early in the third quarter with a 77-yard touchdown strike from Milton to Gabe Davis. The rest of the game was simply window dressing, with Daryl "Moose" Johnston plunging in for a late-game score to cut it to an 11-point UCF lead with 4 minutes remaining. The Knights would recover the ensuing onside kick and run out the clock behind five straight Otis Anderson carries.

(2) '13 Florida State vs. (15) '97 Washington State
Scott Stadium | Charlottesville, Virginia

Florida State 41 – Washington State 24
(FSU) Nick O'Leary 6 REC, 51 YDS, 2 TDs | (WSU) Leaf 30 for 42, 311 YDS, 3 TDs, 2 INTs
ADOT Champ: Winston Finished 7 For 10 For 137 Yards And 2 TDs On Passes Over 15 Yards

---

Things got off to a great start for Mike Price's team. After hitting four straight plays of 10 yards or more on their opening drive, the Seminoles' Devonta Freeman was stripped by Steve Gleason, and the ball hit the pylon for a touchback. Ryan Leaf rode that early momentum and opened the game 5-for-6 through the air. He found Kevin McKenzie in the corner of the end zone to grab a 7–0 lead for the Cougs midway through the first quarter. After that, the Seminoles imposed their will. Jameis Winston would throw for 377 yards and four scores on the day, targeting tight end Nick O'Leary twice for 6. Defensively, Jalen Ramsey cashed in a "scoop and score" off of a Mario

Edwards Jr. strip-sack late in the first half. The Noles finished the game with six sacks in total while forcing three turnovers. The closest the Cougs would get in the second half was 34–24. Following an explosive, 44-yard Shawn Tims punt return, Michael Black scored from 14 yards out on a draw play. Down 10, Wazzu's Lamont Thompson would be called for a critical pass interference on 3rd and 7 at the FSU 28-yard line. Given a second chance, Winston and the Seminoles would march down the field, capping a 13-play drive with a Winston-to-Benjamin touchdown score with 6 minutes remaining. After a turnover on downs, Jimbo Fisher would dial up seven runs on the final drive before kneeling out the clock.

Round of 64 - West

(1) '04 USC vs. (16) '15 Navy
Martin Stadium | Pullman, Washington

> USC 49 – Navy 20
> (USC) Bush 193 All-Purpose Yards, 3 TDs | (Navy) Reynolds 24 CAR, 91 YDS, TD
> Explosiveness Gap: USC 13 Plays Of 20+ Yards From Scrimmage | Navy 3.8 Yards Per Carry

If you tuned in for the Reggie Bush Show, you were in luck. The future Heisman winner scored three different ways. He returned a kickoff 97 yards for 6, took a screen pass 46 yards to the house, and ripped off a 35-yard rushing touchdown on a reverse. Navy was successful in playing keep away with two long scoring drives in the first half. The first was a 14-play, 68-yard drive that resulted in an Austin Grebe field goal. The second was an equally methodical 11-play, 82-yard drive that ended in a Keenan Reynolds rushing touchdown on 4th and goal at the 2. But the optimism of a manageable 21–10 halftime deficit gave way to despair when Leinart opened the second half 5-for-5 for 56 yards, complete with a perfectly lofted pass in the corner for Dwayne Jarrett. The following drive, USC recovered a Quentin Ezell fumble, and the floodgates opened. USC would score touchdowns on six of its nine drives, and aside from a 64-yard run from Chris Swain, the Trojan defense did an excellent job corralling Navy in the final 30 minutes.

(8) '10 Stanford vs. (9) '10 Boise State
Martin Stadium | Pullman, Washington

Boise State 32 – Stanford 31

(BSU) Moore 27 for 40, 308 YDS, 3 TDS | (Stanford) Luck 366 Total Yards, 3 TDS (2 RUSH)

Captain(s) Clutch: Moore And Luck Combined To Go 5 For 5 On Fourth Down Conversions

---

Strictly based on seeding, this was the third upset of the first round, but it was the first true classic of the tournament. Andrew Luck and Kellen Moore combined for 637 yards passing and six total touchdowns, all without turning the ball over a single time. The quarterback clinic got started early, with the Cardinal and Broncos trading touchdown drives in the first 9 minutes of action. Luck found Coby Fleener on a play-action pass in the back of the end zone to cap a nine-play, 82-yard drive in which he converted two third downs with his legs. Moore responded with a surgical 7-for-7 start, heavily featuring the quick passing game. The Broncos would cap off their rebuttal drive with a touchdown out of the wildcat formation. Jeremy Avery faked the ball to Doug Martin on a jet sweep and took it in untouched from 6 yards out. The next two quarters didn't feature a lot of defensive answers, setting up a riveting fourth quarter with the game tied at 24 apiece. After a Doug Martin fumble foiled a promising Boise drive, Jim Harbaugh got aggressive, hoping to close the game out. First, he opted for a quarterback sneak on 4th and 1 at his own 47-yard line with 5:17 remaining in the game. Then he would leave his offense on the field even though they were well within Nate Whitaker's range at the Boise 21-yard line. Boise sold out to stop the run with Stanford in a jumbo package, but Luck found sophomore Zach Ertz on a rollout pass in the flat. Three plays later, Luck pushed his way into the end zone on a quarterback sneak, giving Stanford a 31–24 edge with 1:02 remaining. Boise wisely used two of its three remaining timeouts on Stanford's drive to conserve time. Kellen Moore hit back-to-back out routes to Austin Pettis to move the ball up to the Boise 41-yard line with 39 seconds remaining. After a near interception on a tipped pass at the line of scrimmage, Kyle Efaw secured a pass near midfield and broke a tackle, but was brought down in bounds at the Stanford 42-yard line. Boise burned its last timeout and needed a chunk play with only 26 seconds remaining in the game. Pettis was well covered by Richard Sherman on a first down incompletion, and Moore threw the ball away on second down after Stanford dropped 8 in coverage. With the game hanging in the balance, Moore stepped up in the pocket and attacked the middle of the field. Titus Young made a diving catch on a crossing route and slid down at the Stanford 8-yard line in the closing seconds. Boise would spike the ball with 3 seconds remaining, setting up the final play of regulation. With the ball on the right hash, the Broncos lined up with trips left. Moore would take the snap from under center, roll out left, and force the ball into coverage. Pettis made a contested catch a yard deep in the end zone and survived a big hit from Shayne Skov. Boise would opt to end the game there, trying for a 2-point conversion. A fake reverse to Young impacted the Stanford linebacking corp just enough for Doug Martin to bull his way into the end zone. The play would be reviewed and the successful conversion was upheld. Boise advances to play top-seeded USC in the Round of 32.

LEGENDARY BOWL

(5) '02 Ohio State vs. (12) '84 Boston College
Albertsons Stadium | Boise, Idaho

> Ohio State 24 – Boston College 20
> (OSU) Clarett 29 CAR, 139 YDS, TD | (BC) Flutie 332 Total Yards, 2 TDs, 1 Lost Fumble
> Silver Bullets: Ohio State Defense 10 TFLs, 3 FFs, 5 Sacks, 6 PBUs

As the saying goes, "Styles make fights," and that was absolutely true in this matchup between the Buckeyes and Eagles. Boston College would throw the ball 43 times on the day, while Ohio State ran the ball on 71% of its plays from scrimmage. The end result was an exciting stat line from BC's Doug Flutie and a physically imposing performance from Maurice Clarett. Ohio State opened the scoring with a 12-play, 82-yard drive that was capped with a Craig Krenzel quarterback sneak at the goal line. The Eagles responded with a kickoff return for a touchdown by Ken Bell, but the game-changing play was called back due to a block in the back. After trading field goals, Flutie tied the game with a highlight reel play. On 3rd and 3 at the Ohio State 29-yard line, Flutie broke free from a Darrion Scott sack attempt, rolled toward the sideline, and heaved a pass across his body toward the end zone. Kelvin Martin made a diving catch 2 yards deep in the end zone with Mike Doss draped all over him. Tied at 10, Ohio State rode Clarett in the third quarter, feeding the freshman 11 carries over two drives. He responded with 55 yards and a rushing touchdown. Up 17–13 late in the third, Chris Gamble high-pointed a pass along the sideline, stealing it away from Tony Thurman. Gamble would tight-rope walk down the sideline before getting pushed out at the 2-yard line. Three plays later, Lydell Ross took a pitch from Krenzel, cut back at the 2, and followed lead blocker Branden Joe into the end zone. Flutie converted two fourth downs on the following drive and kept it himself on a QB draw at the 5, finding the end zone and drawing BC within 4 at 24–20. Ohio State nearly drained the clock completely on the following drive before settling for a Mike Nugent field goal attempt. The winds in Boise pushed his kick wide right from 44 yards away, leaving the door open for Flutie and the Eagles with 51 seconds remaining. With no timeouts, BC would work the sidelines and move it to the Ohio State 35 for one final play with 7 seconds remaining. Mark Dantonio dialed up a gutsy blitz on the final play, bringing six while dropping five. The gamble paid off as Flutie was sacked by linebacker Matt Wilhelm on the final play, preserving a 4-point win for Ohio State.

(4) '23 Michigan vs. (13) '98 UCLA
Albertsons Stadium | Boise, Idaho

UCLA 27 – Michigan 24

(Michigan) Sainristil 86-YD INT TD | (UCLA) McNown 26 for 34, 289 YDS, 2 TDs, INT

Red Zone Woes: Michigan Scored 9 Points On Four Trips Inside UCLA's 20-Yard Line

---

Michigan came from behind to beat Alabama in the 2024 Rose Bowl and found themselves in a one-possession game midway through the fourth quarter against Washington in the national title game, so they were accustomed to pressure down the stretch. What they weren't prepared for was a star turn from Cade McNown, who shook off an ugly first-quarter pick-six and got into a groove, particularly in the second half. Michigan grabbed a 24–17 lead early in the fourth quarter thanks to its bruising All-American tailback Blake Corum. Michigan's primary offensive weapon pinballed off of a hit from Bruins' linebacker Tony White, stiff-armed Larry Atkins at the second level, and carried Marques Anderson the final 6 yards into the end zone. Just for good measure, Corum plunged into the end zone for the 2-point conversion on the very next play. From there, UCLA's Chris Sailer inched the Bruins closer with a 44-yard field goal halfway through the fourth to make it 24–20 Wolverines. Michigan would march deep into Bruins' territory before a fumble by tight end Colston Loveland gave UCLA the ball back with 3:02 remaining. McNown converted a pair of fourth down attempts and coaxed a roughing the passer call from the referees after a late hit from Braiden McGregor. This set UCLA up at the 13-yard line with 42 seconds remaining. After overshooting Deshaun Foster on a swing pass and scrambling out of bounds following a 4-yard carry on second down, McNown found Brian Poli-Dixon over the middle for the game-winning score.

(6) '84 BYU vs. (11) '13 Michigan State
Folsom Field | Boulder, Colorado

Michigan State 17 – BYU 13
(Michigan St) Dennard 2 INTs, 3 Pass Breakups | (BYU) Bosco 23 for 40, 288 YDS, 3 INTs
8 Michigan State Pass Break-Ups

The Cougars were accustomed to tight games, having won 5 games in '84 by a single possession. In four of those five tight games, it was BYU scoring late to pull out a victory. The same script was playing out in this one, with Michigan State scoring the first 10 points of the game. Leading 10–0 late in the first half, momentum shifted when a 44-yard Michael Geiger field goal was blocked by Kyle Morrell. On BYU's following drive, a roughing the passer penalty on Marcus Rush set up a 53-yard Lee Johnson field goal just before the end of the half. Unfazed, Michigan State wrestled control of the game away from BYU, picking off Robbie Bosco early in the fourth quarter. With solid field position, Jeremy Langford squirted through the line and broke off a 47-yard touchdown run, giving Sparty a 17–6 lead with 10:22 remaining. A Kurtis Drummond pass interference call in the red zone set up a Bosco to David Mills touchdown connection with 4:17 left, keeping BYU's hopes alive. Down 17–13, BYU's defense coaxed a three-and-out from Connor Cook and MSU, setting up a final drive with 2:10 remaining on its own 22-yard line. Bosco would convert a pair of third downs, one through the air to Glen Kozlowski and a second on a scramble up the middle. BYU would march down to the Spartan 14-yard line before falling apart. Bosco was sacked twice (Denicos Allen, Shilique Calhoun), before a deflected pass was corralled by Darqueze Dennard at the goal line. Michigan State would run the clock out to advance to the Round of 32.

(3) '91 Washington vs. (14) '11 Baylor
Folsom Field | Boulder, Colorado

Washington 45 – Baylor 27
(WASH) Emtman 3.5 TFLs, 2 FFs, FR | (BU) RGIII 288 Total Yards,
2 TDs, 1 INT, *Injured*
Bryant/Barry/Kaufman: 30 Carries, 229 Yards,
4 Rushing Touchdowns

The chess match between Art Briles and Washington defensive coordinator Jim Lambright was worth the price of admission in itself. Lambright matched Baylor's four-receiver sets by abandoning his traditional eight-man front in favor of sub-packages with five and six defensive backs. The result was haymakers from both the Bears' offense and the Huskies' defense in the first half. The Huskies struck first when Steve Emtman broke through the interior of the BU line and essentially tackled both Robert Griffin III and Terrance

Ganaway on the read option. Ganaway was docked for the fumble, and Dave Hoffmann came out of the pile with the football. Beno Bryant broke three tackles en route to a 27-yard rushing touchdown two plays later, helping UW grab a lead they wouldn't relinquish. Despite digging an early 0–10 hole, Baylor still hit the Dawgs with a flurry of big plays. Kendall Wright had receptions of 27, 38, and 61 yards on the day, the latter of which was a touchdown. Down 24–14 at halftime, RGIII entered the locker room with 262 total yards in the first 30 minutes. But the Heisman Trophy winner wouldn't get to do much more damage in the second half after a brutal hit from Donald Jones knocked him out of the game. The blindside hit broke RGIII's collarbone and sank Baylor's comeback bid. On the following drive, freshman Napoleon Kaufman salted the game away when he exploded through the line, tearing off a 65-yard rushing touchdown run. His long score stretched the lead to three touchdowns. Nick Florence led a pair of scoring drives in relief of Griffin III in the fourth quarter, helping to make the final score a little more respectable.

(7) '11 Oklahoma State vs. (10) '13 South Carolina
Aloha Stadium | Honolulu, HI

Oklahoma State 38 – South Carolina 21
(OSU) Blackmon 7 REC, 109 YDS, 2 TDS | (USC) Davis 109
All-Purpose YDS, 2 TDS
Pistols Firing: Oklahoma State Was 5 for 5 in The Red Zone
(4 TDs, 1 FG)

The Pokes must have paid close attention to the game tape from South Carolina's loss to Georgia in 2013 because they nearly replicated the Dawgs' offensive success. Brendon Weeden was dealing from the get-go. Oklahoma

State's 28-year-old quarterback opened the game 8 for 10 for 151 yards with a pair of touchdown strikes to Justin Blackmon. Two early Gamecock drives stalled in the red zone, ending in Elliot Fry chip-shot field goals. Leading 14–6, Oklahoma State hit its first bumpy patch of the half when Jadeveon Clowney sacked Weeden at his own 15-yard line. Facing a 3rd and long, Weeden checked it down to Joseph Randle, who picked up half of the yardage before going down. But a facemask call would extend the drive, which ultimately broke South Carolina's back. Three plays later, Tracy Moore caught a perfectly placed ball from Weeden and walked into the end zone. Trailing 21–6 at halftime, Steve Spurrier's team needed a spark to get things going again. They got it on the opening kickoff of the second half when Pharoh Cooper returned the ball all the way down to the Oklahoma State 36-yard line. But two plays later, Connor Shaw overshot Damiere Byrd on a crossing route, resulting in an interception for OSU's Daytawion Lowe. That red zone turnover demoralized USC, and the blowout was on. South Carolina would score touchdowns on its final two drives, but they served as nothing more than window dressing.

(2) '21 Georgia vs. (15) '93 Arizona
Aloha Stadium | Honolulu, HI

Georgia 20 – Arizona 12
(UGA) Ringo 2 INTs, 3 PBUs, FR | (U of A) Waldrop 3.5 TFLs, 1.5 Sacks, 2 FFs, Safety
Access Denied: Arizona Only Ran Seven Plays in UGA Territory

Two elite run defenses took the field, and neither gave up a single carry of more than 8 yards in this game. Playing through temperatures in the low 90s, fatigue was a concern and favored the deeper Bulldogs squad. Georgia's Zamir

White and James Cook combined for just 43 yards on 16 carries (2.7 ypc), and Arizona's backfield duo of Chuck Levy and Ontiwaun Carter also found the sledding nearly impossible (51 yards, 2.5 ypc). Instead of the ground game, this matchup swung on special teams. Arizona's Matt Peyton boomed a punt over Kearis Jackson's head midway through the first quarter. The ball rolled dead at the Bulldogs' 2-yard line, pinning Kirby Smart's team in the shadow of their own end zone. Two plays later, Rob Waldrop sacked Stetson Bennett in the end zone to give Arizona a 2–0 lead. After a 47-yard Jack Podlesny field goal, Chuck Levy would put UGA on upset alert with a 101-yard kickoff return for a touchdown. Down 9–3, Bennett and the Dawgs would respond with a clinical drive. Georgia's QB1 extended the Dawgs' drive on third down four times, twice with his legs. His final third down conversion on 3rd and 11 in the U of A red zone came on a back-shoulder fade to Brock Bowers. On 1st and goal at the 2, White powered his way into the end zone and gave the Dawgs their first lead of the game. Up 10–9 in the third quarter, Georgia's defense pinned Arizona with back-to-back sacks by Nakobe Dean and Robert Beal. Punting from his own goal line, Peyton shanked it off the side of his foot, setting UGA up just outside of the red zone. Bennett cashed in immediately with a well-placed ball on a crossing route to Jermaine Burton for 6. The teams would trade field goals in the fourth quarter before Keelee Ringo picked Dan White off for the second time in the game with 5:01 remaining. Georgia would pick up three first downs and kneel out the clock to preserve a surprisingly close victory in the Round of 64.

Round of 64 - South

(1) '19 LSU vs. (16) '20 Coastal Carolina
Sanford Stadium | Athens, GA

> LSU 65 – Coastal Carolina 21
> (LSU) Chase 8 REC, 169 YD, 3 TDs | (Coastal) McCall 277 Total YDS, 3 TDs, 3 TOs (2 INTs)
> Middle 8: LSU Scored 17 Pts in Final 4 Mins Of The 1st Half + First 4 Mins Of The 2nd Half

Coastal Carolina finished 32nd in pass defense, 10th in sacks, and third in interceptions in 2020. So the hope was that the Chanticleers' pass defense would somewhat hold up against Joe Burrow and company. So much for that. Burrow completed touchdown passes of 36, 31, and 72 yards on LSU's first three drives. By the time Burrow was knocked down for the first time, he had opened the game 11 for 12 for 197 yards and three touchdowns. Defensively, LSU made big plays and gave them up. After Derek Stingley Jr. intercepted Grayson McCall on Coastal's opening drive, the redshirt freshman passer settled in and found some success. Coastal strung together an eight-play, 75-yard touchdown drive after digging a 0–14 hole to the Bayou Bengals in the first quarter. The critical play of the drive came on an option from McCall out of the pistol. The Chants' full house formation confused LSU, giving McCall enough room to operate on the edge. As he was being wrapped up by Damone Clark, McCall flipped it out to C. J. Marable, and the veteran back took it 28 yards for a touchdown. This would be as close as Coastal would get, thanks to highly disruptive play from Dave Aranda's defense the rest of the way (12 TFLs, 4 Sacks, 4 Takeaways). The knockout punch for Coach O came from Clyde Edwards-Helaire when he broke three tackles inside the 10 before diving for the pylon. His score gave LSU a 44–14 lead early in the second half and allowed LSU to empty its bench in the fourth quarter.

(8) '82 SMU vs. (9) '96 Arizona State
Sanford Stadium | Athens, GA

> Arizona State 26 – SMU 23 (OT)
> (ASU) Tillman 8 TK, 1.5 TFLs, FF, INT | (SMU) Dickerson 24 CAR, 188 YDS, 2 TDs

Ball security was the headline in this game between the Sun Devils and Mustangs. Running the option, the Pony Express put the ball on the turf four times but only lost one of them. Defensively, SMU was all over Jake Plummer, harassing him with constant pressure inside the pocket. Jake "The Snake" lost two fumbles, both of which were recovered by Michael Carter. Neither team could build more than a one-score lead, but SMU was clinging to a 23–20 advantage halfway through the fourth quarter. Bobby Collins opted to punt on 4th and 1 at his own 37 with a chance to salt the game away. This would prove to be a critical error as ASU's J. R. Redmond returned the punt 45 yards. With 12 seconds remaining in regulation, Robert Nycz confidently drilled a 33-yard field goal to send the game to overtime. Arizona State won the coin toss and elected to play defense first. After three Dickerson carries, SMU was already knocking on the door at the ASU 8-yard line. On 1st and goal, catastrophe struck for the Mustangs when a Lance McIlhenny swing pass to Craig James out of the backfield bounced off his fingertips and fell to the ground. It was ruled a backward pass and a live ball, which was recovered by the Sun Devils All-American linebacker Derrick Rodgers. Three Terry Battle carries later, and Arizona State brought Nycz back on the field for a game-winning field goal attempt. His 28-yard kick was nearly blocked by Russell

Carter off the edge, but it squeezed inside the right upright, sending Arizona State to the Round of 32.

(5) '00 Oklahoma vs. (12) '97 North Carolina
Alamodome | San Antonio, Texas

> North Carolina 17 – Oklahoma 10
> (UNC) Bly 4 TK, 3 PBUs, 1 Pick-Six | (OU) Griffin 23 CAR,
> 93 YDS, 1 TD (REC)
> North Carolina Fourth Down Gambles: 3 For 4

A pair of elite defenses locked horns on the fast track down in San Antonio. The first half featured nine total punts, just seven third down conversions, three fumbles, and one pick-six for North Carolina's Dré Bly. Oklahoma's miscue was particularly damaging because Josh Heupel's interception came in the red zone at the end of the Sooners' most effective drive of the half (7 plays, 77 yards). Leading 10–3 at halftime, the Tar Heels still had to figure out how to move the football because they gained just 89 total yards in the first half. Oklahoma responded in the third quarter, scoring a touchdown on its opening drive. Curtis Fagan got open on a skinny post on the opening play of the second half, burning UNC for 28 yards. Five plays later, Quentin Griffin took a screen pass from Heupel and split a pair of defenders in the backfield before taking it to the house for a 36-yard score. With the game tied at 10 early in the fourth quarter, Alge Crumpler made a diving reception on 3rd and 16 near midfield, setting up a 4th and 1 at the OU 46-yard line. Mack Brown gambled and went for it, and Jonathan Linton rewarded him by squirting through the line past a loaded box for a long touchdown run. Oklahoma would get one last chance to even things up in the closing minutes before a

Heupel pass sailed on him, falling into the arms of safety Omar Brown and sealing the upset win for UNC.

(4) '10 Auburn vs. (13) '98 Tulane
Alamodome | San Antonio, Texas

> Auburn 56 – Tulane 34
> (AU) Newton 382 Total YDS, 6 Total TDs | Dawson 9 REC, 106 YDS, 2 TDs
> Ahead Of Schedule: Auburn Averaged 6.8 Yards Per Play On First Downs

The Green Wave offense, with RichRod calling plays, certainly belonged on the field with this former national champion. Tulane would rack up 404 yards offensively, and had it not been for a lost fumble at the Auburn 8 and a Shaun King interception in the end zone, they could have thrown a real scare into the Tigers. The problem, however, was its defense, which was completely overwhelmed by Gus Malzahn's hurry-up, no-huddle attack. Cam Newton was in complete control, and when Auburn wasn't pushing Tulane around between the tackles, it was breaking runs on the perimeter. Onterio McCalebb, in limited work, was a home run hitter in this game. He finished with six carries for 109 yards and two touchdowns. His highlight reel run came early in the second quarter on a jet sweep. The Auburn running back took it 75 yards untouched along the sideline, leaving Tulane's Tellius Carr in his wake. Trailing 35–21 early in the third quarter, Tulane bowed its neck a bit, forcing a 3rd and short for Auburn at its own 29-yard line. Malzahn opted to go play-action, but a free rusher got to Newton, hitting him from behind. The Heisman winner staggered, regained his footing, and fired a wobbly ball into the seam, targeting Darvin Adams. Auburn's top pass-catcher won a

50/50 ball, stiff-armed the defender, and was off to the races. He would be pushed out of bounds at the Tulane 15-yard line, but this constituted the back-breaking play of the game for Auburn. Tulane would score late to make things more respectable, but this was one of the first round's biggest blowouts.

(6) '99 Virginia Tech vs. (11) '00 Oregon State
Neyland Stadium | Knoxville, Tennessee

Virginia Tech 27 – Oregon State 17
(VT) Stith 20 CAR, 106 YDS, 2 TDs | (OSU) Simonton 22 CAR, 101, TD
Beamer Ball: 3 Takeaways, 0 Giveaways, 9 TFLs,
1 Blocked FG Returned For TD

The Hokies didn't need much Michael Vick magic to comfortably dispense with the Beavers. It started on the opening drive when Corey Moore caught Jonathan Smith's elbow in the pocket, forcing a wobbly pass and an interception. Four plays later, the Hokies cashed in on the ground when Vick flipped it out to Shyrone Stith on the speed option. Stith took it up the sideline for a 22-yard score. Oregon State found some success on the ground with Ken Simonton but couldn't get the passing game going. It wasn't until late in the first half, trailing 10–0, that the Beavers hit their first completion over 10 yards. That 27-yard hook-up between Smith and T. J. Houshmandzadeh set Oregon State up for a 35-yard field goal attempt with 3 seconds remaining in the half. Instead of drawing within a touchdown, disaster struck on the attempt. Carl Bradley blocked Ryan Cesca's attempt, and Ike Charlton returned it all the way for a touchdown. That 10-point swing handed Va Tech a 17-0 halftime lead and let Bud Foster's defense tee off on Smith in the second half. Had it not been for a garbage-time touchdown with 6 seconds remaining in the game, this would have been one of the most dominant first-round defensive performances.

(3) '18 Clemson vs. (14) '07 Hawai'i
Neyland Stadium | Knoxville, Tennessee

> Clemson 49 – Hawai'i 14
> (Clemson) Etienne 194 All-Purpose YDS, 3 TDs | (Haw) Brennan 33 for 52, 282 YDS, 2 TDs
> Moving Forward/Moving Backward: Clemson 10 Plays Of 20+ Yards | Hawai'i 9 Off Penalties

The high-flying Warrior passing attack ran into a buzzsaw following their dream regular season in 2007 when they drew a motivated and supremely talented Georgia defense in the Sugar Bowl. Their reward for making this tournament? Facing a steady rain and a championship defense built specifically to stop spread attacks. To Colt Brennan's credit, he protected the football despite the sloppy conditions and being under constant duress in this game. Clemson sacked him seven times and pressured him on nearly every attempt. But June Jones' team won the turnover battle 2-0, which kept things close in the first 20 minutes. A Brennan-to-Bess touchdown connection got Hawai'i on the board and made things interesting at 14-7 early in the second quarter. Then Clemson started connecting with a few haymakers. It started with a 77-yard Travis Etienne rushing touchdown. The following drive, Trevor Lawrence bombed a pass down the sideline, hitting Justyn Ross in stride for a 61-yard gain. Leading 28-7 early in the third quarter, Tee Higgins made a highlight reel one-handed catch over the middle, absorbed a big hit delivered by Jacob Patek, spun, hurdled, and dragged another defender, racking up an additional 25 yards. Etienne would score on a swing pass two plays later, putting the game officially out of reach. Kelly Bryant and the second string played most of the fourth quarter while the starting defense continued to put the shackles on the Hawai'i offense. Isaiah Simmons was Clemson's defensive player of the game, finishing with eight tackles, 2.5 tackles for loss, three pass breakups, and a forced fumble.

(7) '04 California vs. (10) '94 Colorado
Kyle Field | College Station, Texas

> Colorado 38 – California 20
> (CU) Westbrook 7 REC, 115 YDS, 2 TDS | (Cal) Rodgers 25 for 33, 306, 2 TDs, 2 INTs
> Stampede: Buffaloes Havoc Numbers – 8 TFLs, 5 PBUs, 2 INTs, 2 FFs, FR

Under the scorching Texas sun (97°) this game required both teams to rotate players along the line of scrimmage. Luckily for both the Buffs and Bears, this was a strength vs. strength matchup in the trenches. Cal finished second nationally against the run in 2004, allowing a measly 82.5 yards per game on the ground. Colorado ranked third nationally, with 291.5 rushing yards per game at a D-1A best of 6.2 yards per carry. Colorado was bottled up between the tackles in this one (22 carries, 47 yards) but found success on the perimeter, particularly when they ran speed option. Offensive coordinator Elliot Uzelac called seven option runs for Kordell Stewart and Rashaan Salaam, and those plays arguably swung the game. Stewart kept it on three of them, scampering for 51 yards and a score. On the other four, Stewart pitched it out to the Heisman Trophy winner, who consistently found the open field. Salaam broke runs of 10, 14, 22, and 55 yards on those option pitches. Cal pulled within 7 midway through the third quarter, at 24–17, but would turn the ball over on its next two possessions. The first came on a big hit delivered by Steve Rosga. He separated Geoff McArthur from the football, and Ted Johnson scooped it up at Colorado's 45-yard line. The Buffs cashed in on the short field to extend their lead to 31–17. The next turnover would be the nail in the coffin for the Bears. Aaron Rodgers threaded the needle on a pass in the seam, placing it perfectly on tight end Garrett Cross inside the 10-yard line. But Cross bobbled it, got lit up by Matt Russell, and the ball popped up into the air. Chris Hudson snatched the ball out of the air and returned it 35 yards before Rodgers made a shoestring, touchdown-saving tackle. Those turnovers sealed Cal's fate and sent the Buffaloes to the next round.

(2) '20 Alabama vs. (15) '91 East Carolina
Kyle Field | College Station, Texas

> Alabama 59 – East Carolina 24
> (Bama) Smith 7 REC, 177 YDS, 3 Total TDs | (ECU) Blake 288 Total YDs, 3 TDs, 3 INTs

The Pirates had a perfect photo op after they scored the opening touchdown of the game. Framing that 7-0 lead over Nick Saban and Alabama would be as good as it was going to get for ECU. Even its opening touchdown drive was aided by a bit of luck. An interception by Patrick Surtain II was overturned by a roughing the passer penalty, and Alabama committed 35 yards of penalties on ECU's opening drive alone. Jeff Blake would connect with tight end Luke Fisher for an 8-yard touchdown to cap its opening drive. Then, Alabama went to work. The Tide scored on all five of their first half possessions (4 TDs, 1 FG). DeVonta Smith got things started with a 56-yard catch, mossing Chris Hall and nearly taking it the distance on the Tide's first offensive snap of the game. Four plays later, Najee Harris bulled his way in for a score, carrying

ECU linebacker Robert Jones into the end zone. Mac Jones completed passes to seven different players in the first half and was in complete control working from a clean pocket. Leading 17–7 in the second quarter, Jaylen Waddle one-upped his Heisman-winning teammate by taking a bubble screen 67 yards for a score on a catch-and-run up the sideline. Leading 38–10 at half, Alabama was content to run the ball repeatedly in the second half and play prevent against ECU's spread shotgun attack. Blake would rack up yardage, but a pair of third quarter interceptions by Brian Branch put this game on ice.

Round of 64 - Midwest

(1) '95 Nebraska vs. (16) '12 Northern Illinois
Camp Randall Stadium | Madison, Wisconsin

Nebraska 52 – Northern Illinois 17
(NU) Frazier 227 Total Yards, 3 Rushing TDs | (NIU) Lynch 20 for 36, 247 YDS, 2 Total TDs
First Four Nebraska Drives: 20 Plays, 263 YDS, 4 Touchdowns

The Cornhuskers are not a team you want to fall behind, but that's just what the Huskies did in this one. On the third play of the game, Tommie Frazier faked to Jeff Mackovicka on a dive and turned the corner before pitching it off to Lawrence Phillips at the numbers. The Cornhuskers' I-Back stiff-armed Demetrius Stone and raced down the sideline for a 64-yard touchdown. Before NIU could even settle in, it was already 28–0 Nebraska halfway through the second quarter. Jordan Lynch succeeded with a pair of fourth down conversions on the Huskies' final drive of the first half to make things respectable. Lynch found Tommylee Lewis on a Tebow-esque jump pass at the goal line to make it 28–7 with 2:02 remaining in the half. That is as close as the Huskies would get to Big Red. The second half was a Blackshirt showcase. The Nebraska defense ended the game with 11 TFLs, three coming from Jared Tomich. Leading 45–17 in the waning minutes of the game, Lynch was picked off by Michael Booker, and he returned it all the way down to the NIU 3-yard line. Frazier would dive into the end zone on the following play, capping a banner day for Nebraska.

(8) '04 Utah vs. (9) '07 Mizzou
Camp Randall Stadium | Madison, Wisconsin

> Mizzou 42 – Utah 41 (OT)
> (MU) Maclin 227 All-Purpose YDS, 3 TDs | (UT) Weddle 6 TK,
> 1 PBU, 1 Scoop 'n' Score
> Seesaw Battle: 4 Lead Changes in Fourth Quarter/Overtime

This game had it all. There were five touchdowns of 50 yards or more. A special teams score for Mizzou and a defensive touchdown for Utah. Seven fourth down attempts in total. And the game came down to a 2-point conversion in overtime. The scoring got started on the opening drive when Marty Johnson burst through the line, spun out of a Sean Weatherspoon tackle attempt, and dragged Carl Gettis the final 5 yards into the end zone. Mizzou's Jeff Wolfert knocked home one of his two attempts from 50+ yards away on the Tigers' opening drive. From there, Utah's Alex Smith and Mizzou's Chase Daniel engaged in the best quarterback duel of the opening round. Smith finished with 287 passing yards, 77 rushing yards, and four total touchdowns. Daniel was more prolific through the air (303 yards) but was merely a facilitator for Jeremy Maclin. The redshirt freshman scored three touchdowns, all coming in the second half and overtime. He took a kickoff 98 yards to the house, a swing pass out of the backfield 51 yards for a score, and a jet sweep in for 6. The Utes had a chance to win it in regulation, but David Carroll's 54-yard attempt came up just short. In overtime, Mizzou struck first on a Maclin rushing touchdown. Utah would score on its very first play, a 25-yard hook-up between Smith and Steve Savoy in the back corner of the end zone. Urban Meyer would opt to go for 2, but the shovel pass was sniffed out, and Paris Warren was gang-tackled a yard and a half shy of the goal line. Mizzou will draw an old Big 8/12 foe in the next round, hoping for better success than they had in the '90s against Nebraska (0–10, average margin 13–48).

(5) '80 Pitt vs. (12) '99 Wisconsin
Rynearson Stadium | Ypsilanti, Michigan

Pitt 17 – Wisconsin 13

(Pitt) Green 6 TK, 2.5 TFLs, FF, FR | (UW) Dayne 35 CAR, 117 YDS, TD

"Puntapalooza": 14 Punts in Total, 4 Downed Inside The 5-yard Line

---

Outside of '93 Arizona-'21 Georgia, this was the best defensive matchup in the Round of 64. Wisconsin was rated the third-best defense of the 1990s by ESPN's Bill Connelly. And Pitt countered with a star-studded defense that unleashed a record-setting pass rush. Hugh Green finished second in the Heisman race after a 17-sack season in 1980, and Rickey Jackson collected 12 sacks before embarking on a Hall of Fame career in the NFL. Both defenses wreaked havoc for four quarters, suppressing the scoring while elevating the importance of both punters. Trailing 13–10 with 7:05 remaining in the game, Pitt's David Hepler executed a perfect coffin corner, pinning UW down at its own 2-yard line. After three Ron Dayne runs, the Badgers punted out of their own end zone. The Panthers' fair caught the ball at their own 39-yard line and put together the game-winning drive. On 3rd and goal at the Wisconsin 3, Dan Marino rolled right and fired a perfect pass to tight end Benji Pryor 1 yard deep in the end zone. Leading by 4 in the closing minutes, Hugh Green would end the game with a strip-sack of Brooks Bollinger. Green emerged from the pile with the football, and Marino kneeled out the clock to preserve a one-score win.

(4) '98 Tennessee vs. (13) '15 Houston
Rynearson Stadium | Ypsilanti, Michigan

> Tennessee 20 – Houston 17
> (Tenn) Martin 187 Passing, 64 Rushing, 0 Turnovers | (UH) Taylor 11 TKs, 3.5 TFLs, FF
> Bend But Don't Break: Houston Had six Trips Inside UT's 30-Yard Line, Only Scored 17 Points

This was a very physical game in the first half. Neither team exceeded 140 yards of total offense, and had it not been for a muffed punt by Demarcus Ayers, Tennessee would likely have trailed as the favorite in this game. But Ayers's fumble set UT up in the red zone, and Jamal Lewis scored on a sweep from 8 yards out. Leading 13–7 at halftime, Tennessee needed a spark offensively. They got it from Peerless Price on the opening kickoff of the second half. Price returned it 58 yards, and two plays later, he made a diving catch along the sideline on a play-action pass from Tee Martin. Martin would keep it on an option two plays later, helping Tennessee extend its lead to 13. Trailing 20–10 in the fourth quarter, Houston mounted its comeback. Greg Ward had scrambles of 12, 14, and 27 yards on the Cougars' touchdown drive. He capped off the one-man show by spinning away from Corey Terry, rolling to his right, and firing a pass into the back corner of the end zone. Chane Allen hauled in the pass and survived a big hit from Deon Grant. Trailing by 3 with two timeouts and 2:17 remaining on the clock, Houston had a decision to make: kick it deep or go for broke with an onside kick. Tom Herman opted for the onside kick, and Ty Cummings executed it to perfection. The second hop on his onside kick hit off Cedrick Wilson's shoulder pad, and after a pileup, Houston's Steven Dunbar emerged with the football. Trailing by 3, Houston would convert a pair of third downs to move to the Tennessee 29-yard line with less than 45 seconds remaining. Back-to-back run stuffs by Al Wilson backed them up to the 32-yard line, and a near interception by Dwayne Goodrich on third down set the stage for a long field goal from the left hash for Cummings. If he made it, it would be the longest of his career. He didn't. Cummings's kick sailed wide right, and Tennessee dodged a big bullet.

(6) '14 Oregon vs. (11) '07 Kansas
Yager Stadium | Oxford, Ohio

Kansas 41 – Oregon 30

(KU) Reesing 30 for 42 for 317 YDS, 4 Total TDs | (UO) Mariota 404 Total YDS, 4 TDs, 2 INTs

Track Meet: 1,204 Total Yards, 7.2 Yards Per Play, four Touchdowns of 40+ Yards

---

Neither defense strung together back-to-back stops in this game, that's the kind of offensive showcase we saw at Yager Stadium. The difference was Kansas's inspired play in the red zone. Oregon broke off a 75-yard touchdown run (Marshall) and an 82-yard Mariota-to-Carrington catch-and-run on the day, but inside the red zone, it was the Jayhawks defense making memorable plays. On 3rd and goal at 4 at the end of the first half, Mike Rivera made a shoestring tackle on Mariota with nothing but green between the Heisman winner and the end zone. The opening drive of the second half was similar in that Oregon moved the ball quickly down-field only to stall out when Pharaoh Brown was separated from the football by a victorious hit from Darrell Stuckey in the end zone. That would-be touchdown catch would loom large as Oregon settled for its second straight field goal. Leading 31–23, Todd Reesing and the KU offense converted a pair of third downs before he uncorked a deep pass to Marcus Henry. The 6'5" receiver snatched the jump ball away from Troy Hill and regained his balance to walk into the end zone from just 5 yards out. His highlight-worthy grab gave KU a 15-point lead late in the third quarter. Mariota and the Ducks wouldn't go quietly in the fourth. They answered with a seven-play touchdown drive, capped by a 24-yard touchdown pass from Mariota to Charles Nelson. The Ducks drew within 7 when Devon Allen took an end around in for 2. But an illegal chop block took the points off the board, and Oregon settled for an extra point from Aidan Schneider. Trailing 38–30, Oregon forced a long field attempt from Kansas's Scott Webb. His 49-yard kick grazed the inside of the left upright, extending the KU lead to 11 points with 4 minutes remaining. Two plays into the following drive, Mariota would be picked off by Aqib Talib at midfield. Kansas's dream run continues to the Round of 32.

(3) '94 Penn State vs. (14) '14 Mississippi State
Yager Stadium | Oxford, Ohio

Penn State 37 – Mississippi State 31
(PSU) Carter 27 CAR, 139 YDS, 2 TDs | (MSU) Prescott 317
Total YDS, 3 Total TDs (2 Rush)

These two elite offenses lived up to the hype in this game. Kerry Collins and Dak Prescott both completed north of 70% of their pass attempts, and their running backs kept them in 3rd and manageable all game long. The Nittany Lions relied heavily on Ki-Jana Carter in the first two drives, feeding the Heisman runner-up with 11 touches. Prescott wasn't asked to carry the Bulldogs early on, thanks to big chunk runs from Josh Robinson. He scored from 58 yards out on the opening drive and broke a 44-yard run on MSU's second drive. With the game tied at 24 in the third quarter, the game swung on a penalty and ejection. Penn State's drive was extended by a Preston Smith roughing the passer call, and he would be ejected due to a helmet-to-helmet hit on Collins. With new life, Collins would find Kyle Brady in the back of the end zone four plays later, giving Penn State its first lead since 10–7 in the first quarter. On the ensuing drive, Prescott took a deep shot and connected with De'Runnya Wilson. The 6'5" receiver skied over Tony Pittman and reeled it in. But as Wilson continued upfield, Kim Herring punched the ball free from behind. Phil Yeboah-Kodie recovered the fumble, and Penn State used the turnover to extend its lead to 34–24 on a Brett Conway field goal. Mississippi State traded a touchdown for a PSU field goal in the fourth, setting up the final drive for Prescott. Trailing by 6 in the waning minutes, Prescott converted two fourth downs with his legs, moving the ball down to the Penn State 18-yard line. On first down, Fred Ross failed to complete a toe-tap in the end zone. On second down, with less than a minute remaining, Prescott was sacked by Jeff Perry. On third down, Prescott found Fred Brown on a crossing route, but he was taken down at the 10, 2 yards short of the first down. On 4th and 2, with the game on the line, Prescott took it himself and was stood up at the line of scrimmage by Brian Gelzheiser. The red zone stop secured the win for Penn State.

(7) '10 TCU vs. (10) '98 Kansas State
Kinnick Stadium | Iowa City, Iowa

> Kansas State 21 – TCU 18
> (KSU) Bishop 293 Total YDS, 2 TDs, INT | (TCU) Kerley 188
> All-Purpose YDS, 2 TDs
> Little Man, Big Plays: Lockett four Targets, 3 Receptions, 110 Yards,
> 2 TDs

The Horned Frogs jumped out to a 10–0 lead thanks to an opening drive field goal from Ross Evans and a first quarter interception from Tejay Johnson. But then Michael Bishop and the K-State offense started to settle in a bit. Bishop capped a 10-play, 76-yard drive with a 3rd and goal touchdown run from 7 yards out. The following drive, K-State's Mark Simoneau punched the ball away from Ed Wesley, creating a short field for the Wildcats. After an offensive pass interference call on Darnell McDonald, Bishop connected with Aaron Lockett on a 48-yard bomb down the middle of the field. Leading 14–10 at half, the Wildcats kept the pressure on via another Bishop-to-Lockett deep shot to open the second half. Lockett caught a pass over the middle at the TCU 45-yard line, and he ran past two defenders on his way to the end zone. With virtually no answers offensively, it would be a Jeremy Kerley punt return that breathed life back into TCU in the fourth. Kerley fielded the ball at his own 18-yard line, spun away from a tackler, stiff-armed another, and weaved his way through traffic before hurdling KSU's punter James Garcia at midfield. His long punt return touchdown brought TCU within 5, and a successful 2-point conversion run by Matthew Tucker cut the lead to 3 with 6 minutes left. Kansas State was unsuccessful in its attempt to run out the clock, opting to punt on 4th and 2 at the TCU 40-yard line with 1:27 remaining. Andy Dalton would lead TCU into Wildcat territory, but a pair of drops by

Josh Boyce and Waymon James left TCU out of field goal range on 4th and 10 near midfield. Mike Stoops opted not to sit back on fourth down, bringing six rushers. Darren Howard got home and wrapped up Andy Dalton, sealing the 3-point win for Kansas State.

(2) '05 Texas vs. (15) '00 Purdue
Kinnick Stadium | Iowa City, Iowa

Texas 55 – Purdue 31

(UT) Charles 17 CAR, 217 YDS, 2 TDs | (Purdue) Brees 32 for 50, 378 YDS, 3 TDs, INT

Room To Graze: Texas Running Game – 51 Carries, 303 Yards, 6 Touchdowns

---

The first half was an offensive showcase for the Longhorns and Boilermakers. Two different styles, moving the football effectively, while avoiding negative plays and protecting possession. Drew Brees led four scoring drives in the first 30 minutes, and the two-time Heisman finalist was particularly impressive on third downs (6 for 7, 49 yards, TD). Vince Young wasn't asked to do as much in the early going because the running game was popping big plays left and right. Jamaal Charles and Ramonce Taylor both hit 50+ yard rushing touchdowns in the first half, helping UT enter the locker room with a narrow 27–24 lead at the half. The Longhorns' running game continued to gouge the Purdue defense in the second half, and their defense finally started to get to Brees. A fumble by Montrell Lowe on Purdue's first drive of the second half dug Purdue a hole, but the Boilermakers still had life trailing 34–24 midway through the third quarter once they started to drive down the field. At the UT 15-yard line on 3rd and 5, Brees dealt with a blitz straight up the middle by Aaron Harris. Brees sailed a throw off his backfoot, airmailing it over Tim

Stratton and into the arms of Michael Huff. The Jim Thorpe Award winner returned the interception 87 yards before being pushed out of bounds at the Purdue 10. Two plays later, Vince Young took a QB power into the end zone, officially ending Purdue's upset bid.

Round of 32 - East

(1) '01 Miami (FL) vs. (8) '12 Texas A&M
Michie Stadium | West Point, New York

Miami (FL) 34 – Texas A&M 17

(Miami FL) Reed 7 TK, 2 TFLs, 1 INT, 1 Scoop-n-Score | (A&M) Evans 7 REC, 94 YDS, TD

Punches Landed: Dorsey 2 Knockdowns, 1 Sack | Manziel 14 Knockdowns, 4 Sacks, 3 TOs

---

This is a matchup that perfectly explains why the Hurricanes entered this tournament as the odds-on favorite to win it all. Miami possesses the kind of depth in its secondary to match modern spread offense's four and five-receiver sets while still generating pressure on the quarterback. Case in point, Alphonso Marshall and Sean Taylor were each on the field for over 40% of the Canes' defensive snaps, and both backup defensive backs made a big impact. Marshall broke up three passes out of the slot, and Taylor made a diving interception when a Manziel throwaway attempt failed to reach the sideline. Offensively, Ken Dorsey was lights out when Rob Chudzinski dialed up play-action passes. Dorsey completed seven passes off of play-action for 128 yards and two touchdowns (Shockey, Johnson). The Canes were workmanlike in their approach, converting 53% of their third down attempts, scoring all four times they entered the red zone (3 TDs, FG), all while avoiding a single turnover. Manziel had his moments, namely a 44-yard scramble that set up a Christine Michael touchdown and a 61-yard touchdown strike to Mike Evans in the third quarter. That third quarter score brought A&M within 7 at 24–17. But the fourth quarter was a house of horrors for Aggie fans. Manziel ducked out of a sack attempt by Jerome McDougle only to get rocked by Jonathan Vilma and cough up the football. Ed Reed scooped it up and stiff-armed E. Z. Nwachukwu to the turf before returning it 38 yards for a touchdown. The next drive was another addition to Reed's highlight reel when No. 20 pulled it away from Ryan Swope in traffic for a game-sealing interception. On the day, Manziel accounted for 271 total yards and two scores (one rush, one pass), but he would be responsible for three turnovers, all of which came in the second half.

(4) '88 Notre Dame vs. (12) '21 Cincinnati
Lane Stadium | Blacksburg, Virginia

Notre Dame 23 – Cincinnati 21

(ND) Reggie Ho 3 for 3 on FGs | (Cincy) Sauce Gardner 3 PBUs, 1 Pick-Six

Two-Thirds Of The Game: ND And Cincy Special Teams/Defense Accounted For 30 Of 44 Points

---

For the second straight game, Barry Alvarez's defense was forced to deal with an RPO-heavy attack. And just like their opening round game with '15 Ole Miss, it took a handful of drives for the Irish's defense to settle in. The Bearcats averaged 6 yards per carry, and Desmond Ridder completed five of his first six attempts on UC's first two drives. The Bearcats' opening drive was undone by a holding penalty in the red zone, and Luke Fickell settled for 3. On the second drive, Ridder pulled it away from Jerome Ford on the mesh and broke off running. His 45-yard run set up a Ford rushing touchdown, giving UC a 10–0 early lead. After a Reggie Ho field goal, Notre Dame's defense caught a break when Alec Pierce failed to drag his foot on a would-be 35-yard completion. Forced to punt, Rocket Ismail swung the game back in the Irish's favor. He received the punt at ND's 22-yard line, split a pair of defenders, sidestepped a 3rd, and cut it back outside for an adrenaline-pumping 78-yard punt return score. Tied at 10 at halftime, Notre Dame would feature more from Tony Rice in the option game in the second half. On its opening drive of the second half, Rice had the ball in his hands on five option plays. He picked up 30 yards on keepers and sprung two long runs by Mark Green when he pitched the ball to his top back. Tony Brooks scored from 3 yards out to give ND its first lead of the game at 17–10. After a three-and-out, Notre Dame hit its biggest pass play of the afternoon when Rice found Ricky Watters on a post pattern. The 38-yard hookup led to Reggie Ho's second field goal of the day, this time from 42 yards out. Cincy would use two Notre Dame penalties (def P. I., roughing the passer) to move into field goal range. Cole Smith would hook his kick wide right, but a third penalty of the drive, this time an offside infraction, gave Smith a do-over, on which he capitalized from 37 yards out. Trailing 20–13, with 9 minutes remaining in the game, Notre Dame had a chance to extend its lead when Tony Rice was intercepted in the end zone by Sauce Gardner. The future NFL All-Pro took it 102 yards to the house and put the Irish on upset alert. A roughing the kicker call on the extra point emboldened Fickell to go for 2, which was successful thanks to a Ridder quarterback sneak. Leading 21–20, Notre Dame turned to Rice and the running game once more. Three third down conversions put Notre Dame at the Cincy 35 with just over 4 minutes remaining in the game. A Rice sideline shot to tight end Derek Brown on a wheel route was broken up near the goal line by Coby Bryant. On 3rd and 7 out of a split-back formation, Rice scrambled up the middle but was tackled a yard short of the first down. Lou Holtz opted for a 46-yard field goal attempt. Reggie Ho's attempt just cleared the crossbar, giving Notre Dame a 23–21 lead with 3:05 remaining in the game. After a pair of first down completions to Tyler Scott, all Cincy needed was one more chunk play to get into field goal range. Ridder had Tre Tucker open at the 25-yard line, but he was pressured in the pocket by Frank Stams and forced to throw off his back foot. Without enough oomph on the ball, Notre Dame's Todd Lyght cut in front of Tucker and picked it off, sending the Irish to the Sweet 16.

(3) '96 Florida vs. (6) '07 West Virginia
The Bounce House | Orlando, Florida

> Florida 31 – West Virginia 27
> (UF) Hilliard 8 REC, 127 YDS, TD | (WVU) White 194 Pass,
> 136 Rush, 3 TDs, 2 Lost Fumbles
> Pin Your Ears Back: WVU And UF Combined For Nine Sacks

The first quarter promised a shootout, but it would be the defenses that took center stage in the fourth quarter. Florida struck first on its opening drive when Danny Wuerffel connected with Reidel Anthony for a 36-yard score. West Virginia responded on its third play from scrimmage. Steve Slaton took a handoff from Pat White, broke through an arm tackle at the line of scrimmage, and hurdled over a diving tackle attempt by Tony George near midfield. Slaton's 68-yard rushing touchdown sent the crowd into a frenzy. After trading field goals, the defenses really settled in on both sides. Deadlocked at 17, special teams played a pivotal role in the third quarter. A muffed punt by Vaughn Rivers was recovered by Florida, setting up a Fred Taylor rushing score from 2 yards out. Then a roughing the punter penalty extended a West Virginia drive, which ended in a Pat McAfee field goal. The referees would once again take center in the fourth quarter when James Bates was ejected for targeting. West Virginia used that 15-yard penalty as a springboard and capped a 10-play drive with a touchdown plunge from Owen Schmitt. Leading 27–24, WVU forced a three-and-out after Ike Hilliard dropped a deep pass along the sideline. Florida would punt with 4:09 remaining in the game. After Steve Spurrier exhausted his timeouts, West Virginia went for the kill shot, dialing up a play-action pass on second down near midfield. Jevon Kearse came off the edge unblocked and hammered White, forcing a fumble. Ed Chester dove on the ball, giving Florida a chance to win the game with 1:55 remaining. Wuerffel was perfect on the final drive, completing all five attempts including the go-ahead score to Hilliard. A sack and three incompletions later, and the game was in the books, sending the Gators to the Sweet 16.

(2) '13 Florida State vs. (10) '17 Central Florida
Scott Stadium | Charlottesville, Virginia

Florida State 59 – UCF 28

(FSU) Winston 25 for 31, 394 YDS, 5 TDs | (UCF) Milton 287 Total YDS, 2 TDs, 3 INTs

Stretching The Field: Winston 4 For 6 On Pass Attempts Of 25+ Air Yards For 137 YDS, 2 TDs

---

The game within the game between the Seminoles and Knights was the battle at the line of scrimmage. Central Florida needed to get to Jameis Winston if it was to have any hopes of holding up against the pass. And UCF was dead in the water offensively if it failed to open some holes in the running game. The Knights went zero for two in this department. Playing through light rain and breezy conditions, Winston was knocked down just twice all game long. The FSU offensive line was successful in limiting negative plays on the whole. Central Florida registered just two TFLs and finished with zero sacks. In the run game, UCF hit two plays of 20+ yards, but outside of those two long runs from Adrian Killins Jr., it averaged just 2.3 yards per carry. This made UCF one-dimensional offensively and allowed FSU's edge rushers to tee off on McKenzie Milton. The Knights QB1 was sacked seven times, threw six "turnover worthy" passes, and ended the game with four turnovers (3 INTs, 1 lost fumble). With time to operate, Winston was in complete command. He spread the ball out to nine different receivers and locked in on Kelvin Benjamin in the red zone. The Noles' largest receiver (6'5", 242 pounds) caught four passes in the red zone for 29 yards and two touchdowns. And to add insult to injury, UCF's best defensive play of the game, a 67-yard scoop 'n' score by Mike Hughes, was overturned due to a face masking penalty. Hughes would exit the game with an ankle injury suffered during the return. The Seminoles 31-point blowout win sets the stage for a Sunshine Showdown with '96 Florida.

Round of 32 - West

(1) '04 USC vs. (9) '10 Boise State
Martin Stadium | Pullman, Washington

USC 28 – Boise State 17
(USC) White 22 CAR, 106 YDs, 2 TDs | (BSU) McClellin 7 TK,
2.5 TFLs, 2 Sacks, FF, FR
Moore Was Less: Kellen Moore Held To 5.8 Yards Per Attempt
(10.0 YPA in 2010)

Sustained winds in the 15 MPH range had an impact on the passing attacks in this game. Matt Leinart was just four of 10 on attempts that traveled over 10 yards through the air in this game. Similarly, Kellen Moore struggled with the downfield passing game, overshooting Titus Young on two deep shots in the first half. Norm Chow made adjustments and leaned on his power running game to move the sticks. As a result, LenDale White toted the rock 12 times more than he did in the Trojans' opening round win over Navy. Steve Smith was a valuable weapon for USC in 3rd and manageable situations, hauling in five receptions that resulted in first downs. It wasn't as flashy as USC fans were used to, but the offense still managed 28 points and 414 total yards. The defining moment of this matchup came early in the third quarter, when Boise State's Shea McClellin stripped Leinart and recovered the fumble. At the time, Boise was trailing 21–10 and had a chance to make it a one-score game. But USC's Darnell Bing perfectly broke up a pass intended for Austin Pettis in the end zone, knocking the ball up into the air in the process. Dallas Sartz made a full-extension interception before the ball could hit the turf. On the very next play, Reggie Bush would take a reverse 55 yards, and USC wouldn't look back. The Trojans 11-point win was a reminder that their defense could win them games as well.

(5) '02 Ohio State vs. (13) '98 UCLA
Albertsons Stadium | Boise, Idaho

> Ohio State 20 – UCLA 17
> (OSU) Jenkins 6 REC, 67 YDS, TD | (UCLA) Farmer 4 REC, 107 YDS, 2 TDs
> 3rd and Manageable: Avg. Yards To Go On Third Down – Ohio St 3.1 YDS | UCLA 6.2 YDS

The Bruins and their 70th-ranked run defense had a choice to make in this game: Sit back and get gouged by Maurice Clarett, or stack the box and leave their cornerbacks on islands. UCLA's defensive coordinator, Nick Aliotti, opted for the latter. UCLA allowed just one run of over 10 yards in this game and held Clarett in check for four quarters (21 carries, 90 yards). But Ohio State was successful when it took shots down the field. Krenzel hit three deep pass plays, one to Michael Jenkins for a 28-yard score and two to Chris Gamble for 71 yards combined. The Buckeyes won the field position battle by protecting the football (0 turnovers) and pinning the Bruins inside their own 10-yard line three times thanks to a phenomenal game from punter Andy Groom. Despite nearly perfect game management from Jim Tressel and his staff, UCLA wouldn't go away. Trailing by 3, the Bruins had the ball at their own 7-yard line with a little over 2 minutes remaining in the game. A Will Smith sack backed UCLA up to its own 2-yard line on first down. Cade McNown refused to go down quietly, connecting on back-to-back 25-yard completions. The first, out of his own end zone, was a jump ball brought in by Danny Farmer. The second was a deep back-shoulder fade to Brian Poli-Dixon. Now in Ohio State territory, UCLA just needed another 20 yards to get into Chris Sailer's field goal range. But Ohio State's defense would make a stand. A sack and two incompletions left the Bruins staring down the barrel of a 4th and 17 at their own 45-yard line. McNown avoided an A-gap blitz by Cie Grant, but he still forced the ball into double coverage. His pass sailed a few feet over Farmer's outstretched hands and UCLA's Cinderella run came to an end.

(3) '91 Washington vs. (11) '13 Michigan State
Folsom Field | Boulder, Colorado

Washington 16 – Michigan State 13
(UW) Bailey 5 REC, 97 YDS | (MSU) Cook 17 for 24 for 199 YDS, TD
Ground And Pound: Both Teams Ran It On Over 65% Of Their Plays

Despite less than 30 points on the scoreboard, this game was packed with drama. After five consecutive punts to start this Round of 32 matchup, big plays began to swing the momentum back and forth between the Huskies and Spartans. Bennie Fowler made a one-handed catch over the middle to extend Michigan State's first promising drive. Two plays later, Jeremy Langford followed his blockers on a screen pass all the way down to the Washington 8-yard line. On 3rd and goal from the 5, Connor Cook found Josiah Price in the end zone for 6. Facing a 3rd and long on the ensuing drive, Washington's Mario Bailey caught a deep pass in the middle of the field, ducked under the outstretched arms of Darqueze Dennard, and picked up another 15 yards before getting pushed out of bounds. Later in the drive, Billy Joe Hobert would keep it on an option down near the goal line and tie things up at 7 before the break. After a clipping penalty derailed a potential touchdown drive for Michigan State in the third quarter, Michael Geiger curled a 44-yard field goal attempt inside the right upright, reclaiming the lead for the Green and White. The Huskies turned the ball over on the following drive when Kurtis Drummond intercepted a wounded duck of a pass from Hobert. Another drive stalled in the UW red zone, and Geiger tacked on 3 more points, giving MSU a 13-7 lead. Midway through the fourth quarter, the Huskies leaned on their power running game, picking up three first downs on 3rd and less than 3. With the ball just outside the Michigan State red zone, Hobert fired it into Orlando McKay who broke an arm tackle, raced down the sideline, and leaped into the end zone for a touchdown. The extra point would be blocked by Shilique Calhoun, keeping the game knotted at 13. In crunch time, Michigan State converted four first downs before facing a 3rd and 5 at the UW 24-yard line with just 1:15 remaining in the game. Facing a blitz, Cook dumped it off to Langford in the flat, but he was tackled right along the line of scrimmage by Jaime Fields. Washington, out of timeouts, was powerless to stop the clock. Mark Dantonio ran it down to 31 seconds before calling timeout and sending out his field goal unit. The Huskies, having been nipped by a blocked extra point earlier in the fourth, returned the favor. Shane Pahukoa blocked the kick, and Tommie Smith returned it nearly to midfield. With no timeouts and 22 seconds remaining in the game, Hobert found tight end Aaron Pierce in the middle of the field at the Michigan State 29-yard line. The Huskies raced up to the line and spiked the ball with 6 seconds remaining in the game. Travis Hanson's 46-yard attempt from the right hash split the uprights as time expired, giving the UW faithful a heart-stopping win.

(2) '21 Georgia vs. (7) '11 Oklahoma State
Aloha Stadium | Honolulu, Hawai'i

> Georgia 38 – Oklahoma State 17
> (UGA) Bennett 307 Total YDS, 2 Rush TDs | (OSU) Gilbert 99-YD Kickoff Return TD
> Pressure Cooker: UGA D vs. Weeden – 11 Knockdowns, 5 Sacks, 2 FFs, FR, 3 INTs

The story of this game was the Dawgs' defensive line. For 60 minutes, the Bulldog front got after Brandon Weeden, who never really settled in after turning the ball over twice in the first quarter. The first turnover came off of a batted ball at the line of scrimmage. Travon Walker's deflection landed right in the lap of Nolan Smith for the easy interception. Later in the quarter, pressure up the middle from Jordan Davis drove center Grant Garner back into Weeden, causing him to fall backward into a hit from Robert Beal. The collision caused Weeden to twist awkwardly and cough up the football. The Pokes dug themselves a 17-point hole before Justin Gilbert took a kickoff 99 yards to the house early in the second quarter, but that would be as close as Mike Gundy's team would get. Todd Monken—who pulled off the rare feat of calling plays for both Oklahoma State and Georgia—rode the hot hand in the second quarter, which in this game meant lots of touches for James Cook. The senior back had runs of 13, 18 and 24 yards in the second quarter alone and took a screen pass 17 yards in for a score just before halftime. In the third quarter, Georgia's running game continued to dominate, punching holes in the Oklahoma State front. Leading 24-7, the final blow was landed when Brock Bowers caught a play-action pass from Bennett and raced down the sidelines for a 41-yard score. The booth would rule Bowers out at the 1-yard line before he came into contact with the pylon. Bennett would sneak it in on the next play and put this game to bed before Oklahoma State even had the ball in the second half. The Dawgs are now set for a heavyweight battle in the Sweet 16 against another legendary defense ('91 Washington).

Round of 32 - South

(1) '19 LSU vs. (9) '96 Arizona State
Sanford Stadium | Athens, Georgia

> LSU 40 – Arizona State 31
> (LSU) Jefferson 7 REC, 122 YDS, 2 TDs | (ASU) Plummer 311 Total Yards, 3 TDs (2 Rush)
> Joe Cool: Burrow On 3rd and 4th Downs - 7 for 8, 77 Yards, TD (1 Rushing First Down)

Jake Plummer and the Sun Devils had an upset on their mind and came out of their corner swinging in this one. Dan Cozzetto called a perfect opening drive, helping ASU march it 72 yards over 11 plays. The drive culminated with a vintage Jake "The Snake" rushing touchdown. Plummer spun out of a tackle and dove into the end zone for 6. On the following drive, Derrick Rodgers tracked down Clyde Edwards-Helaire from behind and punched the ball out. Scott Von der Ahe scooped up the fumble just outside the LSU 35. Two plays after the turnover, fullback Jeff Paulk climbed to the second level, pancaked Damone Clark, and opened a big hole for Terry Battle. The 27-yard run set ASU up at the LSU 4-yard line. But the LSU defense dug in and forced the Sun Devils to settle for a chip-shot field goal from Robert Nycz. Joe Burrow and the Tigers got the ball trailing by 10 with 6:55 remaining in the first quarter, and it wouldn't take long for the LSU offense to roar. Justin Jefferson made a spectacular over-the-shoulder catch along the sideline and managed to get one foot down despite being crowded by Jason Simmons. Terrace Marshall Jr. moved the sticks with a third down reception, and then Edwards-Helaire atoned for his earlier mistakes by breaking an 18-yard run inside the ASU red zone. Burrow fired a pass into the end zone on the following play, and Jefferson skied over Pat Tillman and came down with the football. LSU would tack on two more touchdowns (CEH, Chase) before Arizona State responded with a drive just before halftime. Plummer completed four of five attempts in a 2-minute drill and rainbowed a perfect post corner to Keith Poole for a touchdown. Trailing 21–17 in the third quarter, Arizona State caught a break that had the potential to swing the game in its favor. On 3rd and 4 at midfield, Thaddeus Moss, wide open, dropped an easy pass and forced Ed Orgeron to send out the punting team. After two first downs, the Sun Devils were threatening but Plummer made his lone mistake of the game when he forced the ball into double coverage. Derek Stingley Jr. picked it off in stride, picked up a convoy along the sideline, and took it 48 yards for a touchdown, upping LSU's advantage to 28–17. The only other play of note in the second half came midway through the fourth quarter when Arizona State was called for holding its own end zone. A garbage-time touchdown run for Plummer in the final 30 seconds of the game made it look a little bit closer on paper, but LSU was never in danger of being upset down the stretch.

(4) '10 Auburn vs. (12) '97 North Carolina
Alamodome | San Antonio, Texas

> Auburn 23 – North Carolina 16
> (AU) Fairley 6 TK, 4 TFLs, 1 Sack, 2 FFs, FR | (UNC) Crumpler 4 REC, 47 YDS, 2 TDs
> Medical Bills: Hits By Fairley Temporarily Knocked Out A QB, RB and FB For UNC

Auburn was on upset alert and trailed by as much as 10 in the second half. The issue for Gus Malzahn's team was turnovers. Seemingly when anyone other than Cam Newton broke a big play, they were putting the ball on the Alamodome carpet. In total, Auburn fumbled the ball five times and lost three of them. It started on the very first drive when Onterio McCalebb burst around the corner on a jet sweep. He raced past Robert Williams on the perimeter but was forced to cut back by the angle taken by safety Omar Brown. That cutback gave Brian Simmons enough time to make a diving tackle, which knocked the ball free from McCalebb's grasp. North Carolina capitalized on four Auburn turnovers, cashing those mistakes in for 16 points. Offensively, North Carolina had two flavors of drives: Effective and Fairley-Wrecked. Auburn's All-American defensive tackle registered four tackles for loss and spread those out across four separate drives. Whenever he brought a Tar Heel down in their own backfield, something good happened for Auburn. His TFLs led to two punts, a lost fumble, and an arm punt (downfield interception) by Chris Keldorf following a 10-yard loss on a sack on the previous play. North Carolina would play two quarterbacks after Fairley bruised Oscar Davenport's ribs in the first half. Suffice it to say, he was a menace. Auburn finally stopped fumbling in the third quarter and began to chip away at North Carolina's 16–6 lead. Newton ran it four straight times for

33 yards before he uncorked a deep ball to Emory Blake. The ball would be overthrown, but Greg Williams was called for pass interference. Later in the drive, Newton would bully his way in from 3 yards out on a quarterback counter. After a three-and-out, Auburn went back to work on the ground. Its seven-play drive ended when Michael Dyer burst through the line and trucked Dré Bly on his way to the end zone. Auburn tacked on three more in the fourth when a holding call on left tackle Lee Ziemba derailed a red zone trip. Leading by 7 in the closing minute, Fairley would put the Tar Heels to bed. Jonathan Linton broke two tackles in the backfield on 3rd and 1 near midfield but was buried by Fairley as he came out of a spin. Fairley's helmet slapped the ball out of his grasp and shot it 5 yards downfield. A pile-up ensued, but Josh Bynes came away with the football and the win for Auburn. To put the Tigers' second half dominance in perspective, they erased a 16–6 deficit and outgained UNC 228 yards to 88 yards in the final two quarters.

(3) '18 Clemson vs. (6) '99 Virginia Tech
Neyland Stadium | Knoxville, Tennessee

Clemson 27 – Virginia Tech 26
(CU) Lawrence 24 for 30, 287 YDS, TD | (VT) Vick 257 Total Yards,
3 TDs (1 Rush), INT
Clemson Didn't Lead in This Game Until 1:13 Remaining
in The Fourth Quarter

Two elite defenses met in Knoxville, but it would be the expert quarterback play from both sides that defined this game in the early going. On the opening drive, Mike Vick connected on four of his first five attempts, including a skinny post to Ricky Hall at the Clemson 17-yard line. Hall was spun back toward the sideline by A. J. Terrell but refused to go down, regaining his balance before racing in for 6. Clemson responded with a nine-play drive that ended in a 36-yard field goal from Greg Huegel. After trading punts, the Hokies marched the ball down into the Clemson red zone, thanks to three consecutive third down conversions. With the ball at the Tigers' 12-yard line, Vick took a speed option down the line of scrimmage, ducked under a hit from Kendall Joseph, backpedaled, and fired a high-arcing pass to the back corner of the end zone. Emmett Johnson's diving catch was ruled incomplete by the side judge. The review, however, showed that Johnson's left foot touched down in bounds before his right knee was ruled out. That touchdown call gave Virginia Tech a 14-3 lead early in the second quarter. On Clemson's only two drives of the quarter, Trevor Lawrence was spectacular, barring one near-fatal mistake. The Tigers freshman phenom avoided disaster when he was stripped by Corey Moore, recovering his own fumble. From there, he completed eight straight passes, including a 34-yard bomb to Justyn Ross. That deep pitch and catch set up a Tavien Feaster touchdown run from 3 yards out. After a lengthy Va Tech drive ended with a short field goal from Shayne Graham, Clemson closed out the half with a nine-play, 82-yard touchdown drive. Lawrence used his legs to pick up two first downs, and Travis Etienne took a draw 23 yards for the score with 41 seconds remaining in the half, pulling the Tigers into a tie with the Hokies at 17. Both defenses made sufficient second half adjustments, and the third quarter became a bit of a "punt-fest." But it was Jimmy Kibble's second punt of the quarter that turned into a big play when Clemson's Amari Rodgers muffed the punt at his own 6-yard line. He was lucky to recover it with three Hokies bearing down on him. After two negative rushing plays, Clemson tried to throw out of its own end zone on 3rd and 12. Michael Hawkes raced in and sacked Lawrence for the safety. With VT leading 19–17, it appeared that Clemson was ready to regain control after three chunk plays from Etienne. But a fumble by Tee Higgins on the sideline took a short hop and didn't make it out of bounds. Cory Bird recovered the football and returned it 20 yards for the Hokies. The following drive ended in a Mike Vick rushing touchdown, pushing VT's advantage to nine with 3:07 remaining in the third quarter. Etienne once again took center stage for Clemson, taking two swing passes for big yardage before a clipping call derailed its drive inside the Hokies' 10-yard line. Huegel's second field goal of the day made it 26–20 with plenty of time left in the fourth quarter. The defining moment of this game came with 7 minutes remaining after Andre Kendrick was tripped up on a 3rd and short sweep. There was nothing but green grass in front of Kendrick, and instead of a game-sealing touchdown run, his knee touched down short of the first down marker. At the Clemson 41-yard line, Frank Beamer opted to punt and rely on his defense. The ensuing 10-play drive was dramatic and a bit controversial. Things got started quietly, as Clemson used three runs to pick up its initial first down of the drive. Then a deep incompletion from Lawrence brought up a 2nd and 10 at the Clemson 27-yard line. Lawrence forced a pass into Hunter Renfrow, but the ball was dislodged by a big hit from Nick Sorensen. Renfrow was knocked out of the game with a concussion, and the play was reviewed for targeting. The booth confirmed the targeting call and ejected Sorensen, and Clemson had momentum with a fresh set of downs nearing midfield. Lawrence would complete three more passes on the drive, including the go-ahead score to Diondre Overton, with a little over a minute remaining in the game. Vick would move the ball to VT's 40-yard line on the final drive before he overshot a deep pass to Andre Davis in the middle of the field. Tanner Muse just got both hands under the football, securing the interception and the 1-point win for Dabo Swinney and the Tigers.

(2) '20 Alabama vs. (10) '94 Colorado
Kyle Field | College Station, Texas

> Alabama 42 – Colorado 28
> (CU) Salaam 18 CAR, 140 YDS, 2 TDs | (UA) Jones 23 for 29, 311 YD, 3 TDs
> Clean Sheet: Alabama 0 Sacks Allowed, 0 Penalties

The Crimson Tide passing attack was clicking from the very first drive of the game. DeVonta Smith set the tone when he made a leaping grab over Chris Hudson on Alabama's second play from scrimmage. He followed that 32-yard chunk play up with a 19-yard touchdown grab to cap the drive. Colorado would attempt to play "keep away," running it seven times on their opening drive. The Buffs' game plan was successful, shaving 7 minutes off the clock and finding paydirt on a 4-yard Rashaan Salaam touchdown run. The problem was that they just couldn't stop Alabama in the first half—or even slow them down all that much. Najee Harris opened the Tide's second touchdown drive with a 46-yard run. Two plays later, Mac Jones surveyed the field from a perfect pocket and hit Jaylen Waddle in stride over the middle. Waddle weaved through traffic, untouched, for the touchdown. By the third quarter, Alabama's offensive dominance was undeniable. The Tide would rack up 517 total yards of offense and 42 points on their first seven drives of the game. Interestingly, Alabama would go scoreless in the fourth after losing a Brian Robinson Jr. fumble and failing to convert a 4th and 1 at the Colorado 38-yard line. But even with a goose egg in the final quarter, Colorado could only draw within 14 before a late comeback bid was ended on a Kordell Stewart interception in the end zone. The Buffs were successful offensively, but Stewart couldn't hit the big play through the air for much of the game. He would finish just 2 of 11 on passes that traveled more than 10 yards through the air downfield.

Round of 32 - Midwest

(1) '95 Nebraska vs. (9) '07 Mizzou
Camp Randall Stadium | Madison, Wisconsin

> Nebraska 41 – Mizzou 27
> (NU) Green 10 CAR, 118 YDS, TD | (MU) Daniel 24 for 37, 276 YDS, 2 TDs, 2 INTs
> (Big) Red Zone: NU 5 for 5 (4 TDs, FG), MU 4 for 6 (2 TDs, 2 FGs)

The Cornhuskers jumped on the Tigers by parlaying an opening three-and-out by Chase Daniel and company with an explosive scoring drive of their own. Ahman Green took a Tommie Frazier pitch 67 yards for a touchdown on the Cornhuskers' fourth play from scrimmage. Leading 7–0, Nebraska put Mizzou behind the eight ball thanks to an incredible defensive stand in the red zone. After the Tigers converted three third downs and one fourth down, they found themselves at the Nebraska nine with a 1st and goal. Daniel rolled to his right and targeted Martin Rucker on a corner route in the end zone. Tony Veland dove and deflected the pass, which ricocheted off of Rucker's facemask back into the end zone, where a diving Terrell Farley secured it before it hit the turf. A 10-play drive followed, ending in a Kris Brown field goal. Leading 10–0, it appeared the rout may have been on, but Mizzou's Jeremy Maclin took the kickoff 102 yards for a touchdown. Nebraska would trade a touchdown for a Jeff Wolfert field goal and enter the locker room leading 17–10. The big play of the third quarter came on a Frazier play-action bomb to Brendan Holbein. Holbein's 39-yard catch-and-run set up a

Lawrence Phillips touchdown run from 11 yards out. Phillips bowled over three defenders on his way to the end zone. Mizzou's last chance to make it a game came with 9 minutes remaining in the fourth. A steady drive from Daniel brought the Tigers deep into Nebraska territory, trailing by 11. But back-to-back sacks (Winstrom, Tomich) rattled Mizzou's Heisman finalist. On fourth down at the NU 12-yard line, Daniel misfired, overshooting Tommy Saunders in the middle of the end zone. Mizzou's red zone woes would define this game, which otherwise could have been a compelling shootout.

(4) '98 Tennessee vs. (5) '80 Pitt

Rynearson Stadium | Ypsilanti, Michigan

Pitt 14 – Tennessee 10

(Pitt) McMillan 13 CAR, 47 YDS, TD | (UT) Wilson 14 TK, 3 TFLs, 2 FF, 1 PBU

Longest Play From Scrimmage: Pitt 13 Yards | Tennessee 14 Yards

---

Big hits, rattled quarterbacks, and defining moments delivered by special teams were the story in Ypsilanti. Both the Panthers and Volunteers failed to clear 300 total yards in this game and combined to punt the ball 12 times. Pitt's Dan Marino was knocked out of the game in the second quarter but returned after halftime with Pitt trailing 10-0. But it wasn't Marino who ended up playing hero. Hugh Green got Pitt on the board in the third quarter when he hammered Tee Martin, separating the junior passer from the football. The former walk-on Sal Sunseri recovered the fumble and returned it 57 yards for a scoop 'n' score touchdown. On the following kickoff, Peerless Price returned it 83 yards before getting tracked down inside the Pitt 15-yard line, but an illegal block in the back negated the game-changing return. After trading punts, Tennessee put together its longest drive of the game, a 12-play, 67-yard masterpiece that included three 3rd and short conversions. But the Vols ran into a wall at the Pitt 5-yard line. On first down, Carlton Williamson broke up a pass intended for Jeremaine Copeland. On second down, an option play was blown up by Rickey Jackson, wrapping up Martin for a 4-yard loss. On third down, a wide receiver screen to Cedrick Wilson was a little too well blocked, with the sophomore walking it into the end zone. A holding call took that score off the board and set Tennessee up at 3rd and goal at the Pitt 19. The third down do-over didn't go well for UT. Martin dealt with a blitz off the edge, and he was swarmed by three defenders at the 25-yard line. It got worse for Tennessee on the field goal attempt, which was deflected by Hugh Green and fell short. Pitt ran the ball on six of their next nine plays and were the beneficiaries of two penalties (offsides, pass interference). Jackie Sherrill put the game on his fullback's shoulders at the 3-yard line. Randy McMillan was stopped at the line of scrimmage on 1st and goal by Al Wilson and stopped on second down by Wilson again, but he pushed the pile on his third straight attempt and found the end zone. Leading by four late in the fourth quarter, Lynn Thomas shoved a leaping Peerless Price out of bounds on a third down, preventing him from getting a foot in bounds. With the game hanging in the balance, Martin attempted to pick up a 4th and 6 near midfield with his legs, but he was wrapped up short of the marker. Pitt would convert two first downs before kneeling the clock out. Pitt's elite defense is set to meet one of the greatest offenses of all time in the Sweet 16.

(3) '94 Penn State vs. (11) '07 Kansas
Yager Stadium | Oxford, Ohio

> Kansas 44 – Penn State 41
> (KU) Henry 8 REC, 122 YDS, 2 TDs | (PSU) Ki-Jana Carter 27 CAR, 287 YDS, 3 TDs
> Game Of Runs: Unanswered 2nd Half Points: Penn State (21) | Kansas (20)

No one could get a stop in this game. Penn State couldn't slow down the Kansas passing attack, and Ki-Jana Carter obliterated his collegiate rushing record. Carter got the scoring started 71 seconds into the game when he took a handoff from Kerry Collins, broke through a James Holt arm tackle, and outran Chris Harris to the edge. His 74-yard touchdown run was just the beginning of the fireworks. Todd Reesing threw three first-half touchdowns, including a 52-yard dime to Marcus Henry that perfectly split Kim Herring and Tony Pittman. Trailing 24–20 at the break, it was clear that Penn State needed to be perfect offensively in the final 30 minutes to win the game. The lone offensive mistake in the first half came from Kerry Collins when he was picked off by Aqib Talib, so it was on the Nittany Lions' senior leader to make up for his rare error in judgment. In the second half, Collins was on fire, completing 14 of his 19 attempts for 179 yards and two scores with zero turnovers. And a Jake Sharp fumble early in the fourth quarter that erased a potential score for KU helped Penn State extend its scoring run to 21 straight points. Leading 41–24 with 13:02 remaining in the game, Penn State opted to run a soft zone against Reesing and Mark Mangino's passing attack. It was successful in making Kansas earn its first score. It took nine plays and four and a half minutes off of the clock. Trailing 41–31, Kansas kicked it deep and hoped their defense could make a stop. But the defense didn't even make it onto the field because Mike Archie exploded through a crease in the KU kickoff coverage and was quickly to midfield with one man to beat. Archie cut back against the grain but was knocked off balance by kicker Scott Webb. Dakota Lewis ripped the ball away from Archie, and a mad dash for the football ensued. Micah Brown slid down and recovered the ball in one motion at the Kansas 39-yard line, giving KU a massive momentum boost. Surprisingly, KU was unable to capitalize and suffered the only three-and-out of the entire game. After a Kyle Tucker punt, Penn State had a chance to bleed the clock. The Nittany Lions picked up two first downs and ran the time down to 4:41 seconds before booting it back to Kansas. Trailing by 10 with just one timeout remaining, Reesing and his receiving corps went to work. A 15-yard out for Dezmon Briscoe got things started. Then a clutch third down conversion to tight end Derek Fine over the middle. Moderate gains to Kerry Meier and Dexton Fields set Kansas up at the Penn State 21 with 2:31 left in the game. Reesing apparently had had enough of the dink and dunk opportunities being served up by Jerry Sandusky's defense, and he went for broke. He hurled two straight pass attempts into the end zone. With the first, he slightly overshot Briscoe, but he placed the second perfectly on Marcus Henry in the front corner of the end zone. Trailing by three with 2:18 remaining, Webb attempted an onside kick. The ball traveled exactly 10 yards and was bobbled by the Penn State hands team and recovered by KU. After a first down, Kansas was on the edge of field goal range with under a minute remaining and the clock running. Reesing dropped back on 3rd and 4 at the Penn State 36-yard line, faked a wide receiver screen, and wound up for a deep throw down the sideline. The play was well covered by Brian Miller, but 6'3" Briscoe won the jump ball, and the pair rolled into the end zone in a heap. Penn State would block the extra point, adding a bit of drama to the final 39 seconds of the game. Kerry Collins completed three passes to midfield before burning Penn State's last timeout. Needing 15 more yards to reach the edge of Brett Conway's range, Collins hit Bobby Engram on a crossing pattern. But Engram would be tripped up just short of the first down marker. Penn State scrambled to the line of scrimmage and spiked it with 4 seconds left in the game. With the ball sitting at the 41, Joe Paterno opted for a Hail Mary instead of a 58-yard attempt to tie the game. Collins's last-gasp attempt sent the ball through the end zone over the outstretched arms of Freddie Scott. With their 3-point upset of Penn State, Kansas became the first double-digit seed to make it to the Sweet 16.

(2) '05 Texas vs. (10) '98 Kansas State
Kinnick Stadium | Iowa City, Iowa

Texas 45 – Kansas State 24

(UT) Thomas 5 REC, 75 YDS, TD | (KSU) Bishop 299 Total Yards, 2 TDs, 2 INTs

Longhorn Havoc: UT Defense – 9 TFLs, 5 Sacks, 2 FFs, 2 INTs, FR, 4 PBUs

---

Any hopes of a Sunflower State showdown in the Sweet 16 were quickly put to bed once Vince Young got rolling in this game. After an opening drive punt, Young and the Longhorns scored 24 points on their other four drives of the first half. He beat them with his legs on a 46-yard rushing touchdown in which he emptied his bag of tricks. Young stiff-armed Mark Simoneau at the line of scrimmage, timed a cut behind a downfield blocker perfectly, and then ran through Lamar Chapman before walking into the end zone. He would toss two touchdown passes in the first 30 minutes as well, the first to a wide-open David Thomas off of a play-action fake and the second on a deep post to Limas Sweed. Kansas State moved the ball effectively for most of the first half, ending with 207 total yards, but a pair of turnovers were too much to overcome. An end zone interception by Michael Huff prevented the Wildcats from tying the game at 17, and a late-first-half fumble by Eric Hickson allowed Texas to tack on another touchdown before the break. The closest Kansas State would get in the second half was 38–24, with a little over 7 minutes remaining in the game. Michael Bishop scored on a red zone draw, but by the time he and the Wildcats offense got the ball back, there was just 2:03 remaining in the game and a 21-point hole. Vince Young would take home offensive MVP honors, but the best performance may have come from Texas's middle linebacker Aaron Harris. The third team All-American had 10 tackles, 3.5 tackles for loss, a forced fumble, a fumble recovery, and a fourth down stop that resulted in a turnover on downs for KSU. He was all over the field and helped corral Michael Bishop for most of the game.

Sweet 16 - East

(1) '01 Miami (FL) vs. (4) '88 Notre Dame
Hard Rock Stadium | Miami, FL

Miami (FL) 28 – Notre Dame 13
(Miami, FL) Johnson 4 REC, 99 YDS, TD | (ND) Watters 3 CAR, 22 YDS, 3 REC, 48 YDS, TD
DBU: Zero Irish Receivers Exceeded 28 Yards

Both defenses showed off their speed in this game. The Hurricanes' secondary was wildly disruptive, making it nearly impossible to complete any pass more than 10 yards down-field. In fact, the Canes had more pass breakups (5) than Tony Rice had completions of 10+ yards (3). Notre Dame's front seven was super active, racking up seven tackles for loss and providing their fans with hope early in the game. Early in the first quarter, on a 3rd and 5 at their own 32-yard line, Chris Zorich collapsed the pocket and pushed Brett Romberg back into Ken Dorsey as he was loading up to throw the football. Dorsey crumbled, and the ball shot backward out of the pile. Michael Stonebreaker recovered it and set Notre Dame up with a short field. Four plays later, Rice rolled and found Ricky Watters on a whip route a yard deep in the end zone. Larry Coker's team responded with a heavy dose of Clinton Portis and Jeremy Shockey, these being the only Canes to touch the football on a seven-play touchdown drive. Shockey's third catch of the drive was a diving one-hander at the Irish three. Portis walked in untouched, thanks to a pancake block from the Canes' pulling guard Sherko Haji-Rasouli. With the game tied at seven midway through the second quarter, Notre Dame was faced with a 3rd and long near midfield. Rice was a hair late on an out route to tight end Derek Brown. Chris Campbell deflected the bullet pass, which skimmed past Brown and into the lap of Phillip Buchanon for an interception. The Canes' top corner immediately put on the jets and returned it 55 yards for a score. Reggie Ho would connect on a 40-yard field goal to end the first half, but it was clear that Notre Dame was simply trying to keep the dam from breaking on a play-by-play basis. That dam broke wide open on the third play of the second half when Dorsey lofted a fade to Andre Johnson down the sideline. Johnson made the catch and stiff-armed Todd Lyght all in one motion before breaking away for a 61-yard score. Leading 21–10, Miami forced three straight Notre Dame punts before putting together their best drive of the game. The Canes' 10-play, 77-yard march was capped by a touchdown pass from Dorsey to Najeh Davenport on a perfectly executed wheel route in the red zone. The Irish would tack on one more field goal, but they wouldn't get back into Miami territory after that. Instead of running up the score, Miami opted to kneel the clock out inside of the Irish 5-yard line in the final 2 minutes of action.

(2) '13 Florida State vs. (3) '96 Florida
Hard Rock Stadium | Miami, FL

> Florida State 35 – Florida 28
> (FSU) Edwards Jr. 3.5 TFLs, 2 Sacks | (UF) Wuerffel 29 for 46,
> 340 YDS, 3 TDs, INT
> Special Seminoles: Aguayo FGs (55 yds, 53 yds) | Beatty 3x Punts
> Inside UF 10-Yard Line

This Sunshine State battle was more of a pillow fight in the early going. Both teams punted on their opening drives, and Florida State was lucky to cash in a 55-yard field goal from Roberto Aguayo on its second drive. Florida was bogged down by Florida State's pressure, with one moment really standing out. Trailing 3–0 late in the first quarter, Florida State's Terrance Smith got home on a blitz and threw Danny Wuerffel to the Orange Bowl turf. But the replay revealed that Reidel Anthony had beaten P. J. Williams's jam at the line of scrimmage and was wide open down the sideline. Missed opportunities like that one would come back to haunt Steve Spurrier and the Gators. The scoring started to heat up in the second quarter, with the teams trading touchdowns on four straight drives. Jameis Winston connected with his favorite target, Nick O'Leary, in the red zone for 6, and Karlos Williams followed Chad Abram through the B-gap for a rushing touchdown just before halftime. Florida's attack was all aerial, as Wuerffel spread the ball out to six different receivers in the first half alone. His touchdown strikes came to Jacquez Green and Ike Hilliard. Hilliard's deep touchdown from 35 yards out was nearly intercepted by Jalen Ramsey, but the future top-ten NFL Draft pick was able to reel in the deflected pass for the score. Leading 17–14 in the third quarter, Winston found his groove. The Heisman winner completed nine of 10 passes in the quarter and scored on a broken play down near the goal line. It looked like Jimbo Fisher had dialed up a reverse to Rashad Greene, but the timing was off, and Winston took the de facto naked boot into the end zone. The next drive for FSU could have put the game to bed, but Kenny Shaw's right foot came down out of bounds on a would-be 45-yard completion near the end zone. Aguayo would bang home his second 50+ yard field goal of the game, extending the Noles' lead to 27–14. Fred Taylor provided the answer for Florida on the next drive, toting the rock for 37 yards on five carries, including a 12-yard score on a stretch in the red zone. After both teams punted on their first drives of the fourth quarter, Winston put the game to bed with a brilliant throw under pressure. Facing a six-man blitz, Winston reared back and fired a deep pass just before getting knocked to the ground by Jevon Kearse. Kelvin Benjamin had slipped free from Anthone Lott on a post corner and made a catch in stride along the sideline. Benjamin jogged in from 24 yards out for a touchdown and also completed the octopus with a 2-point conversion on a fade route the very next play. Refusing to go down without a fight, Wuerffel mounted a final touchdown drive, which included a 4th and goal touchdown pass to Reidel Anthony. Trailing by seven, Florida's onside kick was not successful, setting the stage for a Miami–FSU showdown in the Elite Eight.

Sweet 16 - West

(1) '04 USC vs. (5) '02 Ohio State
Rose Bowl | Pasadena, CA

> USC 24 – Ohio State 17
> (USC) Leinart 22 for 28, 268 YDS, 2 TDs | (OSU) Gamble 139
> All-Purpose Yards, 3 TK, PBU
> Swiss Army Knife: Bush 17 Yards Per Reception, 8 Yards Per Carry,
> 136 Return Yards

The underdog Buckeyes got a huge boost early in this game when Chris Gamble returned a Trojan punt 55 yards, setting Ohio State up deep inside USC territory. Five plays later, Maurice Clarett bullied his way in from 2 yards out to give Brutus something to cheer about. Trailing 7–0, the USC offense failed to convert a third down at midfield, forcing their punting unit to take the field for the second straight series. After a defensive stand, Matt Leinart and the offense finally found some success through the air. A Reggie Bush swing pass got the Trojans' offensive engine out of neutral. Then, a deep fade to Dwayne Jarrett sparked a 28-yard gain. LenDale White converted a pair of 3rd and shorts before Leinart found Dominique Byrd in the flat near the goal line. Byrd walked it in for 6, and USC had tied the game at 7 apiece. Ohio State's special teams lived up to their name once again when Mike Nugent bent home a 53-yard field goal attempt near the end of the first half. But Ohio State left USC enough time, and three timeouts to work with. Reggie Bush opened the drive with a pulse-stopping catch-and-run off of a screen pass. He weaved between his offensive lineman and Ohio State defenders before he was shoved out of bounds by Mike Doss. His explosive 30-yard play allowed Norm Chow to use his entire playbook with the ball at midfield and 1:18 remaining in the half. LenDale White would receive two carries, and Leinart worked the quick game to move the ball down the field to the Ohio State 16 with 28 seconds remaining in the half. After two incompletions, one that Leinart short-armed to Steve Smith in the end zone, USC had time for one more shot at a touchdown before the half. Smith spun Dustin Fox around with a double move before securing the pass 3 yards deep in the end zone. Leading 14–10 at the break, it seemed as though USC just needed to avoid any big mistakes in the second half. Ohio State had failed to generate any big plays outside of Gamble's punt return in the first half. As it would turn out, Ohio State was the team that made the big blunder in the third quarter. After picking up three first downs on the opening drive of the second half, Ohio State was knocking on the door at the USC 29-yard line. On first down, Craig Krenzel rolled out of the pocket. But he held the ball too long and took a wicked blindside shot from Frostee Rucker. Krenzel coughed the ball up, and it was recovered and returned for a touchdown by Dallas Sartz. His 66-yard scoop 'n' score was made worse by the news that Krenzel was lost for the game due to a back injury. From there, it was a defensive showcase for USC against a one-dimensional Ohio State offense operating with a backup quarterback. Scott McMullen was actually serviceable for the Buckeyes, but they couldn't hold up against the Trojan pass rush in obvious passing situations. The Trojans would sack McMullen four times in relief of Krenzel, and outside of a pass interference call in the end zone that resulted in Clarett's second touchdown of the game, USC was nearly flawless on defense in the final 30 minutes of action. After securing Nugent's onside kick, White salted the game away with a 31-yard run in which he broke three tackles, along with the Buckeyes' spirit.

(2) '21 Georgia vs. (3) '91 Washington
Rose Bowl | Pasadena, CA

> Washington 17 – Georgia 16
> (UW) Brunell 18 for 24, 220 YDS, 2 TDs (1 Rush) | (UGA) Bowers 8 REC, 97 YDS, TD
> Red Zone, Purple Reign: UGA Ran 6 Plays Inside UW 9-YD Line in 4th Qtr (0 TDs)

This was *the* defensive matchup of the entire tournament. Both teams were vicious run-stuffers in their day, and neither offense offered a unique schematic threat through the air or on the ground. So with their chin straps buckled tight, the Dawg Fight began in Pasadena. After two drives, the total offensive yardage between UW and UGA sat at -1. After four drives, it had bubbled up to 7 total yards thanks to a Brock Bowers's end around, which went for a whopping 9 yards. It wasn't until Beno Bryant's 27-yard punt return that either team even passed the 50-yard line. After two short gains on the ground, Washington's Billy Joe Hobert airmailed a pass over a wide-open Mario Bailey's head. Washington would punt, and Hobert (0 for 5) would head to the bench for the rest of the game. Georgia, aided by a 22-yard Bowers catch-and-run, moved the ball to midfield and got the first big break of the game. On 3rd and 2, Todd Monken dialed up a read option out of the shotgun for Stetson Bennett. He was swarmed in the backfield, but Chico Fraley was nailed for a facemask. That 15-yard penalty created a field goal opportunity for UGA, which Jack Podlesny converted from 40 yards away. Mark Brunell led the Huskies' next drive, and it turned out to be an inspired move by Don James and his staff. Brunell was 2-for-2 on third downs on that opening drive, and he scrambled for another first down. On a 2nd and 4 at the Georgia 25-yard line, Brunell drew the Bulldogs offside and took a shot downfield with a back-shoulder throw to Orlando McKay in the seam. McKay adjusted to the football perfectly. He caught the ball and allowed his momentum to spin him away from the defender and into the end zone. Georgia, looking to regain the lead, suffered the game's first turnover when Bennett was stripped by Steve Emtman on a designed quarterback draw. Dave Hoffmann recovered the fumble, and four plays later, Travis Hanson connected on a wobbly 41-yard kick that just grazed the right upright. Leading 10–3 at the break, UW had actually been outgained 129 to 89 in the first half. The sledding would get a little bit easier for both teams in the third quarter. Dueling touchdown drives got things started, with Stetson Bennett making the best throw of the game on a wheel route to James Cook. Bennett took a shot right as he released the ball, but he worked the football upfield beyond Jamie Fields in man coverage and in front of Shane Pahukoa sitting back in a cover-two zone. Cook made the catch, juked past Pahukoa, and was off to the races. He would be pushed out at the Huskies' 7-yard line after a 65-yard gain. Brock Bowers hung on to a pass with two defenders draped all over him in the middle of the end zone to tie things up at 10. Brunell and the Huskies used every trick they had to move the football on the next drive. An unbalanced line helped them pick up a 3rd and 2 when Jay Barry burst through the pile for a 9-yard gain. After Barry limped off, Napoleon Kaufman took a screen pass 27 yards, showcasing his acceleration and agility while evading a handful of Georgia defenders. A Mario Bailey reverse was sniffed out later in the drive, but he would get one more opportunity to make a big play. On 3rd and 7 at the Georgia 40-yard line, Brunell faked to Beno Bryant, climbed the pocket, and found Bailey on a deep crossing route near the Bulldog 10. Bailey slowed as he caught the football, slipped underneath Derion Kendrick's tackle attempt, and darted into the end zone, giving UW a 17–10 advantage midway through the third. That's when the pads really started popping. Five players in total would leave the game due to injury in the final 19 minutes of action, including Georgia's Zamir White and Washington's Walter Bailey. With UW's second corner sidelined, Georgia found some success throwing at William Doctor. A.D. Mitchell made two contested catches over Doctor to help move UGA into field goal range late in the third quarter. Doctor would get his revenge in the end zone, preventing a Ladd McConkey touchdown reception on a pivotal third down just three plays later. Podlesny drew Georgia within 4 points on his second field goal of the game. A three-and-out from Washington brought us to the fourth quarter and set the stage for maximum drama, with a berth in the Elite Eight on the line. Bennett connected with Brock Bowers on a 17-yard comeback route before Georgia put its most exciting offensive highlight on film. On first down at their own 45-yard line, Jermaine Burton made a full extension grab on the sideline. He gathered himself, stepped over Dana Hall, and scooted another 20 yards before finally getting tracked down by Tommie Smith at the Washington 5-yard line. The following plays would define the game. On first down, an RPO led to Bennett finding Bowers in the flat, but he was gang-tackled by a host of Huskies at the 2-yard line. James Cook ran into a brick wall at the line of scrimmage on second down, with Emtman tossing him back out of the pile. On third down, Georgia rolled Bennett out to his right. The seasoned quarterback had two passing options in his line of vision. Bowers was doubled in the flat near the goal line, and A. D. Mitchell hugged the back line of the end zone. Bennett opted to throw it to Mitchell 9 yards deep in the end zone. He dragged both feet in the back of the end zone while reeling in the pass. But Mitchell had stepped out of the back of the end zone before catching the football, so Georgia was flagged for illegal touching. They would settle for 3, bringing the UW advantage down to one (17–16). After two first down throws by Brunell to tight end Aaron Pierce, Washington punted it back to Georgia with 6 minutes and change remaining in the game. Starting from their own 13, Georgia would nickel and dime their way down the field, converting two third downs and a 4th and 1 at the Washington 44-yard line with 3:56 remaining. Bennett and company would get as close as the 22-yard line before they started moving backward. First, a false start penalty, then a batted ball at the line of scrimmage set up 2nd and 15 at the 27. A double-covered Bowers was unable to make a contested catch at the Washington 11-yard line. And then, on 3rd and 15, Emtman collapsed the pocket, forcing Bennett to scramble—right into the arms of Tommie Smith on a delayed safety blitz. The sack moved the ball back to the Georgia 35 and, critically, placed it on the hash. Podlesny's 52-yard kick had the leg but straightened out and passed a few feet to the right of the upright—no good. Washington used its short passing game to pick up a first down. And then, with Georgia out of timeouts, Brunell scrambled up the middle on 3rd and 6, picking up the game-ending first down.

Sweet 16 - South

(1) '19 LSU vs. (4) '10 Auburn
Sugar Bowl | New Orleans, LA

> LSU 52 - Auburn 38
> (LSU) Edwards-Helaire 139 All-Purpose YDS, 2 TDs | (AU) Zachery 99 All-Purpose YDS, TD
> Pass To Run: Runs of 10+ - LSU (6) | Auburn (9)

Two of the most prolific offenses the SEC has ever seen locked horns on the fast track in the Big Easy. Cam Newton was sharp from the get-go, demonstrating his mastery of Gus Malzahn's offense. Equal parts finesse and power, Auburn's 8-play, 82-yard opening touchdown drive was a thing of beauty. The big play of the drive came on an option reverse to Terrell Zachery. With the defense overcommitting to Newton, Zachery found nothing but open field on a 34-yard explosive run. Three plays later, Newton ran over JaCoby Stevens at the goal line before unveiling his vintage Superman touchdown celebration. It took five plays for LSU to even the score. After a 6-yard Clyde Edwards-Helaire run, Burrow hit four straight passes to help get LSU into the end zone. His final pass of the opening drive was a sideline strike to Ja'Marr Chase, who caught it in stride on his way to the end zone. Auburn blinked first in this shootout when Onterio McCalebb fumbled the football after taking a speed sweep from Newton. With a short field, LSU faced a bit of adversity after Burrow was sacked by Antoine Carter. Undeterred, Burrow came back the very next play with a 30-yard touchdown pass to Justin Jefferson. By halftime, LSU was leading 28–17. Edwards-Helaire and Tyrion Davis-Price found running room on the opening drive of the second half, allowing Burrow and the passing game to take a back seat. Despite just two pass attempts, LSU was already at the Auburn five before CEH got the corner and crashed into the front pylon for 6. With it clear that Auburn couldn't get any stops, the rest of the game turned into a Cam Newton showcase and four AU onside kick attempts. To his credit, Newton wouldn't go down quietly. He accounted for 411 total yards and was a part of all five Tiger touchdowns (3 pass, 2 rush). His final rushing score came after Auburn recovered an onside kick in the fourth. This cut the lead to 14, but an onside recovery by LSU sewed the game up late in the fourth. Burrow finished the Heisman duel with a "quiet" 329 total yards and four scores (3 pass, 1 rush). Aside from that first quarter sack, Burrow was only hit one more time in the pocket the rest of the game. For comparison's sake, Newton carried the ball 17 times, absorbed 10 knockdowns, and took three sacks while carrying the AU offense.

(2) '20 Alabama vs. (3) '18 Clemson
Sugar Bowl | New Orleans, LA

> Clemson 30 - Alabama 27
> (CU) Simmons 9 TKs, FR, INT | (UA) Harris 96 All-Purpose Yards, 2 Total TDs
> Turnover Worthy Throws: Mac Jones in all of '20 (10), Against CU (5)

Both teams succeeded in critical elements of their game plans. Clemson was able to pressure Mac Jones, forcing him to throw into tight windows all game long. Alabama was successful in containing the versatile Travis Etienne both as a runner and receiver. Clemson knocked Jones down on 11 drop backs, sacking him three times. These pressures led to a game-changing pick-six in the third quarter, with Alabama leading 20–10. Clelin Ferrell forced Jones to quickly step up in the pocket, while Tre Lamar pressured the Alabama senior passer up the middle. The result was an underthrow from Jones across the middle and an interception by K'Von Wallace. The Clemson safety cut in front of Jaylen Waddle and had a head of steam once he secured the interception. His 58-yard return touchdown breathed life back in the Tigers, who were suddenly down 3. A three-and-out on Alabama's next drive kept the Clemson sideline fired up. Tony Elliott put the ball in Trevor Lawrence's hands on the final drive of the third quarter. The true freshman ran it three times, twice on designed runs and once on a scramble along the sideline that helped Clemson convert a critical third down. Deep in Alabama territory, Lawrence found fellow freshman Justyn Ross on a skinny post in the end zone. The Crimson Tide responded with an explosive play from their Heisman Trophy winner. After a few short completions and a 13-yard Najee Harris run, Alabama was set up with a 1st and 10 at their own 49-yard line. Steve Sarkisian kept Miller Forristall and Brian Robinson Jr. in to block on a max protect and sent DeVonta Smith and Waddle deep on crossing patterns. Tanner Muse shaded towards Waddle, prompting Jones to uncork a bomb (55 air yards) to Smith. He made a full extension effort, reeled it in, and rolled down at the Clemson 2-yard line. Najee Harris ran it off tackle on the next play and into the end zone, giving Alabama a 27–24 advantage. Needing a score, Clemson got some help from their superstar and the referees. Travis Etienne's longest play from scrimmage came the following drive on a swing pass in the flat. He raced out to the sideline, cut it back inside, and picked up 23 yards. Two plays later pass interference was called on Josh Jobe on a bang-bang play near the sticks. Clemson would be stuffed on 3rd and 1 at the Alabama 27-yard line. Instead of leaving his offense on the field, Swinney opted for the field goal, and Greg Huegel split the uprights from 44 yards out, tying the game. Time was becoming a factor with just 9 minutes remaining in the game. Alabama bled the clock with three straight first downs, the last of which came on a blown coverage, leaving Slade Bolden wide open in the middle of the field. Alabama, now in Clemson territory, looked primed to take the lead. But a bull rush from Austin Bryant forced Jones to flee the pocket to his left, and before he could escape, Christian Wilkins slapped the ball out of his hands and onto the turf. Landon Dickerson had a shot at the ball but kicked it along the ground and into the grasp of Isaiah Simmons. The Tigers' linebacker/nickelback superstar returned it 27 yards, shrugging off two tackles in the process. Clemson would use the short passing game and a critical third down run by Adam Choice to move the ball down to the Alabama 10-yard line with just 90 seconds remaining. Alabama exhausted all three timeouts and kept Clemson out of the end zone, but Huegel's chip shot was perfect, giving the Tigers a 3-point edge with a little over a minute left. The final drive didn't have much drama when Jones's first pass over the middle was bobbled by John Metchie III and ripped out of his hands by Isaiah Simmons. He earned Defensive MVP honors and was credited with two turnovers on his final two plays of the game.

Sweet 16 - Midwest

(1) '95 Nebraska vs. (5) '80 Pitt
AT&T Stadium | Arlington, Texas

> Nebraska 31 – Pitt 7
> (NU) Booker 9 TK, 2 PBU, FF, INT | (Pitt) Jackson 7 TK,
> 1.5 TFLs, FR
> Playing It Safe: Neither Team Attempted A Fourth Down Conversion

There was bound to be a game where Nebraska needed more from its "Blackshirt" defense, and this was it. The Cornhuskers managed just 10 points in the first half, punting more times in the first 30 minutes than they had in the previous two games combined. Pitt's five-man front, all of which are seniors, gave Nebraska some issues in the running game. Their experience against Army's option attack in 1980 seemed to give them a leg up early on against Nebraska. Three drives in, and Nebraska had just 3 points and zero carries over 7 yards. But Pitt's offense was in far worse shape. Dan Marino went down with a knee injury on the first drive, although he would return in the second quarter. Rick Trocano went 2-for-6 for 14 yards in relief while taking two sacks. This defensive snoozer of a game got a jolt in the third quarter when Clinton Childs returned the opening kickoff into Pitt territory. After Lawrence Phillips took a sweep for 15 yards, Tommie Frazier lofted a first down pass over linebacker Steve Fedell and into the hands of Clester Johnson on a deep square in route. Johnson caught the pass in stride and cut upfield and into the end zone, extending the Big Red lead to 17–0. Marino's best pass of the game came on the following drive when he dropped back deep in the pocket and let a deep shot fly (61 air yards) for Dwight Collins. Tyrone Williams tried to swat it away at the last second, but it fell right over Collins's shoulder and into his hands for a 56-yard gain. Four plays later, Marino found Mike Dombrowski in the end zone for Pitt's only score of the game. A Phillips long touchdown run (47 yards) and a Mike Minter fumble recovery deep in Pitt territory sealed the runaway win for Tom Osborne's team early in the fourth quarter. The final tally for Pitt's offense was just 198 total yards and more turnovers than plays run inside the Nebraska 20-yard line (4 to 3). We'll see if any future opponents adopt Pitt's five-man front to slow the Nebraska running game, which was held below 5 yards per carry in this game. It helped that both Hugh Green and Rickey Jackson were lightning-fast bookends capable of bottling up Tommie Frazier.

(2) '05 Texas vs. (11) '07 Kansas
AT&T Stadium | Arlington, Texas

> Texas 56 – Kansas 21
> (UT) Robison 7 TK, 2.5 Sacks, FR | (KU) McAnderson 93
> All-Purpose Yards, TD
> Bigger in Texas: UT Had 3x As Many Plays Of 20+ Yards (9)
> As Kansas Did Touchdowns

Kansas was bound to turn back into a pumpkin at some point. Such is the life of a Cinderella. Vince Young was truly superhuman in this game, terrorizing the Jayhawk defense with big play after big play. He ran 18 times for 209 yards and two scores. He threw for 257 yards and four scores. And just for good measure, he completed an octopus in the third quarter when he ran it in from 11 yards out for a touchdown and then ran it in again on the 2-point conversion. He broke away from defenders in the backfield and made accurate downfield passes; he timed his pitches perfectly. Halfway to the Jerry World turf, he lateralled it to Ramonce Taylor for a 41-yard rushing touchdown early in the second quarter. Later in the game, he pulled off the same trick, flipping it to Jamaal Charles at the last moment and springing the true freshman for a 71-yard touchdown. The Longhorns couldn't be stopped offensively, running up 688 total yards and eight touchdowns. Defensively, Texas blanked Kansas in the second and third quarters before allowing two garbage-time touchdowns to Kerry Meier and Brandon McAnderson. But for seven straight drives, it was nothing but misery for Todd Reesing and KU. Brian Robison finished with 2.5 sacks, Michael Griffin picked off Reesing twice, and Rodrique Wright forced two fumbles. It had the feeling of an All-Star game for the Texas defense, with players in Burnt Orange only truly competing with each other. In the injury department, Texas advances to the Elite Eight with only one player's availability up in the air. Billy Pittman sprained his left ankle early in the game and didn't return. He's listed as questionable for their meeting with '95 Nebraska in the next round.

Elite Eight - East

(1) '01 Miami (FL) vs. (2) '13 Florida State
Hard Rock Stadium | Miami, Florida

Miami (FL) 24 – Florida State 19
(Miami FL) Portis 97 Total Yards, TD | (FSU) Jernigan 5 TK,
1.5 TFLs, 1 Swat, FF
No Fly Zone: Miami (FL) 9 PBUs, Florida State 6 PBUs

This regional final had the feel of a vintage, high-stakes meeting between the Canes and Seminoles from the early 1990s. And just like those meetings nearly 3.5 decades ago, the winner had a direct path to a title while the loser was left with nothing more than what-ifs. The game script, like a heavyweight bout, came with a feeling-out period, complete with body blows and precise counter punches. Both teams' opening drives were undone with holding penalties. Miami's infraction knocked the Canes back into a 3rd and 14 near midfield, and Larry Coker and his staff chose to play it safe and run. Florida State's hold was more costly because it wiped out a 56-yard touchdown reception. D. J. Williams came on a blitz and was taken down on the edge by left tackle Cameron Erving, giving Jameis Winston enough time to launch a pass to Kenny Shaw downfield. Shaw made the over-the-shoulder catch in stride and jogged into the end zone before the laundry negated the play and stalled the drive. Miami got the scoring started thanks to a Daryl Jones full extension catch on 3rd and 20 at the FSU 22-yard line. Jones's circus grab didn't pick up the first down, but it put the Canes well within Todd Sievers' range. His 39-yard kick split the uprights and opened the scoring. Florida State's next drive nearly ended before it got started when Ed Reed submarined Nick O'Leary along the sideline. The ball popped free as O'Leary's legs flipped over Reed's shoulder pads. Chris Campbell would recover the ball, but his feet were out of bounds, giving the Seminoles a reprieve. This would prove to be a costly missed opportunity for the Hurricanes. Two plays later, Devonta Freeman shot through the line on a lead draw, shed a James Lewis's tackle attempt on the edge, and burst down the sideline for a 40-yard gain. On the edge of the Miami red zone, Winston pushed the ball downfield for Kelvin Benjamin. The 50/50 ball was just beyond Mike Rumph's reach, and Benjamin snatched it out of the air. The Noles' massive red zone threat maintained control as he fell into the front pylon. Leading 7–3, Florida State heated up Dorsey on the following drive. On all three of his pass attempts, FSU brought six or more rushers, getting home twice. The last sack also came with a forced fumble. Timmy Jernigan wrestled the ball away from Dorsey while bear-hugging him to the ground. The Canes would recover but were forced to punt it away to Kenny Shaw. After spreading the ball out to Christian Green, Rashad Greene, and Karlos Williams for their first catches of the game, Winston would come up short on a third down scramble at the Canes' 30-yard line. Roberto Aguayo extended the FSU lead to 10–3 with a kick that would have been good from 60 yards out. Miami finally found success in the explosive department on the next drive. Andre Johnson got things started with a 28-yard reception that could have gone for a touchdown had it not been for a Lamarcus Joyner shoestring tackle. Later in the drive, Jeremy Shockey reeled in a short curl pattern, bounced off of a Telvin Smith hit, stiff-armed Terrence Brooks, and nearly scored from 22 yards out. Shockey stepped out at the 2-yard line before Frank Gore finished off the drive with a power run at the goal line. Tied at 10, with just one timeout remaining, the Seminoles opted to kneel and head into the locker room. Florida State started the second half by grinding out first downs on the ground. A Winston quarterback sneak, a James Wilder Jr.

counter, and a Freeman toss sweep all moved the chains before Jimbo Fisher took his shot. A deep fade to Greene was tipped away at the last moment by Phillip Buchanon. Undeterred, Fisher went right back to the well, this time targeting Greene on a quick slant. In a play reminiscent of his catch-and-run in the waning moments of the BCS National Championship Game, Greene took the slant, broke through an arm tackle, high-stepped away from a diving defender, and broke off downfield. Reed would track him down at the Miami 7-yard line. Two plays later, Winston hit O'Leary in the back of the end zone, but a crushing shot from Jonathan Vilma dislodged the ball. Florida State would settle for a field goal and a 13–10 lead. Andre Johnson once again proved to be too dynamic to handle. First, he took the kickoff out of the end zone and returned it to the FSU 37-yard line. Then on 3rd and 4, he worked back into the middle of the field on a broken play, and Dorsey found him for a pivotal first down. But the play of the game came two plays later when Dorsey threw caution to the wind and forced a deep post to Johnson near the goal line. Johnson caught the ball and collided with Jalen Ramsey in midair. Ramsey hit the turf, but Johnson maintained his balance and dove towards the goal line. The play would be reviewed, and it was determined he broke the plane of the end zone. With the Canes leading 17–13, both defenses stiffened for the next 8 minutes of game action, taking us to the game's final 10 minutes. Florida State's most promising drive of the fourth quarter fizzled at the Miami 48-yard line when Freeman dropped a pass in the flat that would have been an easy first down. Instead of punting and playing field position, Fisher went for it on 4th and 3. And with the gutsiest call of the game, he went with a slant-and-go to Greene. Buchanon bit on the pump fake, and Winston perfectly lofted a pass into his number one target. Florida State would bleed the clock on the next seven plays before Karlos Williams was pushed into the end zone by his offensive line. Leading 19–17, Miami's Ed Reed busted through the line and blocked the extra point. This changed the complexion of the ball game with 3:55 remaining and Miami just needing a field goal to advance to the Final Four. Rob Chudzinski didn't panic as a play-caller and balanced the run and the pass on the final drive. Clinton Portis picked up a first down on his second carry of the drive, a play that looked like it was bottled up until Portis kept spinning away from tacklers. His 8-yard run set the Canes up with a new set of downs at their own 36-yard line. A Kevin Beard reception over the middle picked up another first down, and then an offside penalty on Florida State moved Miami into Seminoles territory with 1:58 left on the clock. On 3rd and 6, just outside of Sievers's range, Florida State brought seven, but Miami countered with a screen pass to Najeh Davenport. The big fullback allowed his linemen to clear a path, and he nearly found the end zone before getting dragged down from behind. A horse-collar penalty at the end of the run moved the ball inside the Florida State 3-yard line. The Seminoles, left with just one timeout, were powerless to stop the clock after first down. On 3rd and goal with 17 seconds remaining, Portis crashed into the end zone, giving Miami a 24–19 lead. After a touchback, Florida State would get off just three more plays. The first was a quick out route to Greene for 11 yards. Then, a post corner to Benjamin would fall incomplete along the sideline. On the final play of the game, Jerome McDougal sacked Winston from behind. Miami will now face the West champion in the Final Four.

Elite Eight - West

(1) '04 USC vs. (3) '91 Washington
Rose Bowl | Pasadena, California

Washington 34 – USC 24
(UW) Hoffmann 10 TK, 1 TFL, FF, FR | (USC) Bush 154
All-Purpose YDS, PR TD
Bend But Don't Break: UW Defense Allowed 435 Yards,
2 Red Zone Takeaways

The San Gabriel Mountains served as the iconic backdrop to this Elite Eight matchup. But if you were tuning in for picture-perfect offensive play, you left disappointed in this one. These two defenses traded highlight reel plays for 60 minutes, never allowing either offense to string together enough positive plays to fully capture the momentum. Don James opted to stick with Billy Joe Hobert at quarterback, but was true to his word and gave Mark Brunell the third drive of the game. Hobert was sacked as many times (2) as he completed passes (2) in the first quarter. Brunell found more success, leading the Huskies on a touchdown drive. He scrambled in from 6 yards out to give UW a 7-6 lead and would finish the game as Washington's QB1. Matt Leinart would be snakebit by deflections in this game, the first coming deep in the Washington red zone. Jamie Fields tipped a pass intended for a wide-open Dominique Byrd near the goal line, and Shane Pahukoa made a diving interception. Washington would punt out of their own end zone on the following drive, and we got Reggie Bush's most electric return of the entire tournament. He would field the punt, absorb a hit immediately, spin forward, and stiff-arm a defender all in one motion. From there, it was a foot race that ended with him dusting Washington punter John Werdel. The 48-yard punt return touchdown gave USC a 13-7 lead. USC smothered UW on the ensuing drive, forcing a three-and-out. Washington would punt it out of bounds this time, avoiding Bush altogether. The Trojans started to click offensively, picking up two first downs, but then Washington's pass rush swung the game back in the Huskies' favor. Steve Emtman collapsed the pocket, forcing Leinart to roll out to his right. That gave Andy Mason enough time to track Leinart down, sack him, and knock the ball free. Dave Hoffmann scooped the ball up and advanced it to the USC 39-yard line with under 2 minutes remaining in the half. Brunell found Mario Bailey along the sideline for a critical third down conversion and then connected with fullback Matt Jones inside the USC 10. In the waning moments of the first half, Beno Bryant took a toss sweep into the end zone, giving UW a 14-13 lead at intermission. USC's best drive of the entire game came on the opening series of the second half. Leinart was 6-for-

6 for 59 yards and a touchdown strike to Steve Smith. LenDale White carried Chico Fraley into the end zone for the 2-point conversion. With both Ryan Killeen's kickoff and the USC fight song hanging in the air, it appeared that USC had righted the ship and wrestled control of this game away from the Huskies. But Napoleon Kaufman took the wind right out of the Trojans' sails with a 97-yard kickoff return for a touchdown. Tied at 21, USC's Dwayne Jarrett would drop a critical pass on third down, forcing them to punt it right back to UW. Brunell and Mario Bailey hooked up twice on the drive, and Travis Hanson converted an attempt from 42 yards out. Reggie Bush put the offense on his back, rushing for 27 yards and turning a well-defended screen into 17 yards by juking away from three defenders. But Washington would bow its neck in the red zone, forcing USC to settle for 3. Early in the fourth quarter, tied at 24, USC would be called for a series of costly penalties. Matt Grootegoed was flagged for a facemask. Then, an overly aggressive pass breakup by Kevin Arbet resulted in a 15-yard penalty for pass interference. Toss in an offside penalty, and USC gave Washington 35 free yards on one drive alone. The Trojan defensive line dug in once Washington got to the 15-yard line, creating three straight negative plays. Mike Patterson had two TFLs, and Lawrence Jackson brought down Brunell on third down for a sack. Hanson made his second 40+ yard field goal of the game, giving the Huskies a narrow 27–24 margin with 7:55 remaining in the game. Just like the opening drive of the second half, Leinart calmly answered the call. The Trojan captain was 5-for-5, including a perfectly placed go-route to Dwayne Jarrett at the UW 18-yard line. After a LenDale White carry, USC was knocking on the door at the Washington 12 with under 4 minutes remaining in the game. Leinart's first incompletion of the drive seemed imminent when a quick out was deflected by Andy Mason. But Chris McFoy ran back to the football and made the catch. The ball hung in the air long enough to allow Dave Hoffmann to tee up McFoy, and his bone-rattling hit created a fumble. The ball took two hops before Walter Bailey scooped it up clean. A questionable block by Donald Jones along the sideline cleared the path for Bailey along the sideline,

and the junior took it all the way for a touchdown. A deflated USC offense would turn it over on downs at midfield the following series, clinching the upset for Don James and the Dawgs.

Elite Eight - South

(1) '19 LSU vs. (3) '18 Clemson
Sugar Bowl | New Orleans, Louisiana

> LSU 38 – Clemson 21
> (LSU) Chase 9 REC, 144 YDS, 2 TDs | (CU) Etienne 177
> All-Purpose YDS, 2 TDs
> Joe Cool: Burrow Facing 6+ Man Blitz: 7 for 11, 139 YDS, 2 TDs,
> 0 INTs, 2 Sacks

This Tiger Tussle in the Big Easy started with a major scare. On the opening drive of the game, Joe Burrow was driven into the turf by Dexter Lawrence, landing with all 350 pounds of his weight on top of the Heisman winner. Burrow would be helped off the field by the LSU staff and taken directly into the medical tent. Travis Etienne got the first Clemson drive started when he took a wheel route up the sideline for 33 yards. Trevor Lawrence would run it three times on the opening drive, including a quarterback counter at the goal line for 6. But despite the early hole they'd dug, LSU was the big winner midway through the first quarter when it was announced that Burrow had avoided a broken collarbone. With a bruise to his non-throwing shoulder, he would reenter the game and go to work. Ja'Marr Chase and Justin Jefferson each caught six passes apiece in the first half, but Jefferson outshone Chase in the circus catch department. With Mark Fields draped on his arm, Jefferson made an over-the-shoulder one-handed snag in the end zone. This gave LSU a 24–14 advantage going into the break and firmly swung momentum in the Bayou Bengals' favor. Trailing by 10 in the third quarter, we got a little bit of everything from Trevor Lawrence. He continued to burn the LSU defense on third downs with his scrambling ability, converting a pair of 3rd and mediums. He and fellow freshman Justyn Ross flashed their chemistry with an impressive 27-yard connection on the fringe of the LSU red zone. But then Lawrence had his first true freshman moment of the ballgame. On 2nd and 3 at the LSU 15, a free blitzer had Lawrence dead to rights. Lawrence, to his credit, ducked under the hit at the last second but quickly forced a throw into the end zone. His pass was off-target and easily intercepted by Kristian Fulton. Reeling, Clemson would opt to blitz Burrow on the following series, bringing five- and six-man pressures on every third down. Burrow would pick up two first downs on those plays and cap the drive with a back-shoulder fade to Terrace Marshall Jr. for a back-breaking touchdown. Leading 31–14, Clemson did everything it could to avoid a blowout, including five fourth down attempts in the final 18 minutes of action. To Dabo Swinney's credit, they would convert four of those five and climb within 10 halfway through the fourth quarter. But a Ja'Marr Chase go-route put the game on ice with the Biletnikoff winner leaving Trayvon Mullen in the dust for 6. After a turnover on downs, LSU would bleed the clock dry and kneel it down at the Clemson 2-yard line in the closing seconds. Ed Orgeron and his Tigers are on to the Final Four.

Elite Eight - Midwest

(1) '95 Nebraska vs. (2) '05 Texas
AT&T Stadium | Arlington, Texas

> Nebraska 32 – Texas 31
> (NU) Frazier 108 Pass, 88 Rush, 2 TDs | (UT) Young 260 Pass, 109 Rush, 2 TDs, 1 INT
> Ball Security: Nebraska 14 Option Calls, 7 Pitches, 0 Fumbles

Tom Osborne must have had déjà vu bringing him back to the '84 Orange Bowl, right down to the exact score. But we'll get to that in a bit. These two offenses became famous for gouging teams on the ground. Once their offensive lines opened holes, they had speed to burn coming out of the backfield. Nebraska successfully stuck to its script for four quarters, using the "I-Option" to spark big plays. Texas found success on the ground, but it would rely on Vince Young in key moments to transcend the play-call from the sideline. The result was a game that featured 901 total yards, 63 points, and just two turnovers (one from each). Young got things started in the first half, keeping it on a read option and racing past Jay Foreman on the edge. His 21-yard rushing touchdown put Nebraska on its heels early. After picking up two first downs, Clester Johnson found a soft spot in the UT zone on 3rd and 5, but he dropped the would-be first down. Texas balanced zone reads from Young and play-action passes to Brian Carter to move the ball quickly down to the Nebraska 26-yard line. But Nebraska wised up to the zone read and bottled up Jamaal Charles on two straight runs before Young overshot Limas Sweed in the end zone. David Pino's 41-yard attempt sailed wide left, and his miss breathed life back into the Nebraska sideline. After four straight bruising runs between the tackles, Osborne's famed I-formation triple option got a back loose on the perimeter. Tommie Frazier faked to Jeff Makovicka before sprinting down the line of scrimmage. He cut inside Brian Robinson and then, seemingly inside a phone booth, squeezed a pitch out to Ahman Green outside the numbers. Green took the pitch in stride and was off to the races, scoring from 55 yards out. The Longhorns averted disaster when they recovered a Ramonce Taylor fumble on the kickoff. But after just six plays they were punting it back to the suddenly hot Nebraska offense. After stuffing the option the first two times the Cornhuskers used it on the drive, Texas blew an assignment on 3rd and 2 at midfield. The triple option brought Frazier to the edge again, but instead of pitching it, he cut upfield, broke a Robert Killebrew arm tackle, and stiff-armed Cedric Griffin. Michael Huff would chase him down from behind at the Texas 11-yard line after a 39-yard scamper. Two plays later, Lawrence Phillips carried a pile of Longhorns into the end zone. Trailing by seven, Young would complete his longest pass of the game, a 40-yard jump ball to Sweed. This set up Texas to score right before halftime. Henry Melton and the jumbo package punched it in from 1 yard out to even the game at 14 with just 37 seconds remaining in the first half. But a 43-yard kickoff return by Clinton Childs gave Nebraska an opportunity to respond. After failing to connect on his first two pass attempts, Frazier tucked it and ran on third down, picking up 15 yards. With just 20 ticks left on the clock, a short pass to Mark Gilman and a surprising draw to Ahman Green got Nebraska to the UT 30-yard line with 2 seconds remaining. Kris Brown's kick nearly touched the left upright, but Nebraska was back ahead 17–14 at the break. The third quarter belonged to the Longhorns, who scored on all three of their drives. It started with an explosive Jamaal Charles run on the third play of the second half. His 71-yard carry was nearly a touchdown, but he stepped out at the Nebraska 3-yard line. Young would take a QB power into the end zone two plays later, giving UT a 21–17 advantage. After Nebraska's only three-and-out of the game, Texas began picking on Tyrone Williams. First, they pancake-blocked him on a wide receiver screen that went for 20 yards, and then Billy Pittman beat him deep on a post for 27 yards.

Nebraska would hold its ground in the red zone thanks to a Mike Minter deflection in the corner of the end zone. His diving pass breakup held UT to a field goal and a 24–17 lead. Frazier and the offense responded midway through the third with a clutch drive that included four third down conversions. The first two came via the pass, with Texas stacking the box against their famed running game. Reggie Baul got his hands beneath an underthrown ball for a first down, and Brendan Holbein took a slant 22 yards on a 3rd and 1 at the Texas 45-yard line. With the Longhorns off balance, Tom Osborne dug into his bag of tricks. Clester Johnson faked a reverse, and with the Texas defense in man coverage, Frazier tucked the ball and took off down the sideline. He'd make it 20 yards before breaking his first tackle. He was spun down at the 5-yard line by Tarell Brown. Facing a nine-man box, Frazier hit Ahman Green on an angle route out of the backfield, who caught the pass in the middle of the end zone with no defenders within 3 yards of him. Texas continued to move the football on offense, and on a 3rd and 2 at their own 40, Young dropped back to pass with four receivers in the pattern. Nebraska sent Mike Fullman on a corner blitz, and he had Young dead to rights. But Young shrugged him off and broke contain near the numbers, racing out to the Nebraska 15 before Mike Minter and Michael Booker dragged him down. Two plays later, with the Nebraska defense keying on Young, Ramonce Taylor took a jet sweep into the end zone untouched—31-24 UT. After trading punts in the fourth quarter, a critical Texas stop put Nebraska on upset alert with 7 minutes and change remaining. Texas would move the ball out to midfield before a critical third down sequence unfolded. Young would scramble up the middle for an easy first down, but a holding call on Kasey Studdard wiped out the play. On 3rd and 14, Tony Veland jumped a slant to Brian Carter and appeared to get there a hair early. The pass fell incomplete, and the flag stayed in the official's pocket, forcing Mack Brown to send on the punt team. Richmond McGee got a rare chance to impact a Texas game, and he took advantage by angling a punt out of bounds at the Cornhusker 8-yard line. Needing 92 yards to tie the game, Osborne would put the ball in Frazier's hands on eight of the next 11 plays (four options, four pass attempts). It started with an option keeper that resulted in 8 yards, then a play-action checkdown to Clester Johnson for 6. Nebraska moved out of the shadow of its own end zone and had a bit of momentum. After Green and Phillips traded carries, Frazier tucked it and ran on a pass play, stretching out his run to the Texas 37-yard line. Time was melting away quickly, and by the time Nebraska crossed the 50, there were less than 3 minutes remaining. After a first down incompletion, Frazier pulled it from Makovicka's belly, darted down the line, and pitched it perfectly to Phillips on the edge. The burly Phillips ran over Tarell Brown and picked up 12 yards. A few plays later, Nebraska was down to the Texas 5 with under a minute remaining. A first down throw from Frazier to Jon Vedral in the flat was well covered and picked up just 2 yards. Texas would use its second timeout of the game, stopping the clock at 39 seconds. On 2nd and 8, Osborne appeared to dial up yet another option for Frazier, but halfway down the line, he hopped backward and fired a pass between Aaron Harris and Michael Huff. Mark Gilman made the catch while falling to the ground, securing it for the Nebraska score. With 35 seconds remaining, Osborne opted to go for the win. He sent Phillips, Makovicka, and a second fullback (Brian Schuster) out alongside two tight ends for a Power I-formation. With the game on the line, Frazier faked to Makovicka and worked his way down the line only to find Tim Crowder between him and Phillips. Instead of pitching it, he charged full speed into Robert Killebrew and crashed down near the goal line. On the field, they ruled the conversion successful, and the replay booth confirmed it. Trailing 32–31, Young and the Longhorns had time for a last-gasp comeback bid, but it wouldn't last past the first play of the final drive. Nebraska dropped eight and used Grant Wistrom and Jared Tomich to box Young into the pocket. Young took the bait and pushed the ball downfield for Limas Sweed. A Mike Minter deflection turned into a Tony Veland interception, and Nebraska held on for the 1-point decision at Jerry World.

Final Four

First Semi-Final

1995 Nebraska vs. 2019 LSU

Mercedes-Benz Stadium | Atlanta, GA

Vegas Line

Spread: LSU-3

Total: (67.5)

Moneyline: LSU -158 / Nebraska +130

How They Got Here

2019 LSU

Round of 64: LSU 65 vs. ('20) Coastal Carolina 21
Round of 32: LSU 40 vs. ('96) Arizona State 31
Sweet 16: LSU 52 vs. ('10) Auburn 38
Elite 8: LSU 38 vs. ('18) Clemson 21

1995 Nebraska

Round of 64: Nebraska 52 vs. ('12) Northern Illinois 17
Round of 32: Nebraska 41 vs. ('07) Mizzou 27
Sweet 16: Nebraska 31 vs. ('80) Pitt 7
Elite 8: Nebraska 32 vs. ('05) Texas 31

Pre-Game

Unlike most of the pre-2000 teams in the field, Nebraska is well-suited to face a modern offense. They took on Steve Spurrier's "Fun 'n' Gun" in the 1996 Fiesta Bowl and broke the Gators' spirit. While four- and five-wide receiver sets flummoxed Florida opponents for much of the '95 season, Nebraska seemed at ease. Defensive coordinator Charlie McBride played nickel and dime personnel for the majority of the game and still found ways to generate pressure. Tom Osborne's recruitment realignment in the early 1990s had a lot to do with that. Osborne was hoping to replicate Jimmy Johnson's success on the recruiting trail at Miami in the mid-1980s, with a focus on speed. The hulking, plodding Nebraska teams of the '80s and early '90s, which regularly flamed out in postseason play, were suddenly smaller and faster across the board. This was particularly true in the secondary.

Key reserves like safety Jamel Williams and cornerback Eric Warfield played significant snaps against the Gators in the Fiesta Bowl and demonstrated two important elements of the Nebraska defense. They had the size and speed to match up with a record-setting, pass-first offense, and McBride wasn't afraid to bring pressure from all over the field. Both Williams and Warfield, who would spend a combined ten years in the NFL, sacked Danny Wuerffel that night in Tempe, Arizona.

Nebraska enters with potential answers defensively, but can they break through an LSU defense that is better against the run than they are against the pass? LSU gave up 50 pass plays of 20 yards or more in 2019, placing Dave Aranda's defense in the bottom 15 of FBS units when it came to defending aerial explosives. But this same defense was top five nationally in the "stuff rate" metric, which measures the percentage of running plays stopped at or behind the line of scrimmage. Converting third down and manageables, and avoiding negative plays, is what made this Nebraska offense special. It's worth noting that LSU only played four mobile quarterbacks during their run to the national title in 2019, with varied results. They held Oklahoma's Jalen Hurts and Clemson's Trevor Lawrence in check, although the duo scored three rushing touchdowns in total against the Tigers. Texas' Sam Ehlinger nearly upset the Tigers with a 461-yard outburst but wasn't a true game-breaker on the ground (60 rush). The most troubling outcome, from the LSU fans' perspective, was the performance of Ole Miss's John Rhys Plumlee. Running Rich Rodriguez's spread option, JRP ran for 212 yards and four touchdowns while the Rebels piled up 402 yards on the ground. The defensive film from that game was filled with missed assignments and poor tackling at the second and third levels of the defense. That kind of confusion and poor fundamentals are a recipe for a big day for Nebraska's rushing attack.

In this tournament, no one has slowed down Joe Burrow and the Tigers' offense. Ed Orgeron's team is averaging just shy of 49 points per game. But the formula for beating LSU is still on the table: batter Burrow and protect the football. Clemson nearly knocked Burrow out of their Elite Eight meeting by hitting him early. Ultimately, they couldn't force enough turnovers to spark the upset. Flashing back to the fall of 2019, Auburn nearly knocked off LSU by doing three things defensively. They won the turnover battle, they created negative plays (6 TFLs), and they found a way to get off the field in the second half (4 punts, 1 TODs, 1 INT). This allowed them to hang around despite being outgained by 221 yards. If the Blackshirts can generate pressure, the final piece of the puzzle is their backend. Can Nebraska's cornerbacks hold up against Ja'Marr Chase and Justin Jefferson in key third downs? That's the big question.

Nebraska arrives at Mercedes-Benz Stadium with two confidence-building wins on its resumé. The Cornhuskers moved the ball through the air against an elite '80 Pitt defense in a 31–7 blowout win once it was clear that the running game wasn't enough. That Panther front was fundamentally sound and filled with playmakers, so Tom Osborne needed to call more pass plays to soften them up. Frazier was up to the task, throwing for 182 yards and a touchdown. He'll likely need to do the same against an LSU defense that will be daring him to throw the ball downfield. If he plays as he did against Pitt or against Colorado in a top 10 showdown in '95 (241 yards, 2 TDs), LSU could have some real problems getting stops.

What we know for sure is that these two coaches won't shy away from the big moment. Of Ed Orgeron's 51 wins at LSU, 13 were against top-ten opponents. Not to be outdone, Coach Osborne won the last 10 matchups of his career against top-ten opponents.

Starting Lineups

LSU Offense

"I'm not sure either Kirk (Herbstreit) or I have seen an offense this explosive in all our years of covering college football, and I think that's a dimension that LSU teams haven't had in the past."

— *Chris Fowler (Interview With 247Sports, Billy Embody, Jan. 8th, 2020)*

QB	9	Joe Burrow	6'4" 216 lbs. – **Heisman Trophy Winner**	Sr.
RB	22	Clyde Edwards-Helaire	5'8" 209 lbs. – **First Team All-SEC**	Jr.
WR	1	Ja'Marr Chase	6'1" 200 lbs. – **Fred Biletnikoff Award Winner**	So.
WR	2	Justin Jefferson	6'3" 192 lbs. – **First Round NFL Draft Pick '20**	Jr.
WR	6	Terrace Marshall Jr.	6'4" 200 lbs. – **Second Round NFL Draft Pick '21**	So.
TE	81	Thaddeus Moss	6'3" 249 lbs. – **School Records For REC/YDS By A TE**	Jr.
LT	77	Saahdiq Charles	6'4" 295 lbs. – **Fourth Round NFL Draft Pick '20**	Jr.

LG	73	Adrian Magee | 6'4" 343 lbs. – **Second Team All-SEC**	Sr.
C	79	Lloyd Cushenberry III | 6'4" 315 lbs. – **First Team All-SEC**	Jr.
RG	68	Damien Lewis | 6'3" 332 lbs. – **Second Team All-SEC**	Sr.
RT	76	Austin Deculus | 6'7" 322 lbs. – **Sixth Round NFL Draft Pick '22**	Jr.
PK	36	Cade York | 6'2" 189 lbs. – **Second Team All-SEC**	Fr.

Nebraska Defense

"Who would ever have thought a nice man like Tom Osborne would create such a monster? Here he was all these years in Lincoln, turning out nice teams that measured their rushing yardage in miles and their wins in megabunches, but were a little on the slow and stodgy side and seemed to turn into pumpkins at the stroke of midnight every New Year's Eve. But it turns out that was just his day job. By night, he was tinkering away in a secret laboratory building one of the scariest monsters college football has ever seen."

— Joe Gillmartin (The Phoenix Gazette, Jan. 5th, 1996)

DE	98	Grant Wistrom | 6'5" 235 lbs. – **Third Team All-American**	So.
NT	55	Christian Peter | 6'2" 290 lbs. – **Honorable Mention All-American**	Sr.

DT	95	Jason Peter | 6'4" 275 lbs. – **First Round NFL Draft Pick '98**	So.
DE	93	Jared Tomich | 6'2" 250 lbs. – **First Team All-American**	Jr.
SLB	56	Jay Foreman | 6'1" 200 lbs. – **Fifth Round NFL Draft Pick '99**	Fr.
MLB	41	Phil Ellis | 6'2" 225 lbs. – **Team Captain & H.M. All-Big 8**	Sr.
WLB	43	Terrell Farley | 6'1" 205 lbs. – **Second Team All-American**	Jr.
CB	20	Michael Booker | 6'2" 190 lbs. – **First Round NFL Draft Pick '97**	Jr.
CB	8	Tyrone Williams | 6'0" 180 lbs. – **First Team All-Big 8**	Sr.
FS	10	Mike Minter | 5'10" 180 lbs. – **Second Team All-Big 8**	Jr.
ROV	9	Tony Veland | 6'2" 205 lbs. – **Second Team All-Big 8**	Sr.
P	19	Jesse Kosch | 6'0" 180 lbs. – **Academic All-Big 8**	So.

Nebraska Offense

"This was like watching perfection. Nebraska played the kind of football game Tuesday night that coaches script in their endless pregame meetings. This wasn't just football. It was choreography. It was X's and O's coming to life. By the second half of their 62-24 Fiesta Bowl win, the Huskers weren't playing against Florida anymore. They were playing against history."

— *Steve Kelley (The Monitor, Jan. 4th, 1996)*

QB	15	Tommie Frazier | 6'2" 205 lbs. – **First Team All-American**	Sr.
IB	1	Lawrence Phillips | 6'0" 215 lbs. – **First Round NFL Draft Pick '96**	Jr.
FB	22	Jeff Makovicka | 5'10" 215 lbs. – **Honorable Mention All-Big 8**	Sr.
WB	33	Clester Johnson | 5'11" 210 lbs. – **Honorable Mention All-Big 8**	Sr.
SE	5	Brendan Holbein | 5'9" 180 lbs. – **Honorable Mention All-Big 8**	Jr.
TE	87	Mark Gilman | 6'3" 240 lbs. – **Captain/Boyd Epley Lifter Of The Year**	Sr.
LT	77	Chris Dishman | 6'2" 300 lbs. – **Honorable Mention All-American**	Jr.
LG	67	Aaron Taylor | 6'1" 295 lbs. – **Third Team All-American**	So.

C	54	Aaron Graham | 6'4" 285 lbs. – **First Team All-American**	Sr.
RG	69	Steve Ott | 6'4" 290 lbs. – **Second Team Academic All-American**	Sr.
RT	70	Eric Anderson | 6'4" 305 lbs. – **First Team All-Big 8**	So.
PK	35	Kris Brown | 6'0" 190 lbs. – **12-Year NFL Career, All-Pro in 2007**	Fr.

LSU Defense

"There was never any doubt that Joe Burrow & Co. could outscore just about anybody they faced. But when the guys on the other side of the line finally showed up, that's when LSU ensured its place for perpetuity."

— Paul Newberry (Associated Press, Jan. 15th, 2020)

DE	97	Glen Logan | 6'4" 309 lbs. – **UDFA in NFL/UFL Draft Pick**	Jr.
NT	72	Tyler Shelvin | 6'3" 346 lbs. – **Fourth Round NFL Draft Pick '21**	So.
DE	90	Rashard Lawrence | 6'2" 308 lbs. – **Second Team All-SEC**	Sr.
OLB	35	Damone Clark | 6'3" 239 lbs. – **Fifth Round NFL Draft Pick '21**	So.

MLB	8	Patrick Queen | 6'1" 227 lbs. – **First Round NFL Draft Pick '20**	Jr.
MLB	6	Jacob Phillips | 6'4" 233 lbs. – **Third Round NFL Draft Pick '20**	Jr.
OLB	18	K'Lavon Chaisson | 6'4" 250 lbs. – **First Round NFL Draft Pick '20**	So.
CB	1	Kristian Fulton | 6'0" 200 lbs. – **Second Round NFL Draft Pick '20**	Sr.
CB	24	Derek Stingley Jr. | 6'1" 190 lbs. – **First Team All-American**	Fr.
FS	7	Grant Delpit | 6'3" 203 lbs. – **Thorpe Award Winner**	Jr.
SS	3	JaCoby Stevens | 6'1" 228 lbs. – **Second Team All-SEC**	Jr.
P	38	Zach Von Rosenberg | 6'5" 240 lbs. – **Top 3 At LSU in Punts, Yards, Avg**	Jr.

First Quarter

The chess match between LSU play-caller Joe Brady and Nebraska defensive coordinator Charlie McBride would come to define this game. In the early rounds of this game within the game, McBride's willingness to bring pressure paid off. On the opening series of the game, LSU's offensive line was able to open some holes for Clyde Edwards-Helaire. Three carries into his night, and he already had 18 yards on the ground. But a second down drop by Thaddeus Moss gave McBride his first chance to heat Burrow up a bit. An overloaded blitz off of the edge forced Burrow out of the pocket, and his first read, Ja'Marr Chase, was blanketed by double coverage. Jared Tomich would make a diving tackle that tripped Burrow up for a sack. A Zach Von Rosenberg punt set Nebraska up on their own 27-yard line, and a new duo sat down at the chess board. Dave Aranda's 3–4 scheme often simulates pressure and thrives on getting off the field on third down. Tom Osborne's reputation as a skilled play-caller comes from his ability to find a weak spot in the defense and exploit it after the first few drives. The Cornhuskers opted more for the power running game on its opening drive, feeding Lawrence Phillips three times and Jeff Makovicka on a dive once. After picking up a first down, Brendan Holbein would be driven back after making a reception on 3rd and 5. Grant Delpit's big hit forced a Nebraska punt and set LSU up with a fresh set of downs at its own 17. A wide receiver screen to Chase got things started on LSU's second drive, with the lightning-quick receiver gobbling up 13 yards along the sideline. Two plays later, Burrow found Justin Jefferson on a deep crosser near midfield. Jefferson shielded Tony Veland from the football and maintained control of the ball all the way to the ground. Burrow would find CEH out of the backfield for his third completion and a first down on the very next play. Later in the drive, facing a 3rd and 2, Nebraska's Jay Foreman would sniff out a pass in the flat, causing Burrow to pump fake, tuck it, and run for the first down marker. He would be brought down by Grant Winstrom, but he got just enough to move the sticks. Two plays later, he connected with Jefferson on a whip route at the 5-yard line, and he beat Tyrone Williams to the pylon for the opening score of the game. Nebraska's rebuttal would be an 11-play marathon of a drive.

Second Quarter

After a Phillips screen pass moved Big Red out to its own 40-yard line, this drive became a formational showcase for Tom Osborne. Tommie Frazier took a snap from center with five wide receivers on the field, another from the shotgun, and a third with three backs lined up directly behind him in the

Maryland I. Despite the formational diversity, Frazier would run option out of the shotgun and Maryland I sets, so a lot of the exotic looks were nothing more than window dressing. It did have its desired effect on this drive, with Nebraska picking up 71 yards on the ground on nine carries. Down inside the LSU 5, a toss play to Ahman Green nearly got them into the end zone, with the freshman getting stacked up at the 1-yard line by Patrick Queen and Damone Clark. Frazier would submarine into the end zone on the QB sneak on the next play, tying things up at 7. After a series of checkdown throws, Burrow would be sacked by Grant Winstrom, setting up a 3rd and 13 at their own 33-yard line. Burrow stood tall in the pocket, facing down a six-man blitz, and lofted a deep ball down the sidelines for Ja'Marr Chase. His favorite playmaker snatched it away from Michael Booker, broke through a tackle, and raced in for a touchdown from 67 yards out. Five plays into the next drive, LSU seized control of the game with a big turnover. A Frazier pitch to Ahman Green was slightly behind the I-Back, forcing him to spin counterclockwise while receiving the football. Before he could regain his bearings he was lit up by Patrick Queen, fumbling the football into a pack of defenders. JaCoby Stevens came away with the rock, setting LSU up with a 1st and 10 at the Nebraska 32-yard line. Burrow would pull the ball on an RPO on the first play of the series and fire it to Terrace Marshall Jr. on a skinny post. The sophomore broke free from Tyrone Williams and carried the ball inside the Nebraska 5. Two plays later, Edwards-Helaire burst through the B-gap for a touchdown, making things 21–7 to LSU at the break.

Third Quarter

After a 48-yard Cade York field goal extended LSU's lead to 17, the teams traded punts before Nebraska began to mount its comeback. Clester Johnson made a difficult catch along the sideline on an early 3rd and medium, one of NU's few passing game highlights. Derek Stingley Jr. was also flagged for a facemask, moving the ball out to midfield. Two plays later, Frazier broke into the second level of the LSU defense and flipped it out to Ahman Green at the last possible moment. Green sped down the sideline, cut it back inside, and was spun down at the LSU 9-yard line after a 40+ yard gain. Osborne would give it to his workhorse three straight times in the goal-to-go situation. Lawrence Phillips bowled over a pair of LSU defenders at the 1 and inched Nebraska closer on the scoreboard. Trailing 24–14, Nebraska failed to get off the field on back-to-back third downs. An acrobatic reception by Ja'Marr Chase on 3rd and 10 at the Nebraska 27 seemed to secure the Bayou Bengals another first down, but a questionable spot left LSU with a 4th and inches. Coach O didn't hesitate and sent his offense back on the field for what looked to be a quarterback sneak. Right guard Damien Lewis got a head start and was flagged for a false start. LSU would settle for its second field goal of the third quarter and a 27–14 lead with 3 minutes and change remaining in the third. After a 39-yard Clinton Childs return, Nebraska continued to bang away on the ground. Runs of 7, 11, 6, 15, and 16 got the Cornhuskers inside the LSU 5-yard line by the end of the quarter.

Fourth Quarter

On 2nd and goal from the 4, Frazier would keep it on the option and follow Brian Schuster into the end zone. Down by just 6, Nebraska would throw blitz after blitz at Burrow. A sack on first down at the Tigers' own 36-yard line and a deflection by Jason Peter on the following play put Burrow and the Tigers behind the eight ball. On 3rd and 16, Nebraska's Terrell Farley had a free run at Burrow and drilled him just as he released the football. His deep shot to Chase sailed just beyond the Biletnikoff winner's grasp and fell harmlessly to the ground. After nearly getting blocked, Von Rosenberg's punt would bounce out of bounds at the Nebraska 29-yard line. A reverse to Reggie Baul picked up 15 yards on the first play of the series for Nebraska. Then, a tight end screen to Sheldon Jackson tacked on 11 more yards. It seemed as though the LSU defense was gasping for air when they approached the line of scrimmage with 11:02 remaining in the game. A familiar fake to Makovicka got Nebraska's third play of the drive started before K'Lavon Chaisson shot into the backfield. He spun Frazier around but ultimately whiffed on the tackle, setting up No. 15 for a run against the grain. Frazier found the open field and lowered the boom on Grant Delpit near the numbers before breaking away down the sideline. Cary Vincent Jr. tripped him up inside the 5, but Frazier and the football hit the pylon for 6. Trailing 28–27, Burrow and the Tigers settled in for a tense fourth-quarter battle. A tunnel screen to Justin Jefferson neutralized a first down blitz from Nebraska, resulting in 17 yards and a new set of downs. Burrow dissected the cover-two defense on the next play and perfectly dropped his pass down the chimney to Chase, beyond the corner and in front of the safety along the sideline. Already in Nebraska territory, Tyrion Davis-Price and CEH would alternate carries, and before you knew it LSU was down into the NU red zone with 6:27 remaining. At the Nebraska 8, Burrow sat in the pocket, worked through his reads, and found Thaddeus Moss in the back of the end zone for the go-ahead score. LSU would try to extend the lead to 7 on the 2-point conversion, but Phil Ellis deflected a pass intended for Justin Jefferson a few yards deep in the end zone. Trailing by 5, Nebraska marched the ball into LSU's territory with under 3 minutes remaining. The crucial series of plays would unfold at the LSU 22 in the closing minutes. On first down, Frazier would tuck it and run for 6 on first down. But a second down holding penalty moved Nebraska backward and forced them to abandon the run. After a checkdown throw to Mark Gilman, the Cornhuskers were facing a 3rd and 9. With LSU crowding the line of scrimmage, Frazier took a shot at the end zone, finding Reggie Baul open near the goalpost. But a big hit from Grant Delpit broke up the pass and set up a fourth down with the game on the line. Dave Aranda brought pressure and got to Frazier right away. Damone Clark went too high on Frazier and missed the sack, but he successfully kept him in the pocket. With pressure crashing in on him, Frazier fired a ball into the slot, targeting Jon Vedral near the goal line. Cordale Flott undercut the pass, picked it off, and returned it 31 yards before stepping out of bounds. LSU would pick up two first downs before

Burrow took a snap out of victory formation in the closing seconds. The Bayou Bengals are headed to the title game in Glendale.

> LSU 33 – Nebraska 28
> (NU) Frazier 118 Passing, 106 Rushing, 3 Rush TDs | (LSU) Jefferson 8 REC, 101 YDS, TD
> Playing To Their Strengths: LSU 8x 20+ Pass Plays | NU 11x 10+ Rush Plays

Statistical Leaders

LSU Tigers	Nebraska Cornhuskers
Burrow	29 for 39, 379 YDS, 3 TDs	Frazier	9 for 17, 118 YDs, INT
Edwards-Helaire	94 All-Purpose YDS, TD Burrow	7 CAR, 33 YDS	Phillips	15 CAR, 119 YDS, TD Green	9 CAR, 70 YDS Frazier	18 CAR, 106 YDS, 3 TDs
Jefferson	8 REC, 101 YDS, TD Chase	7 REC, 139 YDS, TD Marshall	4 REC, 59 YDS	Ball	3 REC, 39 YDS, 1 CAR, 15 YDS Vedral	2 REC, 29 YDS Gilman	2 REC, 22 YDS
Phillips	12 TK, 1 TFL, 1 PBU Queen	9 TK, 1.5 TFLs, FF Delpit	8 TK, 2 PBUs Stingley Jr.	2 TK, 2 PBUs, 2 REC Allowed	Wistrom	6 TK, 1.5 TFLs, Sack, 1 Swat Minter	7 TK, 1 PBU Veland	7 TK, 1 PBU, FF Booker	5 TK, 1 PBU, 2 DEF P. I.

Second Semi-Final

1991 Washington vs. 2001 Miami (FL)
Mercedes-Benz Stadium | Atlanta, GA

Vegas Line
Spread: Miami-3.5
Total: (45.5)
Moneyline: Miami -180 / Washington +150

How They Got Here

1991 Washington

Round of 64: Washington 45 vs. ('11) Baylor 27
Round of 32: Washington 16 vs. ('13) Michigan State 13
Sweet 16: Washington 17 vs. ('21) Georgia 16
Elite 8: Washington 34 vs. ('04) USC 24

2001 Miami (FL)

Round of 64: Miami (FL) 27 vs. ('99) Marshall 6
Round of 32: Miami (FL) 34 vs. ('12) Texas A&M 17
Sweet 16: Miami (FL) 28 vs. ('88) Notre Dame 13
Elite 8: Miami (FL) 24 vs. ('13) Florida State 19

Pre-Game

The Huskies and Canes were forced to share the national title in 1991, but this time around we'll be settling things on the field. Both defenses were terrifying in their day, and they've continued to dominate during their run to the Final Four. Miami has surrendered less than two touchdowns per game despite playing a pair of Heisman Trophy winners. The Canes battered Johnny Manziel (14 Knockdowns, 4 Sacks, 3 TOs) and flummoxed Jameis Winston

(17 for 30, 238 YDS). They grounded a prolific passing attack (Marshall '99) and boxed in a deep Irish backfield (Notre Dame '88). Washington, not to be outdone, knocked RGIII out of their game with '11 Baylor, forced six punts and blocked a late field goal to sneak past '13 Michigan State, and used a pair of goal line stands to upset Georgia by 1. Even its 34–24 win over USC featured a late-game scoop 'n' score. This defense has made play after play when it's mattered most.

Unlike the contrast of styles we saw in the first semi-final matchup between LSU and Nebraska, there are a lot of similarities between these two offenses. Both operate from under center, rely on deep backfields that feature a fullback, and have a game-breaker on the perimeter. Miami's offensive line touts a pair of All-American bookend tackles and an all-conference middle led by future Rimington Trophy winner Brett Romberg. Washington's line is just a touch below Miami's, but has a College Football Hall of Famer at left tackle (Kennedy), and a pair of third-round NFL Draft picks in Ed Cunningham (C) and Siupeli Malamala (RT). Is this a mirror match? It's shaping up that way.

Miami faced many traditional pro-style offenses during its run in 2001, routinely dominating the less talented teams they faced, like Rutgers (61–0), Temple (38–0), and Penn State (33–7). They also stuffed No. 15 Syracuse (59–0) into a locker and took the ball away from Florida State five times. But the Virginia Tech matchup late in the season provides the '91 Huskies both hope and a blueprint. Grant Noel was nothing more than a glorified game manager for Frank Beamer in the Hokies' first season of the post-Vick era, but the Canes made him look like a Division III walk-on. He completed as many passes to his teammates (4) as he did to the Miami defense (4 INTs). But despite all this, the Hokies were a 2-point conversion away from tying things up with Miami in the fourth quarter because of Kevin Jones and their special teams. Jones ran for 160 yards, and VT blocked both a field goal attempt and a punt, returning the punt for a touchdown. Washington won some games in similar fashion back in 1991, most notably an "underwhelming" 29–7 win over Oregon in which they blocked two punts and forced four turnovers. If it's a rock fight, Washington has the experience, the defense, and the special teams to hang around.

On the personnel front, Coach James was presented with a tricky decision before kickoff. Mark Brunell came off the bench in relief of Billy Joel Hobert in back-to-back games, guiding UW to wins over '21 UGA and '04 USC. Pressed by the media on game day—specifically, Tracy Wolfson outside the Huskies' locker room—James confirmed that he would be going with Brunell as his starter against the Canes. He pointed to Brunell's mobility and natural instincts inside and outside of the pocket as the determining factor in the move at quarterback. Brunell started at quarterback for the majority of the 1990 season and was named Rose Bowl MVP at the end of that campaign before injuring his knee during the spring of 1991. He would come off the bench and account for five touchdowns in eight games during the '91 season as he recovered from his injury.

Miami didn't have any brewing quarterback controversy to deal with. In fact, it was the opposite. After a relatively quiet start to this tournament, Ken Dorsey was starting to heat up. After turning it over early against Notre Dame in the Sweet 16, Dorsey has been a virtuoso in the past seven quarters of football. He's completed 72% of his passes and connected on three touchdowns, all while throwing just one turnover-worthy pass (0 INTs). He has lost two fumbles, which will be something to keep an eye on as Washington's aggressive front looks to create negative plays in Atlanta.

Miami (FL) Offense

"Honest to God, I cut people off mid-sentence when people try to create any type of argument or justification. There is no team ever, or will ever be assembled like that 2001 team."

— Brett Romberg, Starting Center (Interview With Fox Sports, Aaron Torres, Sept. 17th, 2014)

QB	11	Ken Dorsey	6'5" 210 lbs. – **Maxwell Award Winner**	Jr.
RB	28	Clinton Portis	5'11" 195 lbs. – **Third Team All-American**	Jr.
FB	4	Najeh Davenport	6'2" 245 lbs. – **Fourth Round NFL Draft Pick '02**	Sr.
WR	5	Andre Johnson	6'3" 220 lbs. – **Third Overall Pick in NFL Draft '03**	So.
WR	1	Daryl Jones	5'10" 184 lbs. – **Seventh Round NFL Draft Pick '02**	Sr.
TE	88	Jeremy Shockey	6'6" 236 lbs. – **First Team All-American**	Jr.
LT	78	Bryant McKinnie	6'9" 355 lbs. – **Outland Trophy Winner**	Sr.
LG	74	Sherko Haji-Rasouli 6'6" 325 lbs. – **Second Team All-Big East**	Jr.
C	66	Brett Romberg	6'3" 293 lbs. – **First Team All-Big East**	Jr.
RG	65	Martin Bibla	6'4" 300 lbs. – **First Team All-Big East**	Sr.

RT	73	Joaquin Gonzalez | 6'5" 292 lbs. – **First Team All-American**	Sr.
PK	16	Todd Sievers | 6'3" 215 lbs. – **First Team All-American**	Jr.

Washington Defense

"New York has the Empire State Building. Seattle has the Emtman Building. This building is 6-4, 290. It moves, breathes, bleeds and has a first name: Steve. When he is not blocking out the sun, Emtman plays defensive tackle for the Washington Huskies."

— Patrick Reusse (Minneapolis-St. Paul Star Tribune, Jan. 2nd, 1992)

DE	13	Andy Mason | 6'2" 238 lbs. – **Left UW No. 2 On All-Time Sack List**	So.
MG	57	Tyrone Rodgers | 6'3" 265 lbs. – **UDFA in NFL For 3 Seasons**	Sr.
DT	90	Steve Emtman | 6'4" 280 lbs. – **Outland/Lombardi Winner #1 Pick '92**	Jr.
DE	48	Donald Jones | 6'1" 236 lbs. – **First Team All-Pac-10**	Sr.
LB	39	Chico Fraley | 6'2" 210 lbs. – **First Team All-Pac-10**	Sr.
LB	54	Dave Hoffmann | 6'2" 220 lbs. – **Second Team All-American**	Jr.

LB	3	Jamie Fields | 6'0" 230 lbs. – **Fourth Round NFL Draft Pick '93**	Jr.
CB	5	Dana Hall | 6'3" 202 lbs. – **First Round NFL Draft Pick '92**	Sr.
CB	23	Walter Bailey | 5'11" 190 lbs. – **UDFA in NFL/CFL Career**	Jr.
FS	21	Shane Pahukoa | 6'3" 196 lbs. – **Second Team All-Pac-10**	Jr.
ROV	15	Tommie Smith | 6'2" 212 lbs. – **Former 5-Star Recruit, CFL Career**	Jr.
P	98	John Werdel | 6'2" 188 lbs. – **5th Most Career Punts in Program History**	Jr.

Washington Offense

"'Were they the best team you've played this season?' someone asked Coach Gary Moeller, after the Wolverines' worst bowl loss ever, a 34–14 New Years' stuffing. 'This season?' he said. 'That's the one of the best teams I've ever seen.'"

— *Mitch Albom (Detroit Free Press, Jan. 2nd, 1992)*

QB	12	Billy Joe Hobert | 6'3" 225 lbs. – **Third Round NFL Draft Pick '93**	So.
RB	29	Beno Bryant | 5'11" 192 lbs. – **Third Rated Special Teamer of Pac-10 Era**	Jr.

FB	22	Matt Jones | 6'2" 215 lbs. – **Led Pac-10 Fullbacks in Receptions**	So.
WR	5	Mario Bailey | 5'9" 162 lbs. – **First Team All-American**	Sr.
WR	4	Orlando McKay | 5'11" 178 lbs. – **Fifth Round NFL Draft Pick '92**	Sr.
TE	84	Aaron Pierce | 6'5" 240 lbs. – **Third Round NFL Draft Pick '92**	Sr.
LT	75	Lincoln Kennedy | 6'7" 315 lbs. – **Third Team All-American**	Jr.
LG	72	Kris Rongen | 6'5" 280 lbs. – **11th Round NFL Draft Pick '92**	Sr.
C	79	Ed Cunningham | 6'3" 285 lbs. – **First Team All-Pac-10**	Sr.
RG	56	Pete Kaligis | 6'2" 274 lbs. – **All-American in The Shot Put**	So.
RT	70	Siupeli Malamala | 6'6" 300 lbs. – **Third Round NFL Draft Pick '92**	Sr.
PK	4	Travis Hanson | 6'0" 178 lbs. – **Brother Jason is in CFB Hall of Fame**	Jr.

Miami (FL) Defense

"Some things need to be experienced live to get the full effect. The size of the Grand Canyon. The roar of Niagara Falls. And the speed of the Miami Hurricanes."

— *J. A. Adande (Los Angeles Times, Jan. 4th, 2002)*

DE	95	Jerome McDougal | 6'4" 270 lbs. – **Third Team All-American**	Jr.
DT	94	William Joseph | 6'5" 297 lbs. – **Third Team All-American**	Jr.
DT	91	Matt Walters | 6'5" 263 lbs. – **Fifth Round NFL Draft Pick '03**	Jr.
DE	99	Andrew Williams | 6'4" 260 lbs. – **Third Round NFL Draft Pick '03**	Jr.
SLB	48	Chris Campbell | 6'2" 225 lbs. – **Started 30 Straight Games For Miami**	Sr.
MLB	51	Jonathan Vilma | 6'2" 211 lbs. – **First Team All-Big East**	So.
WLB	17	D. J. Williams | 6'2" 244 lbs. – **First Round NFL Draft Pick '04**	So.
CB	31	Phillip Buchanon | 5'11" 182 lbs. – **First Team All-American**	Jr.

CB	8	Mike Rumph | 6'2" 190 lbs. – **First Round NFL Draft Pick '02**	Sr.
FS	20	Ed Reed | 6'0" 198 lbs. – **First Team All-American**	Sr.
SS	23	James Lewis | 5'11" 196 lbs. – **Sixth Round NFL Draft Pick '02**	Sr.
P	13	Freddie Capshaw | 5'11" 190 lbs. – **Ray Guy Award Finalist**	Jr.

First Quarter

Miami didn't pick up a first down until the 4-minute mark of the first quarter, but they were winning the field position battle because of Freddie Capshaw. The junior punter boomed a 54-yard punt and then was the beneficiary of a crazy hop on his second punt. Lining up at his own 22-yard line, Capshaw angled a punt towards the sideline, with UW's return man Beno Bryant waving teammates away from the football. But instead of it bouncing out of bounds, the ball hugged the sidelines for another 16 yards, finally rolling dead at the Washington 14 (64 yards). From there, the action really started to heat up. On 3rd and 7 at his own 17, Brunell targeted Curtis Gaspard over the middle. The pass was on target but a little bit late, and Gaspard was hammered by James Lewis. Gaspard went down in a heap, fumbling the football upfield. Ed Reed scooped it up and advanced it down to the Huskies' 9-yard line. Gaspard was helped off the field and ruled out for the game with a concussion. The play was reviewed for targeting, and Lewis was ejected for the helmet-to-helmet hit. Instead of a 1st and goal, the Canes turned around and put their defense back on the field. Brunell wasted no time taking advantage of the do-over, targeting Mario Bailey on a quick out near midfield. Bailey snatched the ball out of the air, wiggled away from a Mike Rumph arm tackle, and darted down-field. Reed made the touchdown-saving tackle, pushing Bailey out at the 26-yard line. Four plays later, Brunell rolled to his left and fired a pass to the front corner of the end zone. D. J. Williams dove to deflect the pass but was a touch late, and Aaron Pierce got his arms under the football, securing the catch. Leading 7–0, Washington kicked it off to Andre Johnson, and the Canes' big-play machine nearly broke it, stumbling down at the 33 with no one between him and the end zone. On its third series of the game, Miami finally started to settle in offensively. After a Portis first down run, Dana Hall was flagged for pass interference along the sideline while shadowing Daryl Jones. Two plays later, Jeremy Shockey made a contested catch with Jamie Fields draped on his arm. From the Huskies' 23-yard line, Rob Chudzinski dialed up five straight runs, capping the drive with a 6-yard touchdown run from Frank Gore.

Second Quarter

Randy Shannon's defense didn't miss a beat following James Lewis's ejection. Sean Taylor and Maurice Sikes split snaps at strong safety across from Ed Reed. Sikes would make three tackles in the game, but it would be Taylor who would leave a mark—both literally and figuratively. On the Huskies' first drive of the second quarter, Taylor leveled Mark Bruener after the backup tight end caught a dump-off pass from Brunell. Bruener would leave the game and head for the locker room. Four plays later, on 3rd and 7 at the Washington 41, Brunell would pump an out route to Aaron Pierce before loading up for a deep strike to Mario Bailey. The pass hung in the air long enough for Taylor to close the gap, and the true freshman came down with the football, albeit out of bounds. After a punt, Miami went back to work offensively, and Dorsey found a matchup he wanted to exploit. Jeremy Shockey caught passes of 11, 15, and 22 on the drive, the last of which brought the Canes to the Washington 8-yard line. But this is where the Huskies thrived against Michigan State, Georgia, and USC earlier in the tournament. Jim Lambright's eight-man front was tailor-made for goal-to-go football. After stuffing Clinton Portis on first down a yard behind the line of scrimmage, they jammed the receivers at the line and double-covered Shockey on second down. With no one to throw to, the pocket collapsed in on Dorsey, who lunged forward to mitigate the damage. Facing a 3rd and goal from the UW 12-yard line, Dorsey stepped up in the pocket and fired a laser to Kevin Beard in the middle of the end zone. Will Doctor got his hands between Beard's and knocked the ball away as he was going to the ground. The Canes settled for 3 and took a 10–7 lead. A once-promising Washington drive was undone by back-to-back penalties (holding, false start), backing Brunell into a corner on 3rd and 17 at the Miami 49. Brunell would avoid the rush from Jerome McDougal but try to do too much with a cross-body throw in the middle of the field. The pass was behind Orlando McKay and intercepted by Ed Reed. The All-American would break two tackles on the return before stumbling down at the Washington 16-yard line. After a first down, Miami ran the clock down to the final 35 seconds of the half and set themselves up for three cracks at the end zone. An off-tackle carry by Portis brought the ball down to the Dawgs' 2-yard line. Then a pass to Najeh Davenport in the flat was broken up by Chico Fraley. On 3rd and goal, Miami opted to spread the Huskies out with four wide receivers. A slant pass to Ethenic Sands was well-defended and ultimately broken up by Shane Pahukoa. A chip shot from Todd Sievers sent Miami into the locker room up 13–7.

Third Quarter

The third quarter was defined by improvisation on both sides. Brunell continually scrambled away from the Miami pass rush and completed three passes on the move on the Huskies' opening series of the half. Rolling to his left, he hit Orlando McKay on a wheel route for 25 yards. Sean Taylor hammered McKay along the sidelines, popping the ball into the Washington bench. After avoiding an untimely turnover, the Huskies picked up another first down on the ground before facing a critical 3rd and long at the Miami

36-yard line. Brunell lobbed a screen pass over the outstretched arms of Matt Walters, perfectly placing it in Napoleon Kaufman's hands. The freshman stepped out of a shoestring tackle, glided behind his blockers, and burst through an opening along the sidelines. A pair of Miami defenders rode him down inside the Canes' 5-yard line. Beno Bryant bounced a carry outside on the following play for 6, giving UW a 14–13 lead. After a Miami three-and-out, the Canes' pass rush started to turn up the heat. Brunell rushed a second down pass and overshot Mario Bailey on a post. On the following play, Brunell is swallowed up by William Joseph and Andrew Williams for an 8-yard loss. Needing a spark, Phillip Buchanon fielded a punt with two gunners bearing down on him. He split the Huskies' defenders, cut across the field, and picked up two critical blocks before sprinting down the sideline. John Werdel was no match for Buchanon, who blew past the UW punter on his way to the end zone. Miami opted for 1 and reclaimed the lead at 20–14. The remainder of the third quarter was a battle of attrition. Mario Bailey left the game briefly with an ankle injury, and Ken Dorsey would be helped off after a late hit knocked him off his feet. Dorsey would only miss three plays, and Bailey was back by the time Washington's offense retook the field. The alternating injuries were nestled in the middle of a five-punt sequence that took us into the fourth quarter.

Fourth Quarter

Miami's first drive of the fourth could have resulted in points had it not been for two drops. The first came on an otherwise perfectly executed screen pass to Daryl Jones. The second was far more costly when Andre Johnson got behind the defense. His post corner took him to the sideline, and instead of securing the pass first, he worried about getting a foot in bounds. The would-be reception, which would have put Miami inside the Washington red zone, resulted in a pivotal third down drop and a punt. After an 18-yard Jay Barry rush and pass interference flag against Phillip Buchanon, Washington was stonewalled at the Miami 25-yard line. With 9 minutes and change remaining,

Don James opted to kick instead of going for it on 4th and 3. Travis Hanson's 42-yard kick split the uprights and cut Miami's lead in half. The Hurricanes' rebuttal was a reminder that beyond their overwhelming talent, they also had championship mettle. Three third down conversions, including a diving catch by Jeremy Shockey, moved the football down inside the Husky 40 while draining the clock. Dorsey was battered on the drive, absorbing three hits—including a sack. But the Maxwell Award Winner stood tall in the pocket and continued to deliver. That was until a flukey play nearly cost the Canes the football game. With 4:32 on the clock, Miami had a 2nd and 8 at the Washington 18-yard line. Facing a six-man rush, Dorsey quickly threw it out in the flat to Najeh Davenport. The throw was a touch high and would bounce off Davenport's fingertips and right into the waiting hands of Dana Hall, who was sitting in a zone a few yards off the line of scrimmage. Hall would spin out of a tackle attempt along the sideline and return it 86 yards for a touchdown. But a review revealed that Davenport's tackle attempt had pushed Hall close enough to the sideline for the Washington cornerback's left heel to touch down out of bounds. With momentum still in hand, Washington pieced together four first downs, the last of which came on a Brunell fourth down scramble up the middle. With 1:54 on the clock, Washington had marched down to the Miami 22-yard line. A first down pass down the sideline fell harmlessly to the turf. Then a Brunell scramble netted just 1 yard on second down. On 3rd and 9, with a chance to take the lead, Washington went for broke and dialed up a deep passing play. Brunell, on a five-step drop, stepped up in the pocket and floated a pass into the back corner of the end zone for Mario Bailey. Bailey, Ed Reed, and the football all met in the same spot, with the violent collision resulting in an incompletion and no flags. Having made all six of his field goal attempts thus far in the tournament, Hanson took the field for Washington, hoping to force overtime. His only kick thus far that hadn't split the uprights was a blocked extra point against Michigan State. So when his 38-yard attempt cleared the mass of outstretched arms at the line of scrimmage, it appeared the Huskies had found a way to tie things up. But

Hanson's kick was leaking right from the start and sailed outside the right upright by a few feet. With only one timeout remaining, Washington needed to hold the Canes to get a second chance. But a gutsy second down play-action fake by Dorsey left Daryl Jones wide open over the middle. The Big East 100-meter sprint champion caught the pass and raced 46 yards before being shoved out inside the Washington 30-yard line. Three knees later, the game was in the books.

> Miami (FL) 20 – Washington 17
> (UM) Shockey 7 REC, 81 YDS, 5 First Down Receptions |
> (UW) Emtman 5 TKs, 2 TFLs, Sack
> Busy Buchanon: 4 TKs, 2 PBUs, 1 TFL, 72-Yard Punt Return Touchdown

Statistical Leaders

Miami (FL) Hurricanes	Washington Huskies
Dorsey	19 for 28, 251 YDS, INT	Brunell	17 for 30, 199 YDS, TD, INT
Portis	16 CAR, 80 YDS Gore	7 CAR, 27 YDS, TD Johnson	5 REC, 69 YDS	Bryant	15 CAR, 67 YDS, TD Barry	8 CAR, 33 YDS Brunell	9 CAR, 17 YDS
Shockey	7 REC, 81 YDS, 5x 1st Down REC Davenport	2 CAR, 8 YDS, 2 REC, 12 YDS	Bailey	6 REC, 70 YDS McKay	4 REC, 44 YDS Pierce	3 REC, 24 YDS, TD

Jones | 3 REC, 69 YDS	
Reed | 9 TKs, 2 PBUs, 1 INT (FR Overturned) Vilma | 10 TKs, 1.5 TFLs, FF Joseph | 4 TKs, 1.5 Sacks Taylor | 6 TKs, 2 PBUs, FF	Emtman | 5 TKs, 2 TFL, Sack, Swat Hoffmann | 12 TKs, 1 TFL, 1 PBU Bailey | 3 TKs, 2 PBUs Pahukoa | 8 TKs, PBU Hall | 3 TKs, PBU, 1 INT

Legendary Bowl Championship Game

2001 Miami (FL) vs. 2019 LSU

State Farm Stadium | Glendale, AZ

Vegas Line

Spread: LSU-3

Total: (54.5)

Moneyline: LSU -160 / Miami (FL) +135

How They Got Here

2019 LSU

Round of 64: LSU 65 vs. ('20) Coastal Carolina 21
Round of 32: LSU 40 vs. ('96) Arizona State 31
Sweet 16: LSU 52 vs. ('10) Auburn 38
Elite 8: LSU 38 vs. ('18) Clemson 21
Final 4: LSU 33 – ('95) Nebraska 28

2001 Miami (FL)

Round of 64: Miami (FL) 27 vs. ('99) Marshall 6
Round of 32: Miami (FL) 34 vs. ('12) Texas A&M 17
Sweet 16: Miami (FL) 28 vs. ('88) Notre Dame 13

Elite 8: Miami (FL) 24 vs. ('13) Florida State 19
Final 4: Miami (FL) 20 vs. ('91) Washington 17

The Quarterback Battle - Mental Aspect

Ken Dorsey, Miami (FL)

"What separates Kenny (Dorsey) is his ability to think quickly and think accurately. He's one of the smartest college quarterbacks I've been around in recent memory."

— Brent Musburger, ESPN College SportsCentury, Dec 20th, 2001

"He is a superb decision-maker, delivering the football to the right man, in the right spot at the precise moment... Dorsey is the Hurricanes' calm eye, seeing and sensing all around him."

— Chris Fowler, Heisman Presentation, December 8th, 2001

Joe Burrow, LSU

"I love studying quarterbacks and I've never sat down with a guy who's more insightful and more prepared for a defense and what he's facing every week and more just in tune.

— Kirk Herbstreit, Hey Fightin' Podcast Network, Jan. 9th, 2020

"His strength is his brain. The guy has a 4.0, and he can go to medical school if he wants. Very instinctive and what great work ethic. He's kinda OCD in that he wants everything perfect. Film junkie, gym rat."

— NFL GM anonymously quoted by NFL Network's Ian Rapoport, Dec. 14th, 2019

Tools

Ken Dorsey, Miami (FL)

"Some people say anyone could run the exceptionally talented Miami offense, but this Mr. Anyone would not throw with Dorsey's accuracy, nor would he get rid of it so quickly. When a quarterback has great skill athletes, he has to throw the ball on their break while they are running at lightning speed... to say an average quarterback could execute Miami's offense is the height of absurdity."

— Bill Curry, ESPN, Dec. 4th, 2001.

Joe Burrow

"Burrow has the makings of a future NFL star: He boasts incredible precision as a passer and plays with an ice-in-his-veins demeanor that's invited Tom Brady comparisons—and while he's certainly got a long way to go to back up that lofty praise, it won't be too surprising if ten years from now Burrow ends up as the defining player of this (draft) class."

— Danny Kelly, The Ringer, April 23rd, 2020

Overall Talent

Miami (FL)

"You can make the argument it's the most talented team to ever play. Maybe Alabama last year ('20). But the number of great players, first-round draft choices, and players who got drafted, it's amazing really. Vince Wilfork, Frank Gore, Kellen Winslow, and Sean Taylor were all NFL first-rounders and backups on that team. How good is that?"

— Frank Beamer, ESPN Article by Andrea Adelson and David Hale, Nov. 18th, 2021

"Of (Miami's) 38 draft picks, 13 became Pro Bowlers, including 11 with multiple selections. For context, the Jaguars have only nine multiple Pro Bowlers in their entire 27-year history. Three of the four running backs on the 2001 depth chart received at least one Pro Bowl berth (Frank Gore, Clinton Portis and Willis McGahee)."

— ESPN's "Inside The 2001 Miami Locker Room" Virtual Series by Andrea Adelson, Jan. 3rd, 2022

LSU

"Look, they have no weaknesses on offense. They've got a really good runner. They got a really good quarterback. They got really good receivers. They got a good offensive line. They got a system and a scheme that is very sound and solid… and they do a really good job executing. I can't give them enough credit for what they do. It's nothing like what they tried to do a year ago. It's completely different and I think it features their players. I think their players buy into it, have confidence in it and do a great job executing it. I felt like that going into the game and I certainly feel just as strongly now about that after having played them."

— Nick Saban, Postgame Press Conference, Nov. 9th, 2019

"I think we all knew at the time that it was a special team and a magical season, and for it to play out this way now in the NFL only a few years removed has proven just how talented it was. NFL draft picks equate to wins in college football, and that (LSU) team was stacked with high-end talent."

— Jim Nagy, Executive Director of the Senior Bowl and a former NFL scout, NOLA.com, May 20th, 2022

"Jaw-Dropping" Accomplishment

Miami (FL)

"The '01 Miami team finished a perfect 12-0, and even if you took away all 50 touchdowns the offense scored that year, they still would've had an 8-4 record thanks to their dominant defense led by Hall of Famer Ed Reed."

— Daniel Bates, The Spun, July 17th, 2023

LSU

"LSU accomplished something that no other team has ever done in college football, beating seven top-10 teams in the same season while at the same time defeating the No. 1, No. 2, and No. 3 preseason teams as well. It was a historic coaching season, one that earned Orgeron the AP, Home Depot, and Eddie Robinson Coach of the Year Awards."

— Glen West, SI.com, Jan. 14th, 2020

History Lesson

Before we settle the college football G.O.A.T. debate, it's important to note that our venue throws a bit of intrigue into the mix. Strange things seem to happen in the desert when it comes to college football.

As a touchdown favorite, the Miami Hurricanes' Vinny Testaverde threw five interceptions against Penn State in the '87 Fiesta Bowl. That shocking 14-10 upset cost the Canes the national title.

Sixteen years later, the Canes were once again snakebit in the desert, this time by an infamous call. As 11.5-point favorites, the Hurricanes rallied late to force overtime against the upstart Ohio State Buckeyes. And it appeared, after a Dorsey-to-Winslow touchdown, that they had taken Ohio State's best punches and were set to prevail. On 4th and 3 at the Miami 5-yard line, Craig Krenzel's pass to Chris Gamble was on the money, but the ball skipped off his hands and chest and fell harmlessly to the ground. The fireworks went off, Miami's bench stormed the field, and the Canes had won their second straight national title. But a late flag from the side judge, Terry Porter, gave Ohio State second life. The controversial pass interference call against Glenn Sharpe was the beginning of the end for the Miami dynasty. The Canes couldn't recover emotionally, giving up a rushing touchdown to Krenzel and Maurice Clarett over the next eight plays of overtime. With a chance to tie the game in double overtime, Dorsey was blitzed off the edge by linebacker Cie Grant on 4th and goal at the 1-yard line, forcing a desperation pass. It fell to the turf and, without a flag to bail them out, the game and their 34-game win streak were over.

Four years later, the roles were reversed for Ohio State. The Buckeyes entered the BCS National Championship Game as a touchdown favorite, and just like Miami, the Buckeyes were undone by turnovers and poor injury luck. That 41–14 runaway win for Florida came 1 week after one of the most memorable games in college football history.

In the 2007 Fiesta Bowl, the Boise State Broncos knocked off Adrian Peterson and the Oklahoma Sooners using every last trick in the book down the stretch. A 50-yard touchdown in the waning seconds of regulation featured a perfectly executed hook and lateral. But Chris Petersen and the Broncos were just getting started. Trailing by 7 in overtime, facing a 4th and 2 at the OU 5-yard line, Boise opted to take the ball out of their starting quarterback's hands and placed the fate of its season on a direct snap to a sparingly used wide receiver by the name of Vinny Perretta. The converted defensive back had one rushing touchdown out of the formation that season and appeared to be taking a wildcat snap outside on a designed sweep. But instead of following his blockers upfield, he flattened out and lofted a pass to the back corner of the end zone. Tight end Derek Schouman secured the catch and brought the Broncos within a point of forcing double overtime. But instead of kicking the extra point, Petersen decisively sent his offense back on the field. The Broncos personnel package was receiver-heavy, and Oklahoma's Bob Stoops immediately called timeout. As a detail-oriented defensive coach, Stoops undoubtedly had scouted Boise's 2-point attempts throughout the season. The Broncos' two attempts that fall used this exact personnel package, and the two tries were nearly identical—a Jared Zabransky rollout to the right, with receivers flooding three levels of the end zone. Both attempts ended with a Zabransky throw to the back of the end zone. On that magical night in Glendale, Boise gave the Sooners the exact same look following the timeout. But instead of rolling to his right, Zabransky pump-faked out in the flat with an empty hand, sneaking a handoff to Ian Johnson behind his back. Boise's "Statue of Liberty" worked to perfection, and Johnson jogged into the end zone untouched.

The games in Tempe and Glendale are woven into the very fabric of the sport, having produced countless memorable moments. Michael Dyer's late run against Oregon in the 2011 BCS National Title Game, Nolan Turner's game-winning interception against Justin Fields and Ohio State in 2019, and the flurry of big-play haymakers thrown by TCU in their upset of Michigan on New Year's Eve 2022 are just a small sampling of the wild plays that unfold when the Fiesta Bowl is involved. Would we be so lucky as to see game-changing moments like that this time around?

Pre-Game

Miami's path to victory comes on the ground. By controlling the line of scrimmage, they have an opportunity to bully the LSU run defense while keeping the high-flying Tiger offense on the bench. And the Canes have the offensive line to do it. By the end of their careers in Coral Gables, Bryant McKinnie had won the Outland ('01), Joaquin Gonzalez was twice named a First Team All-American ('00–'01), and Brett Romberg had won the

Rimington Trophy ('02). McKinnie's dominance was recognized that fall when he finished eighth in the Heisman race. No lineman has cracked the top 10 since. He was recently enshrined in College Football's Hall of Fame, joining teammate Ed Reed. And just for good measure, along the offensive line, guards Martin Bibla and Sherko Haji-Rasouli each achieved All-Big East First Team honors by the time they graduated. This unit could move mountains and provide Dorsey with Secret Service-level protection. Dorsey played the first two months of the 2001 season without getting sacked a single time.

LSU will counter with a defense that creates havoc and gets off the field on third downs. The Tigers finished fifth in havoc, which means they ranked highly in the percentage of plays in which they recorded a tackle for loss, forced a fumble, intercepted a pass, or broke up a pass. Additionally, they were super elite on third down, allowing opponents to convert just 29.58% of the time (6th).

Offensively, this Miami defense has no appreciable weaknesses, so LSU will likely keep the ball in Burrow's hands and give him every opportunity to win the game. Once he hit his stride in 2019, only Auburn slowed him down. But even in that 23–20 scare, Burrow still completed 78% of his attempts for 321 yards. The game will likely swing in the big play department when LSU is on the field offensively. The Tigers generated 113 plays of 20 yards or more in 2019, the second-highest total in the past 15 years. Miami counters with a defense that takes the ball away while battering your quarterback. If you include their Rose Bowl performance, the Canes sacked opposing passers 42 times while forcing 48 turnovers. Their +2.16 turnover margin average is simply unheard of in modern college football.

First Quarter

LSU won the toss and deferred to the second half. After Avery Atkins's kick sailed over Andre Johnson's head, the Canes sent their offense out onto the field to begin their drive at the 25-yard line. Rob Chudzinski had cycled in running backs throughout this tournament, but it was still surprising to see him utilize both Clinton Portis and Willis McGahee on the Canes' first play of the game. McGahee motioned out of the fullback position and set up just behind Jeremy Shockey on the line of scrimmage. Portis took his opening carry for 6 yards before a violent collision with Patrick Queen brought him to the turf. On second down, Ken Dorsey faked to Portis on a lead draw and found Shockey in the middle of the field. The athletic tight end stiff-armed Jacob Phillips away from him before getting gang-tackled at the Miami 45-yard line. After short gains by Portis and Najeh Davenport, Miami spread the field with four wide receivers on 3rd and 6 at midfield. Dorsey looked to Kevin Beard on a quick slant, but he was locked down by Kary Vincent Jr. Dorsey moved to his right in the pocket and fired a low pass to Ethenic Sands, who made the catch right at the sticks. On first down, Frank Gore patiently waited for a hole to open up on his first carry, following Martin Bibla on a counter. Gore broke into the second level of the defense before being spun down by Grant Delpit at the LSU 34. Later in the drive, Dorsey would face pressure and be lucky to throw it away on third down. He was nearly sacked by K'Lavon Chaisson, who came into the backfield nearly untouched. Todd Sievers's 47-yard field goal split the uprights, and Miami took a 3–0 lead following its 5-minute opening drive. Two things were striking on LSU's opening series: how much time Joe Burrow had to operate and how tightly the Canes defensive backs were playing the LSU receivers. On first down, Burrow checked it down to Clyde Edwards-Helaire for a 4-yard gain. On second down, Mike Rumph closed hard on the football and knocked it away from Ja'Marr Chase. Facing a 3rd and 6, Phillip Buchanon made a similar play on the other side of the field, defending Justin Jefferson a yard beyond the first down marker. His deflection was followed by a flag—pass interference. With a new set of downs, Burrow connected with Chase down the sideline for 17 yards. Ed Reed upended Chase, who would be helped off the field. He would return the next series. Later in LSU's opening drive, Burrow scrambled for a first down, running out of bounds at the Miami 11-yard line. Burrow's only true miscue came on the very next play when he overshot Thaddeus Moss in the end zone. Undeterred, he motioned Jefferson pre-snap on second down and then found him on a crossing route for a touchdown. Cade York's extra point made it 7–3 Tigers with nearly 5 minutes remaining in the first quarter. A six-play drive by the Hurricanes was derailed by a holding call on Jeremy Shockey, which negated a 16-yard Portis run. Backed up behind the sticks, Beard made a catch underneath but was swallowed up by the defense before he could get a first down. After a 44-yard Freddie Capshaw punt was fair caught by Derek Stingley Jr., Burrow and company went back to work. Completions to Terrace Marshall Jr., Racey McMath, and CEH moved the football into Canes' territory before Burrow took a deep shot down in the middle of the field. James Lewis undercut the football intended for Moss and nearly came away with an interception. The first quarter came to a close with LSU facing a 3rd and 7 at the Miami 38-yard line.

Second Quarter

Randy Shannon's defense didn't generate much pressure in the first 15 minutes of the game. So he opened the second quarter with a blitz. Burrow quickly took off running up the middle, but he was tripped up by Jonathan Vilma near the line of scrimmage. His 2-yard gain set up a 53-yard field goal attempt for Cade York. The kick was lucky to make it out of the backfield, nearly getting blocked by a wall of defenders at the line of scrimmage. His kick fluttered to the left and curled away from the upright—no good. Miami wasted no time taking advantage of the momentum swing in the game. Andre Johnson made a leaping grab over Kristian Fulton and spun out of his grasp all in one motion. He would run back across the field before getting tracked down from behind by JaCoby Stevens. His 45-yard catch-and-run put the Tigers defense on its heels. Inside the red zone, Miami would run it four times before Jeremy Shockey slipped behind the LSU linebacking corps on a play-action pass. The First Team All-American snatched the ball out of the air, lowered his shoulder, and bulldozed over Grant Delpit for 6. On the following drive, LSU was expecting a pass interference call on third down when it appeared that Phillip Buchanon had cut off Ja'Marr Chase on a slant pattern. Burrow's pass skidded across the playing surface, and the flag stayed in the referee's pocket. Buchanon would return Zach Von Rosenberg's punt 22 yards, setting up UM just outside LSU territory. The power running game would once again produce first downs, with Miami moving inside the LSU 30-yard line. But a tackle for loss by Rashard Lawrence and a beautiful pass breakup by Stingley Jr. forced Miami to settle for 3. Sievers's second kick of the game made it 13–7 Miami. The two teams would trade punts before LSU took the field with under 4 minutes remaining in the half. On the first play of their drive, Burrow faked a speed sweep to Jefferson and handed it off to CEH. The bowling ball of a back spun out of Chris Campbell's arms and streaked down the sideline for 23 yards. Burrow threaded a ball between defenders to Chase along the sideline for 16 more yards, and LSU was cooking. Two plays later, Burrow targeted Chase again with Mike Rumph in single coverage. He underthrew the fly route, but Chase adjusted, leaped, and came down with the football. Rumph's leaping attempt to swat the ball away left him flat on his back, and Chase walked in for the score. After two first downs, Miami punted it back to LSU. The ball rolled dead at the LSU 3-yard line with under a minute to go in the first half. Two dive plays later the teams jogged off the field for their locker rooms, with the score LSU 14, Miami 13.

Third Quarter

The Tigers' opening drive of the second half seemed a bit conservative at first. Edwards-Helaire carried the ball four times in the first six plays, picking up 17 yards and a pair of short-yardage first downs. Dump-off passes to Moss and Stephen Sullivan helped the Tigers continue to chip away. But once Justin Jefferson found single coverage in the slot against Markese Fitzgerald, Burrow couldn't resist taking a shot. Jefferson shielded Fitzgerald and made the catch for a 27-yard gain in the middle of the field. But Jefferson was held up and was swung around by the Canes' defensive back. Before his knee touched down, the ball came free and was recovered by Ed Reed without an LSU player within 10 yards of him. Reed broke towards the sideline and followed a caravan of defenders turned blockers. Vilma pancaked Marshall Jr., and Andrew Williams sealed off Joe Burrow. Reed nearly took it all the way, but a shoestring tackle by Lloyd Cushenberry III brought the Miami safety down at the LSU 22. Portis nearly scored on the very next play, running behind Bryant McKinney off the left edge. McKinney climbed to the second level and buried Patrick Queen. Portis hurled over Queen, stiff-armed Grant Delpit, and rolled down at the LSU 4-yard line. After another carry, Portis would come off the field, giving Gore a chance to punch it in. After motioning Shockey presnap, Gore was met immediately by Chaisson in the backfield, but bounced off a hit and plunged into the line. He kept his feet churning and broke the plane of the end zone. Coker opted for the kick instead of a 2-point conversion attempt, giving Miami a 6-point edge 20–14. Unfazed by the Tigers' first turnover, Joe Brady would dial up six straight passes on the following drive. Burrow responded by going 5-for-6 for 61 yards, including four first down throws. Inside the Canes' red zone, Tyrion Davis-Price battled through three tacklers to pick up a first down at the Miami 8-yard line. On 1st and goal, some pre-snap motion freed Marshall Jr. up on a fade route into the back corner of the end zone. Burrow's pass dropped in over his shoulder, and despite a strong takedown by Rumph, Marshall maintained control for the score. A three-and-out by Miami gave LSU an opportunity to break the game wide open. Burrow continued to throw in rhythm, and LSU marched into the Miami red zone for the second straight drive. But the Canes' team speed started to show up with tighter passing windows down near the end zone. Burrow fired a deep pass to Chase in the end zone near the goal post, but Reed and Buchanon were all over him, and the pass fell incomplete. On second down at the Miami 14, Jerome McDougle tracked down Burrow from behind for a sack. And on 3rd and long, more pressure forced a quick throw from Burrow. He short-hopped a pass to Jefferson on a curl route, and Ed Orgeron was forced to send out his field goal unit. Cade York's second kick was more successful than his first, splitting the uprights with plenty of leg.

Fourth Quarter

Miami, trailing by four, didn't deviate much from its game plan. Portis, Gore, and McGahee teamed up to carry the ball six times for 35 yards. This softened up the LSU defense and gave the Miami receiving corps a chance to attack man coverage. Daryl Jones did just that on a deep dig at the LSU 20-yard line. The Canes' speedster caught Dorsey's laser without breaking his stride and crossed the field, leaving Fulton in his wake. He would weave in and out of the LSU secondary before running out of bounds at the LSU 6. On 1st and goal, a play-fake to Portis helped Shockey gain a step on his defender, and Dorsey put it right on him for his second touchdown of the game. Leading 27–24, Miami nearly seized control of the game on the following kickoff. Clyde Edwards-Helaire was knocked off his feet by Sean Taylor, and the ball squirted out. A pileup at the LSU 27 ensued. The Tigers' Jontre Kirklin emerged from the pile with the football. Two plays later, a wheel route to Marshall Jr. was violently broken up by Ed Reed. Marshall was helped off the field, and the play was reviewed for targeting. After some time under the hood, the officials returned to the field, and it was reported that there was no targeting on the play, setting LSU up for a pivotal 3rd and 5 at their own 32. D. J. Williams came nearly untouched on a blitz, but Burrow was already off and running on a quarterback draw. He would scamper 14 yards before sliding down. Six plays and 3-plus minutes later, Burrow and the Tigers were inside the Miami 10. A whip route to Jefferson brought them down to the 3-yard line before a pop pass to Moss helped them regain the lead at 31–27. With 5:28 remaining in the game, Miami turned to their two best receiving options: Shockey and Johnson. Shockey picked up a first down a few plays into the drive, but it would be Andre Johnson's big-play ability that burned LSU on this drive. A 33-yard reception on a deep post moved Miami inside LSU's 30. Back-to-back Portis carries generated a first down. On second down, at the

LSU 15-yard line, with just over 3 minutes remaining in the game, Dave Aranda's defense made the play of the game. A five-man rush forced Dorsey to throw it a touch early to Shockey in the seam. JaCoby Stevens was shadowing Shockey in the red zone, and he reached out and deflected the football. But instead of being slapped down into the turf, the ball skipped off his hand and hung in the air. The route combination on that side of the field was a dagger route concept, with Shockey on the seam and Johnson on the deep dagger. As Johnson cut towards the middle of the field, he brought Stingley Jr. with him, so he was in the neighborhood when Stevens deflected Dorsey's pass. The freshman All-American dove and snagged the football just before it hit the ground. The red zone turnover had given LSU a chance to win the football game with two first downs. Two CEH carries, and a Burrow pass out in the flat to Jefferson were enough for a first down. With no timeouts remaining, Miami was forced to watch the clock tick down inside of 2 minutes on the next few plays. On 3rd and 4 at their own 21, Burrow dropped back to pass and wisely tucked it, with no one immediately breaking open. He would be ridden down by Matt Walters short of the first down marker with 55 seconds remaining. A Von Rosenberg punt was angled towards the sidelines and prevented a return. Miami had the ball back with 9 seconds remaining at their own 37. A quick out to Ethenic Sands moved the football to the Miami 48-yard line with 5 seconds left in the game. Down to their last play, Dorsey uncorked a Hail Mary. With Kevin Beard and Andre Johnson in the vicinity, Kristian Fulton would box out the Hurricane receivers and slap the ball down right at the goal line. Ball game.

LSU 31 – Miami (FL) 27

(LSU) Stingley Jr. 5 TK, 2 PBUs, 1 INT | (UM) Shockey 9 REC, 94 YDS, 2 TDs

Pick Your Poison: Touchdown Receptions For Chase, Jefferson, Marshall Jr., Moss

Statistical Leaders

LSU Tigers	Miami (FL) Hurricanes
Burrow | 29 for 39, 337 YDS, 4 TDs	Dorsey | 24 for 33, 270 YDS, 2 TDs, INT
Edwards-Helaire | 20 CAR, 79 YDS Burrow | 8 CAR, 23 YDS Tyrion Davis-Price | 4 CAR, 20 YDS	Portis | 19 CAR, 82 YDS Gore | 6 CAR, 21 YDS, TD McGahee | 6 Touches, 41 All-Purpose YDS
Jefferson | 9 REC, 126 YDS, TD Chase | 6 REC, 111 YDS, TD Marshall Jr. | 5 REC, 71 YDS, TD	Shockey | 9 REC, 94 YDS, 2 TDs Johnson | 5 REC, 103 YDS Jones | 2 REC, 33 YDS
Stingley Jr. | 5 TKs, 2 PBUs, 1 INT Chaisson | 5 TKs, 1 TFL, 3 QB Hurries Fulton | 3 TK, 2 PBUs Lawrence | 3 TK, 1.5 TFLs	Reed | 11 TKs, 1 TFL, FF, FR Buchanon | 5 TKs, 2 PBUs, 1 P. I. Vilma | 7 TKs, 1 TFL, 2 QB Hurries McDougal | 3 TKs, 1.5 TFLs, 1 Sack

Conclusion

After 67 games, we're left with one team still standing. This college football odyssey, which began as a pet project of mine more than a decade ago, is finally complete. Once the simulations began, my only hope was for the virtual results to fall within realistic guardrails. In that regard, I consider the results and the tournament itself to be a great success.

In the "first four" and Round of 64, we struck a balance between compelling games and expected blowouts. Fifteen of the 32 first round matchups were one-score decisions, with two requiring overtime. There were also eight runaways in the first round, with one team winning by three touchdowns or more. The '07 Kansas Jayhawks played our Cinderella, using the Play-In round as a springboard to the Sweet 16. In total, eight double-digit seeds won at least one game. The '98 UCLA Bruins took the cake for the biggest upset (by seed line) when they shocked '23 Michigan in the West Region's 13-4 matchup.

While the early upsets were fun, they didn't prevent us from enjoying a powerhouse Elite Eight. All eight teams that reached their respective regional finals were national champions. Moreover, their collective records were a sterling 106-0.

By the time the Final Four rolled around, I had watched 125 hours of simulations over the course of four months. Between the painstaking note-taking process and serving as a de facto replay official, I was ready for the last three games to deliver. And boy, did they ever. I was on the edge of my seat for LSU-Nebraska, a game that essentially ended with a dramatic red zone interception. Miami and Washington provided wire-to-wire drama fueled by a quarterback controversy, critical special teams moments, and hard-hitting defense. The two semi-finals were decided by just eight points.

As for the title game, I was pleased with the matchup. In my opinion, six or seven teams could have won this tournament, including '19 LSU and '01 Miami (FL). From the get-go, this was going to be a legitimate outcome in my eyes. The game itself was exciting to watch, with tremendous speed all over the field. The second half featured lead changes, a dramatic turnover in the closing minutes, and a Hail Mary with the championship on the line. All in all, I couldn't have written the game script better if I had tried.

I hope you enjoyed this new chapter in college football's G.O.A.T. debate. If we can generate enough buzz for this book, I'll have no choice but to run things back for *Legendary Madness: Deciding College Basketball's G.O.A.T.— stay tuned!*

THANK YOU FOR READING MY BOOK!

Thank you for reading my book! Here are a few free bonus resources.

Scan the QR Codes Here:

Tournament Bracket   **Behind The Scenes Podcast**

Being A De Facto Selection Committee Podcast

I appreciate your interest in my book and value your feedback as it helps me improve future versions of this book. I would appreciate it if you could leave your invaluable review on Amazon.com with your feedback. Thank you!

Made in the USA
Coppell, TX
23 July 2024

35101978R00148